D1202163

# SENSORY ISOLATION
## AND
# PERSONALITY CHANGE

# SENSORY ISOLATION
# AND
# PERSONALITY CHANGE

*Compiled and Edited by*

## MARK KAMMERMAN, Ph.D.

*Director, Labyrinth Corporation*
*Beverly Hills, California*

## CHARLES C THOMAS • PUBLISHER
*Springfield • Illinois • U.S.A.*

*Published and Distributed Throughout the World by*

CHARLES C THOMAS • PUBLISHER

Bannerstone House

301-327 East Lawrence Avenue, Springfield, Illinois, U.S.A.

© *1977, by* CHARLES C THOMAS • PUBLISHER

ISBN 0-398-03581-4

Library of Congress Catalog Card Number: 76-18908

*With* THOMAS BOOKS *careful attention is given to all details of
manufacturing and design. It is the Publisher's desire to present books that
are satisfactory as to their physical qualities and artistic possibilities and
appropriate for their particular use.* THOMAS BOOKS *will be true to those
laws of quality that assure a good name and good will.*

*Printed in the United States of America*
*R-2*

*Library of Congress Cataloging in Publication Data*

Kammerman, Mark.
  Sensory isolation and personality change.

  Includes index.
  1. Sensory deprivation--Therapeutic use.   2. Personality change.   I. Title.
RC489.S44K34        616.8′913        76-18908
ISBN 0-398-03581-4

# CONTRIBUTORS

**HENRY B. ADAMS, Ph.D.**
Psychology Coordinator,
Area C Community Mental Health Center
Washington, D.C.

**HASSAN AZIMA, M.D.**
Allan Memorial Hospital
Montreal, P.Q., Canada

**GEORGE W. BARNARD, M.D.**
Gainesville, Florida

**SIDNEY E. CLEVELAND, Ph.D.**
Chief, Psychology Service, Veterans Administration Hospital,
Houston, and Professor of Psychology, Baylor College of
Medicine.
Houston, Texas

**G. DAVID COOPER, Ph.D.**
Associate Professor of Psychology, George Mason University
Fairfax, Virginia

**ROBERT G. GIBBY, Ph.D.**
Director, Drs. Gibby & Gibby, Jr., Ltd., Consulting Psychologists
Richmond, Virginia

**LEO GOLDBERGER, Ph.D.**
Director, Research Center for Mental Health and Professor of
Psychology, Graduate School of Arts and Sciences, New York
University
New York, New York

**THEODORE F. HENRICHS, Ph.D.**
Professor of Psychiatry and Psychology, School of Medicine,

University of Missouri
Columbia, Missouri

**JOHN C. LILLY, M.D.**
Malibu, California

**MARK KAMMERMAN, Ph.D.**
Director, Labyrinth Corporation
Beverly Hills, California

**MALCOLM ROBERTSON, Ph.D.**
Director, Clinical Psychology Training Program, Psychology
Department, Western Michigan University
Kalamazoo, Michigan

**JAY T. SHURLEY, M.D.**
Senior Medical Investigator, Veterans Administration Hospital, Professor of Psychiatry, Behavioral Sciences and Human
Behavior and Human Ecology, University of Oklahoma
Health Sciences Center
Oklahoma City, Oklahoma

**PETER SUEDFELD, Ph.D.**
Professor and Head, Department of Psychology, The University of British Columbia
Vancouver, B.C., Canada

# PREFACE

SENSORY isolation limits the external stimulation available to a human being. My research has lead me to believe the central and most significant effect of sensory isolation on the mind is the phenomenon of ego diffusion. As the intensity of available stimulation is reduced, there appears a concurrent reduction in certain of the functions that make up the ego. Specifically, there is a diffusion of the processes of testing reality, defense, and cognitive focus. These functions appear to both arise from and be dependent upon a continual interaction with external and somatic sensations.

An individual in sensory isolation finds it difficult, and at times impossible, to maintain a cognitive focus. Thoughts drift through consciousness in free association, unobstructed or little affected by the process of information scanning and selective focus. Body boundaries along with the distinction between internal and external sensation become blurred, as there is little basis for the comparison of inner and outer when virtually all stimulation arises from within. Defensive operations are also diffused, allowing the influx of material that has previously been repressed.

Three specific functions of the ego appear relatively unaffected by sensory isolation. The autonomous and congenital processes including intelligence, memory, and learning ability remain intact. Object relations, the individual's relationships to people and objects are also unaltered. Most importantly, the synthesizing process is present during isolation; the individual's ability to integrate the resources of his personality with efficiency and effectiveness appears to be enhanced both during and after periods of isolation.

This unusual condition in which approximately half of the processes which comprise the ego are diffused creates a situation in which unconscious contents, usually experienced in disguised forms, emerge and become accessible to direct observation. The diffusion invites an intermix of conscious and unconscious material in which autonomy of the ego gives way to a temporary display of unconscious themes, often of startling vividness. In its most dramatic form, the display consists of visual and auditory hallucination combined in eidetic scenes from the unconscious mind. The remaining three functions of the ego provide a locus of perception, memory and organization which in essence provides for an immediate conscious recognition and integration of the experience.

Fortunately, the experience is more than a simple failure of repressive defenses, and less than a psychotic process in which the synthetic functions of the ego are impaired. The unconscious is generally experienced as a series of affect-images ranging from sexual and aggressive to deeply religious and transpersonal themes. The unconscious reveals itself as more than a cellar of pathology and conflict; it is also a reservoir of meaning and energy, and perhaps the creative source itself.

The temporary but often intense collaboration of unconscious and conscious contents allows a glimpse of the psyche as a whole, or the Self. The Self arises from the process of integration; it is neither conscious nor unconscious, but the confrontation and integration of both. The brief and most generally incomplete vision of the Self creates ripples of change which appear behaviorally in the life of the individual. The sudden, conversion-like symptom remissions occurring after periods of isolation demonstrate the immense power of the Self for reformation and transformation even in severely disturbed individuals. Growth, repair, and the developmental process itself is a man becoming what he intrinsically is.

M.K.

# ACKNOWLEDGMENTS

THIS book was written with the help of many people. I am deeply indebted to Dr. Jerome S. Stumphauzer whose encouragement formed the genesis of this work, and whose personal concern made this book far better than it would have been without him. I am most grateful to Dr. James A. Bondell for his immense help with the organization of the manuscript, and to my father, Roy Kammerman, whose diligent reading of rough drafts provided inspiration and perspective. I am also indebted to Mr. Bruce W. Thu, a craftsman of the highest order, who designed and built the water suspension tank used in my research, and to Marshall S. Cherkas, M.D., Dr. Cecil E. Burney, Dr. Kent Candelora, and Dr. John Tholen for the time and considerable insight they gave to the manuscript. Credit is also due Dr. John Curtis Gowan whose ideas and research have contributed immeasurably to my professional development. My deepest thanks go to my contributors, for it was their extensive expertise and generosity with their own research that made this book possible. Lastly, but most important, was the love and support of my wife, Alice, to whom this book is dedicated.

M.K.

# CONTENTS

## PART THREE
### Water Suspension Environments and Ego Diffusion

## PART FOUR
### Water Suspension Isolation and the Induction
### of Ego Diffusion

## Contents

# SENSORY ISOLATION
# AND
# PERSONALITY CHANGE

# PART ONE

## The Effects of Bed
## Confinement on Personality

# INTRODUCTION

CONCERN over reports of Chinese and Korean brainwashing in the early fifties generated the studies with experimental isolation that began at McGill University. Their findings were unusual and provocative. Subjects reported a strong hunger for stimuli, emotional lability, an inability to concentrate, and a variety of imagery and hallucinations similar to those induced by some psychotropic drugs, such as LSD and mescaline.

Within the field of experimental isolation, there has appeared a series of experiments with surprisingly consistent findings. Researchers have found brief periods of reduced sensory input to have psychotherapeutic value. In light of the frightening tales of brainwashing that gave impetus to the study of sensory isolation, the reports of positive personality change appeared paradoxical and did little to offset a generalized negative feeling about experimental isolation.

This book includes seventeen experiments which are, in the editor's opinion, the major studies in the therapeutic use of sensory isolation. The editor has illuminated the experimental variables, theoretical constructs, and the individual differences of subjects which appear to be most influential in the effective use of sensory isolation as a precipitant of personality change.

The most common method of sensory isolation is bed confinement, a procedure in which the subject lies in a quiet, dark room. Ear plugs and blindfolds are generally included to further reduce available stimulation. In addition, movement may be restricted by encasing the arms in cardboard gauntlets and hands in mittens. Although this method of isolation is not as effective in reducing stimuli as water suspension, it is readily available to hospital and experimental settings as it does not require the construction of an elaborate sensory limiting environment. The experiments in this section attempted to accomplish personality change by using the bed confinement method.

## Experimental Variables

### *Degree of Stimulus Reduction*

The degree to which external stimulation is reduced appears to be an experimental variable of primary importance. While the specific reduction in the intensity of stimulation varies in the following reports, one stands out as being significantly different. In this study, "... there was no reduction in the absolute level of stimuli intensity. Instead ... meaningful patterned cues had been minimized," (Cleveland, Reitman and Bentinck, this volume, chapter 4). In other words, although their use of a white noise generator and opaque goggles reduced the patterning of stimulation, there was essentially no stimulus reduction and therefore no true sensory isolation. This lack of stimulus reduction may be the reason this is the only study included in this section that did not produce personality change. Although these authors cited the short time (four hours) as explanation for their failure to replicate previous successes, it appears from the vantage point of subsequent research that homogeneous stimulation is not effective in creating personality change.

### *Time Spent in Isolation*

The length of time a subject spends in reduced contact with external stimuli may have bearing on the experimental outcome, but no substantial conclusions can be drawn at this time. Beneficial effects were found across a wide range of isolation duration (two hours to four days) which prevents a definitive notion of either a minimum or ideal length of time.

### *Experimental Set*

The set given to the subject before his isolation experience seems to have direct bearing on the outcome. Azima and Cramer (1956) were careful to distinguish their work from that of their predecessors who reported largely negative effects in subjects. Although the method of isolation was essentially the same, they told their subjects that the isolation was a form of treatment, and reported, "The patients accepted the isolation mostly with optimism, and as a means for recovery from their psychological handicaps" (chapter 1). This positive set was appropriate and necessary as indicated by the following study. In 1968, Curtis and Zuckerman published a report in which a paid subject developed an acute psychotic reaction during an eight-hour bed confinement study, the effects of which lasted several weeks. Although the isolation in this particular study was more restrictive than the others reported in this section, the subject himself believed his reaction was caused by his being insufficiently prepared for the experience. He had not expected to be strapped down and believed monitoring electrodes were going to burn him.

Most of the studies in this section make no mention of the set that was given to the subjects. However, it seems reasonable to assume the experiments had at least a neutral set since they were conducted in hospital settings and thus probably appeared as a method of treatment to inpatient subjects. Fortunately, Cooper, Adams, Dickenson, and York (chapter 7) demonstrated set could be manipulated therapeutically in a preisolation interview. They concluded:

> The interpersonal set induced just prior to a deprivation experience is critical in determining the interpersonal meaning of such an experience for the individual *Ss*. By eliminating competing stimuli and the possibility of self-initiated correction of incoming data, sensory deprivation makes any social data acquired immediately beforehand far more significant for determining consequent behavior than would otherwise be the case (chapter 7).

## Theoretical Constructs

### *Stimulus Hunger*

Cooper et al. (this volume, chapter 7) stressed the development of a strong stimulus hunger as the vehicle of change. As they concluded above, the preisolation interview was significant in determining consequent behavior due to the elimination of competing stimuli in the isolation environment. This effect was magnified by the strong need for stimuli of the subject in isolation " ... which generally enhances their general receptivity to all environmental influences." The theory that stimulus hunger leads to greater receptivity of an explicit or implied message is predominant in the literature investigating the use of taped messages in isolation and will be discussed in Part Two. It is difficult to separate the effects of the preisolation interview in Cooper et al.'s study from the effects of isolation alone, since they did not have an isolation-only group.

### Psychoanalytic Theory

Most of the following papers advance psychoanalytic constructs to explain changes in personality. This position views sensory isolation as an effective means of inducing regression to the primary process with a concurrent disorganization which leads to the reorganization on a higher level of functioning. Old defensive mechanisms are broken down, making way for a relatively quick reconstruction of personality. This breakdown of ego defenses, or ego diffusion, permits the influx of previously unconscious material into consciousness. Material previously repressed emerges as the individual regresses into the primary process. The strong pull of the primary process under these conditions was explored by Goldberger, who concluded:

> ... the data seem generally to support the psychoanalytically-derived hypothesis that continued contact with the structure of reality is necessary for a person to maintain secondary-process thinking, and to prevent the onslaught of drives in the form of the primary process (chapter 3).

The emergence of novel material into consciousness was demonstrated in the findings of Gibby et al. who reported:

> After the deprivation experience, the subjects expressed in a

variety of ways their increased awareness of inner conflicts and anxieties, and heightened perception of the fact that their difficulties stemmed from inner rather than from outer factors (chapter 2).

## Individual Differences

While general results demonstrated positive effects on personality, each study invariably had subjects who did not improve. Beneficial results appeared to occur more readily in the presence of poorly integrated and unsuccessful psychological defense systems, whereas subjects with rigid and elaborate defenses were found to be uninfluenced (Cooper et al., Chapter 5; Adams et al., Chapter 6). These latter individuals showed an exaggeration of their defenses possibly reflecting their successful resistance to the regressive pull of the environment. Other individual differences that predicted beneficial use of isolation were: low verbal fluency, tendencies to act out, severe presenting symptoms, and a reliance on primary repression as a defense. Several researchers have noted the dissimilarity of this profile with that of persons most likely to benefit from traditional psychotherapy.

## Conclusions

This group of experiments gives some insight into the workings of the mind. When isolated from external stimulation, diffusion of ego processes marked by regression and disorganization permits an influx of previously unconscious material into consciousness. This procedure appears to be a mechanism of psychological growth and repair not only in the isolation laboratory but also in an individual's *in vivo* development. Periods of stress and emotional upheaval very often give rise to spurts of personality growth. A prime example of this sequence is found in puberty during which the child's sense of self is diffused in the turbulence created by new and powerful stirrings within the psyche. Previously unknown content emerges and forces an expanded sense of self that marks the ego of adulthood.

## REFERENCES

Curtis, G. C. and Zuckerman, M.: A psychopathological reaction precipitated by sensory deprivation. *American Journal of Psychiatry, 125*:255, 1968.

# EFFECTS OF PARTIAL PERCEPTUAL ISOLATION IN MENTALLY DISTURBED INDIVIDUALS*

H. AZIMA, M.D., AND FERN J. CRAMER, M.A.

THE purpose of this paper is to present the results of a study of partial perceptual isolation which has yielded some information about the problem of depersonalization and body-scheme.

The impetus for this study came from three different lines of inquiry:

A. The problem of the patient disorganizing in psychotherapy which under certain conditions yields beneficial therapeutic results. Recent experiments with hypnosis,[1] anaclitic therapy,[2] prolonged sleep treatment[3,4] and "regressive electroshock therapy"[5] all have indicated that in an appropriate setting if the opportunity is provided for the organism to regress (in action and in phantasy) to those stages of development where it has been fixated and its growth vitiated, a reverse impetus for progression and reorganization may ensue.

B. Studies of Perceptual Isolation in Hebb's laboratory. Thompson and Heron[6] reporting the effects of restriction of the environment on exploratory activities of dogs, and later experiments of Bexton, Heron and Scott[7] on the influence of decrease variability in sensory environment of "normal" human subjects, demonstrated the disorganizing effects and reduction of partial isolation. The importance of isolation has been emphasized in the reports of political prisoners who have become disorganized and "brain-washed," and in the subsequent reorganization stages have shown an alteration in their former ideational defence

*From *Diseases of the Nervous System*, 17:117-122, 1956. Courtesy of Physicians Postgraduate Press, Inc.

11

patterns.

C. A wide variety of reports have dealt with the problems of body-image, body boundaries, body-ego, social field, deperson-alization, style of being or "being-in-world" (The dasein of Exis-tential Philosophy) or what Scott[8] has reconceptualized as the Body-Scheme. All these problems deal with the relationship of the individual to his world. It was felt that perceptual isolation may allow us to study this relationship under altered conditions.

## Method

Five patients suffering from anxiety states, two obsessive com-pulsives, five depressions and two hebephrenics were put on par-tial perceptual isolation for a period of time ranging from two to six days. Except for two depressed cases whose ages were fifty and sixty respectively, the ages of eleven of the patients were below forty.

The isolation setting consisted of an ordinary single hospital room containing all facilities, and situated farthest from the center of the ward. The room was darkened by means of heavy curtains on the windows. The patient remained in the room throughout the isolation, lying or sitting in bed, wearing translu-cent eye-goggles, and with hands and arms encased to a few inches below the shoulders, in cardboard cylinders. Patients were put on demand feeding and demand evacuation, and if possible they were fed with the apparatus on. Face and teeth were washed once a day. Except for the dark setting and some changes in nursing care the apparatus was quite similar to the one used by Bexton, Heron and Scott.[7] However, the technique used here differs in two major aspects from those of the above mentioned authors: The first is the motivation and psychological attitude of the subjects, and the second the relative decrease of verbal relationship. Before isola-tion the procedure was explained in detail to the patient as a method of investigation and treatment, aiming at cutting down external stimulations. They were told that they could terminate the procedure any time they wished. The patients accepted the isolation mostly with optimism, and as a means for recovery from their psychological handicaps. The decrease in relationship was partially realized by cutting down the verbal exchange with the patient. Patients were checked once every hour, but they were interviewed or tested only once or twice a day for a period ranging from fifteen to thirty minutes, (the glasses were removed during the testing period). This interview was conducted more or less in a psychotherapeutic setting. The changes in psychodynamics were investigated through the analysis of patients' dreams, fantasies, free association, figure drawings and Rorschachs. All the patients were tested before and after the isolation with a partial Wechsler Bellevue scale and figure drawings, (F.D.) Rorschachs were redone on those patients who had had the test prior to the isolation. During isolation, figure drawings were repeated every other day. Three patients were investigated in regard to their vestibular apparatus before and after isolation. The reason for this was the emphasis some of the authors like Schilder had placed on the important role of vestibular apparatus on maintenance of body-image. Most of the patients were on a supportive form of psychotherapy.

## Results

We shall limit ourselves to a few brief case reports in each diagnostic category, with particular emphasis on the changes and emerging processes during isolation. The reasons for our refraining from a detailed discussion of the patients' pre-isolation psychodynamics will be discussed in a later portion of the paper.

In all, eight cases out of a total of fifteen showed a depersonalization state with different degrees in intensity of visual, auditory and gustatory hallucinoses. A beneficial therapeutic effect was observed in the five depressed cases; in two this effect was permanent. The two obsessional neuroses manifested acute psychotic episodes. They were treated later with electric shock, which resulted in improvement in both paranoid and obsessional features. The remaining eight cases showed a moderate increase in motivation, socialization and self-assertiveness.

CASE 1. A nineteen-year-old male presenting a hebephrenic reaction was put on isolation with the purpose of promoting a regressively satisfying environment in which most of his needs would be satisfied, and his anxiety about his relationship with the world reduced. He remained in isolation for four days. During the first two days he appeared restless and manifested increasing withdrawal and blocking. On the second day he experienced an hallucinosis consisting of yellowish spots. On the third day the hallucinosis increased in variety and color, for short periods of time: e.g. "I see flickering of light, sort of yellowish. Sometimes I see different designs." He also reported, "I can't identify what I am drinking any more ... I imagine sometimes that I am not in this room, that my bed is in the hall. It feels funny, I know I am not in the hall." On the fourth day he experienced an increase in both hallucinosis and feeling of estrangement: "I see different objects now, broken down shacks, pen, etc ... (?) sort of imagination I suppose ... I can't feel my arms anymore (?) My hands and legs, I just can't feel them. (What do you think has happened?) I don't know, I just don't feel them. (Patient moves his arms.) Still don't feel them ... Ah! It is coming back now (Where?) My left arm." Although he was quite restless he never felt aggressive and was pleasant. The study of his psychodynamics during isolation through his figure drawing and the analysis of one dream ("My father died."), revealed repression of aggressive tendencies which was particularly evident on the fourth day (absence of hands and feet in figure drawing) associated with some increase in anxiety indices. However, F.D. revealed also some degree of re-organization (better details, better proportion, etc.) increasing need for social contact, and oral demands. Postisolation cognitive tests showed some mild improvement in concentration and intellectual functioning.) Clinically, during the postisolation period he showed a transitory improvement which lasted about four days. He became more communicative, was less vague and more cheerful.

Contrary to the above case, a hebephreno-catatonic girl who remained in isolation for six days showed no perceptual alteration. Behaviorally, she manifested overt hostility, became quite talkative and self-assertive. Her F.D. revealed gradual, but definite emergence of aggressive tendencies. She also experienced several spontaneous orgasms, and verbalized memories of her "sexual adventures."

CASE 2. A thirty-year-old female suffering from a depressive state, which had become manifest a year previously, after the birth of an unwanted illegitimate child. She accepted isolation and tolerated it for six days. During the first two days she felt "lonesome," and tried "to think things over." On the third day, she reported: "My head occasionally starts to spin, and then sometimes I feel I am not here, I don't know where I am (?) I just don't know. It takes about half an hour or more to think back and get my bearings... It is unpleasant, I get scared." She had similar, but more intense experiences on the fourth day. On the fifth day she reported: "Sometimes I don't feel the bed. It goes away (?) I feel that I am in the air floating. I don't like it. It lasts about ten to fifteen minutes. I float lying down as in a cloud (?) I can't explain it, you have to go through it to know. I don't feel anything, my arms weren't there from the shoulder down. . . I feel also that my bed occasionally is rocking, swinging." On the sixth day there feelings began to decrease, the patient became restless, resentful, broke an arm band, and demanded the termination of isolation. Throughout isolation, except for the last day, she has remained calm, rather cheerful, very co-operative, and dependent.

The study of her psychodynamics during isolation, with the aid of five consecutive dreams and her F.D., revealed the emergence of aggressive tendencies in the first few days, and its subsequent suppression and introjection. She dreamed for three nights that she was "in a boat with her father fishing" (with the doctor in isolation). This was followed by the "the doctor eating ... a cow killed, blood on the snow." (She kills the doctor because she feels sexually assaulted by him. Patient is frigid like snow); and afterwards the dream of "going home in a train" (possessing father's penis); ... a train wreck, a woman bleeding (she punishes herself for killing her father, etc.). These dreams were not interpreted. The analysis of figure drawing brought out a rapid withdrawal and depression associated with evidence of repressed aggression (sudden decrease in size, loss of hands and arms, oral amphasis).

In the postisolation period, the patient showed considerable clinical improvement. Her mood changed, she became more communicative and self-assertive, she began to pay more attention to her appearance and manifested a desire to socialize.

Concomitantly, psychological tests showed immediate increase in feelings of well being, increasing desire for socialization. In postisolation there was slightly improved efficiency on the intellectual subtests, and the F.D. were better organized. The improvement continued for four days and then gradually the patient returned to her former state and was put on electric shock therapy.

We draw attention to the difference between the overt behaviour of the patient during isolation (calm, cheerful, dependent) and her overt tendencies of destructiveness. The study of vestibular sensitivity before and after isolation showed no abnormality.

CASE 3. A forty-one-year-old female suffering from recurrent attacks of depression, the last of which had started two months prior to her admission. It was noted that a previous attack had been precipitated when a doctor told her that her son's tooth should be extracted, and a second episode followed the death of her father-in-law.

She remained in isolation for five days. During the first day she was quite restless, and had vivid day-dreams of being or having been home. On the second day she stated: "When I woke up, I didn't know where I was ... I felt quite dizzy." On the third day she reported: "It seems that at times I am losing parts of my body ... my legs, as if there was nothing in bed (?) I thought I went to sleep, but I wasn't. It is hard to describe, I am in bed, then a minute later I am not there anymore ... as if I had lost control of my body. Movement does not bring my body back. I was surprised at first, then I said, 'oh, well!' " During the fourth day these experiences increased in intensity: "I felt I had no body at all, just head and arms. I know I have them ... I wait till it comes back." The patient had no feeling of anxiety, and remained calm throughout isolation, but because of increasing depression, isolation was terminated.

The study of her dynamics (during isolation) through figure drawings showed increasing aggression, (gradual increase in size, the appearance of fingers and toes from the second day on, oral amphasis, etc.) A considerable disorganization in the drawings was noted on the second day just prior to the development of a depersonalization syndrome, followed by a decrease in tension and agitation. On the fifth day the findings in the drawings (appearance of ears), and in Rorschach suggested the beginning of a projection of aggressive tendencies.

In the postisolation period the patient showed a relatively rapid improvement. Her mood changed, she became cheerful and self-assertive, and began to socialize. This improvement continued and the patient was discharged with no further treatment. Her F.D. and Rorschach showed increasing organization, decrease in tension, and reversal of mood. There were no gross changes in other psychological tests.

In this particular case it was felt that the disorganization initiated by isolation was followed, clinically and in psychological tests, by a rapid type of rebound process of reorganization. It seemed that, at least in part, the reorganization and mood changes could have been attributed in part to the projection of aggressive impulses.

It should be noted that of three other depressed cases who accepted isolation, one showed marked improvement leading to her discharge, and another moderate temporary improvement. Behaviorally and psychodynamically, all showed overt and considerable aggression; one of them actually wanted to attack the therapist. The case which recovered under isolation was a thirty-year-old female who manifested, in addition to overt hostility, marked sexual phantasies and daydreams. She perceived isolation as representing a sexual intercourse with the therapist, and brought out vivid daydreams related to pregnancy and childbirth. She showed similar psychodynamics in the figure drawing (the female figure in the drawing became pregnant at the beginning of isolation and at the end of the treatment the female was drawn holding a baby). In this case, it appeared that isolation had resulted in a release of aggressive and libidinal impulses, with considerable gratification in phantasy. These three cases manifested no changes in body-scheme or in perceptual fields.

CASE 4. A thirty-nine-year-old female who was suffering from an obsessive-phobic state with exacerbation and remission since the age of nineteen. At the onset, the phobia was related to having swallowed a fish bone, then a piece of glass, and for the past four years of the fear of dying. This fear had increased gradually, had remained refractory to all types of therapy and had become incapacitating.

She remained in isolation for four days. The first day she experienced an increase in her anxiety and fear ("This is like dying"). She was unsure about continuing isolation, and once came out of the room. However, she persuaded herself to stay in. We draw attention to this fact because it appeared that this acceptance, of what could be interpreted as a symbolic death, might have had some correlation with the depersonalization syndrome which developed the following day. She reported on the second day: "I see silver stuff jumping up and down ... my spine seems to be missing. I know it is there, but I feel I have no bones. I feel myself going up and down, swaying and then I go around ... I feel floating in the air." She also experienced marked sweating of hands, and difficulty in "controlling my thoughts." On the third day, the hallucinations increased, and on the fourth day, she reported in the morning "when I shut my eyes I see foolish looking faces ... then I see flowers of all sorts ... I hear music, too. They stop occasionally. I don't know why I should see them, I know they aren't there." The changes in body feelings continued with additional feelings of "being turned upside down, feeling up in the air, etc." In the afternoon of the fourth day, she developed frank paranoid tendencies. "I see myself dead in a box. I see them looking at me. I think he is going to kill me (who?) my boy friend ... I have no more power to stop my thoughts." The isolation was terminated at this time, and the patient was put on electric shock therapy which resulted in almost complete recovery of paranoid as well as phobic ideation.

The behavior of the patient throughout isolation was indicative of great anxiety, but very little overt aggression. Figure drawings showed immediate denial of aggression on the first day (prior to depersonalization) and evidence of break in the defences and disorganization on the third day. Although in Rorschach, there was evidence of some paranoid tendencies, there were also some signs of reorganization such as increased productivity, and more use of human concepts. The cognitive tests showed somewhat lowered attention and concentration.

Another case of obsession neurosis, suffering from severe motor compulsions, who had not responded to any form of treatment, was put on isolation with the explicit aim of provoking a psychotic disorganization. He remained five days in isolation, began to manifest signs of depersonalization on the second day, and showed several acute psychotic episodes, lasting about three hours on the fourth and fifth days. The disorganization manifested itself, in part, as a marked sexual disinhibition. He experienced many spontaneous orgasms, and manifested overt erotic behaviour toward the nurses. His eating habits deteriorated, and his behaviour was like that of a very hungry child during the feeding periods. In the postisolation period, he showed some reorganization and lost some of his motor compulsions. But because of the appearance of some paranoid tendencies, he was put on the electric shock therapy, which resulted in considerable improvement and subsequent discharge. Analysis of his drawings during isolation, revealed emergence of both libidinal and aggressive tendencies, (appearance of genitals and breasts; increase in size, teeth; disappearance of hands and feet, etc.) A marked disorganization and regression of F.D. occurred (primitivization, simplification, fragmentation) concomitant with the deterioration of his overt behavior. In the postisolation the figure drawings showed increasing reorganization. The status of vestibular apparatus was found within normal limits before and after isolation.

CASE 5. A twenty-five-year-old female suffering from a long standing anxiety neurosis who had experienced an exacerbation of her symptoms associated with some depression for about one year prior to her hospitalization, was put on isolation for the purpose of releasing her repressed hostility, inhibition and depression. On the first day of isolation, she showed some anxiety about sexual phantasies, and expressed her concern about emerging destructive tendencies as follows: "I feel this feeling of hatred inside of me; I don't know how to let it come out." On the second day she lost this feeling completely, and reported: "I feel dizzy again, as if my head didn't belong to me; it rolls back and forth (?) I know it is attached to me, but it rolls around . . . I feel as if I were drunk . . . I saw small circles before my eyes." She talked extensively about her lack of "sexual adventures" brought out phantasies of "vividly seeing myself on my father's knees," and recalled that she had "not felt anything when my mother died." On the third day the feeling of corporeal changes increased in intensity, and she reported "my head feels too heavy for me. At night my arms feel as if they were being lifted by an invisible force ... I was amazed. I felt dizzy ... going round and round the room, I felt in mid air ... I didn't feel the bed ... subconsciously I knew the bed was there." She also experienced paresthesias, such as tingling, pin pricks on her hands, as well as inability to identify some foods. An incidence in her childhood when she was terrified of a dog was recalled. On the fourth day, she occasionally lost the feeling of having a body and saw flashes of light before her eyes. Behaviorally, she remained indifferent and calm until the fourth day, when she became aggressive, quite self-assertive, and terminated the isolation. Concomitantly, with this, she verbalized feelings of resentment against her stepmother and her female boss.

The study of her dynamics during isolation showed a gradual internalization of aggressive tendencies, particularly in her figure drawings (closure of the mouth, decrease and finally the disappearance of hair, decrease in line pressure, etc.) At the same time there was a rather sudden disappearance of the feeling of hatred on the second day. Some degree of suppression of sexual preoccupations was also noted in the drawings.

In the postisolation period, the patient was no longer depressed, felt more self-assertive, and was discharged on follow-up psychotherapy.

Four other neurotic patients accepted isolation. Two of these, both anxiety states, could not tolerate isolation more than two days and became openly resentful and aggressive. They showed no perceptual or bodily feeling changes. Two anxiety hysterics remained in isolation for four and six days respectively. Both showed marked changes in body-scheme, such as the feeling of floating in the air, the absence of body parts, etc. The patient who remained in isolation for six days became gradually depressed, for the first three days clinically, and psychodynamically showed evidence of suppression of aggressive impulses (decrease in size of F.D., thinning of lines, disappearance of feet and hands, etc.) The reverse process occurred in the last three days. The patient became gradually more aggressive, self-assertive, lost her feelings of depression and terminated the isolation herself. In figure drawing she showed a sudden increase in expansivity, increase in activity and a better organization of the self-drawing. It was noted that ideationally she was using her increasing ability and self-assertiveness in a constructive manner (planning for the future, "thinking things over," etc.) It seemed as if the early disorganization tendencies had initiated a rebound reorganization impulse. She had no changes in bodily-feelings on the last day of isolation. A study of vestibular function showed no abnormalities before or after isolation.

## Discussion

The foregoing data demonstrates that perceptual isolation provokes a disorganization of psychic structure which, according to the kind and quality of defenses, may lead to a psychotic state. This disorganization in most cases leads either to a temporary or to a relatively permanent reorganization of some aspects of a previously unsteady psychic state. This disorganization took the form of what is classically called a depersonalization syndrome, particularly effecting body-feelings, body image, and what Scott[8] has designated as body-scheme.

The primary theoretical problem is to determine the etiology of this disorganization and changes in body-scheme. What is the role of the decrease in sensory variability; what is the role of emergent dynamic processes; and how are they correlated? We do not think that the present data, and the information available in this area, can furnish a definitive comprehensive formulation. However, the facts permit some theoretical considerations from three relatively separate points of view: physiological, interpersonal (relationship), and intrapersonal. The separation of these three hypotheses is arbitrary, and made only for the sake of the analytic clarification. No final validity is claimed for any of the following hypotheses.

(1) PHYSIOLOGICAL HYPOTHESES: What isolation produces is a reduction in the variability and kind of sensory input. Bexton, Heron, and Scott have attempted to explain changes in cognitive functions in isolation as related to the nonspecific function of

stimuli, which altered the maintenance of arousal. There were few cognitive alterations in our cases, and in several of them there were some actual improvements, although we did not use all of the same tests as the above authors. However, it may be maintained that it is the quantitative aspects of the stimulus-reduction which is responsible for disorganization. According to the intensity of this reduction, sleep or disorganization may occur. In fact, in some of the patients, the quantity and the pattern of sleep was intensified and disturbed. If variability in sensory input is decreased to a marked degree, one may postulate that it inhibits the integrating activity of the ascending reticular system. This inhibition in turn may release some self-regulating, auto-repetitive neuronal sets[9] of parieto-temporal zones with the resulting activities which are not experienced as belonging to the self. The feeling of the absence of body parts would then be interpreted as a disengagement from the central regulating system whose function is arousal or attentive apprehension[9] of the world, and needs for its activity a constant variation in sensory input. Jasper's studies on diffuse projection system[10] and Penfield's centrencephalic concept[11] have thrown some light on these sub-cortico-cortical connections. Experiences similar to the depersonalization syndrome have been described[13,14] in temporal lobe lesions or stimulations, and the relationship of parietal lobe to asomatognosia is well known.

This hypothesis as such fails to explain the choice of organs from which the feelings are withdrawn, and the process of reorganization which some patients showed during or after isolation. In addition it remains to be proven that the central regulating systems require for their activities constant variations of stimuli, in particular the visual and tactile areas.

(2) RELATIONSHIP HYPOTHESIS: It is evident that in the method of isolation described here, three major areas of relationship to the world, namely visual, tactile and verbal, are being curbed more or less in their activities. If we accept the assumption maintained by Head,[13] Schilder,[14] Lhermitte,[15] Cameron,[16] Scott[8] and others that body-scheme is a dynamic ever changing process, perpetually being altered and reconstructed, it is consistent to state that its integrity depends on a continuous close perceptual and expres-

sional relationship with external objects. As Sullivan[17] and Angyal[18] have stressed, the boundaries of the individual and the world are closely intermingled, and it is extremely difficult to determine a line of demarcation. Total isolation is death. Cameron's concept of "incomplete organism"[19] is such a psycho-biological formulation, which has reached its apotheosis in philosophy of existence where "Dasien"[21] or being-in-world is the unit of experience and inference.

We think that these and other similar concepts can be conceived and linked together in the unifying and unitary concept of "Relationship." We reserve the elaboration of this concept for other occasions, suffice it to say that relationship in this sense may be considered not as a physical linkage, but rather as a concept connoting the way elements or being interconnect, or, as Whitehead has stated,[21] form aspects from the standpoint of one another, constructing orderly or disorderly complexes or organisms.

Isolation disrupts this relationship, prevents interchange, and disorganizes the scheme of the body and its object relationships. However, the disorganization is not random. The prevention of total relationship provokes the emergence of, and a return to less organized levels of relationships — in themselves relatively complete. It should be noted that the isolation setting with the dark room, demand-feeding, and demand evacuation, and ready gratification of oral needs, may be taken as resembling in some respect the situation of infancy. By partially incapacitating the individual's three main areas of relationship, it may be conceived that he is artificially being pushed into the role of an infant whose corresponding three areas are naturally deficient, but without provoking frustration. It can be inferred that this relative anaclitic[2] setting psychologically and somatically pushed the individual into his genetically primitive position wherein the organism is still in parts, and in a state of "natural disembodiment. In psycho-analytic terms isolation stimulates regressive tendencies, and in the Sullivanian formulation it enhances a parataxic mode of experience. The changes in body-scheme may therefore be taken as comparable to the regressively evoked states of infancy where the organism is in "bits and pieces," "Sometimes mostly being good and sometimes mostly being bad"[22]. The second case of

obsessional neuroses described above is a good example of this
primitivization or regression of behaviour. This patient behaved
quite like an infant in his eating and defecating habits.

(3) INTRAPERSONAL HYPOTHESIS: This hypothesis concerns itself
with the psychodynamic changes within the individual emerging
during isolation. We have purposefully refrained from discussing
the preisolation psychodynamics of each patient because (a) from
the range of clinical pictures, it was unlikely that there was any
common dynamic constellation upon which any single conclusion could have been made, or even expected, and (b) a review of
the literature on depersonalization indicates[23, 24, 25] that there are
dynamics referable to almost all stages of development and to
almost all layers of psychic structure in individuals suffering
from this syndrome. It seemed, therefore, that regardless of the
importance of the underlying dynamics, the emerging processes
during isolation would be of greater significance. These
emerging processes were found to be related to the quantity and
direction of aggressive drives. No case which expressed aggression
overtly showed changes in body-scheme. It appeared that when
aggressive tendencies were repressed and turned against the self
the feelings referable to the absence of body-scheme occurred.
There was no constant finding in regard to libidinal tendencies.
The problem arises as to the relationship of this introjection or
turning inward of aggression to the depersonalization states, and
to the etiology of the emergence of aggression. Schematically,
three theoretical formulations can be given: depersonalization as
a defense, as the result of a split in the ego, or as a disorganization
of the self.

Depersonalization has been considered as a *defense* by many
authors,[25-31] whose conceptions imply that the emergence of
intense needs, be it libidinal or aggressive, causes unpleasantness,
anxiety and fear, which results in withdrawal of feelings or interest from the involved organs.

Depersonalization as the result of a split in the ego due to
turning in of aggressive tendencies has been upheld by some
authors.[32, 33]. Freud, in a letter to Oberndorf[31], spoke of depersonalization as a "split in ego." Cameron's conception of the increase
in tension as the cause of the disorganization of the self has

similar implications[16].

It is difficult to find much incompatibility among these concepts. The split in ego or disorganization of the self may be taken as a defense against the anxiety of annihilation or of the confrontation with the drives and their aims. The fact remains that repression of aggression was concomitant with the depersonalization. Why did aggression emerge to begin with? Tentatively one may assume that isolation was a frustrating situation, and aggression was a reaction to frustration. In psychoanalytic terms, isolation provoked frustration of libidinal drives, a narcissistic injury, which evoked aggression. This aggression subsequently was repressed and turned against the self, causing a split in the ego. Or one may say that isolation hindered the expansionistic tendencies of the organism[19] or "power motive"[17] which resulted in an increase in tension and in part disorganized the self and in part enhanced normalization processes and reorganization.

Space does not permit further elaboration of this disorganization-organization sequence. Suffice it to say that one may be able to canalize this reorganization in definite patterns if, during the disorganization, when the organism is most vulnerable in its sets, appropriate modes of action are imposed or suggested to the organism. Cameron's concept of "psychic driving" and "dynamic implant"[34] are useful in this regard.

## Summary

1. The disorganizing effects of sensory isolation on animals and normal human subjects led the authors to study this problem in mental patients for the purpose of gaining some information about the therapeutic value of the disorganization-reorganization sequence of the psychic events and about the problem of depersonalization and body-scheme.

2. Two hebephrenics, five depressions, two obsessive neuroses, and five neurotic anxiety states were subjected to a partial sensory and expressive isolation for an average period of four days (eyes covered, upper extremities maintained in a cardboard cylinder, and no verbal communication except twice a day for interviewing).

3. Two sets of changes occurred:

(a) Disorganization. This consisted of the appearance of a depersonalization state in eight cases; of visual, auditory, and gustatory hallucinoses, and of paresthesias. The two obsessional neuroses developed acute psychotic episodes, were treated with electric shock with subsequent improvement of both paranoid and obsessional states.

(b) Reorganization: This consisted in marked change in mood in almost all of the depressed cases, two of which showed lasting recovery and were discharged without any other therapy. In addition, constructive aggression occurred in most cases with an increasing tendency to socialization and relationship-undertaking. Psychological tests showed no significant impairment in concentration and efficiency.

4. The common emergent dynamic process during isolation which was concomitant with the changes in body-scheme was found to be related to the quantity and direction of aggressive tendencies. It appeared that repression and aggression turned against the self lead to the depersonalization syndrome. The theoretical aspects of the problem are discussed and physiological, relationship, and intrapersonal hypotheses are outlined.

5. It is suggested that the imposition of some action tendencies during the disorganization state may lead to reorganization according to planned patterns, and this may be useful in clarifying the problem of "brainwashing," etc. Further research along the lines described here seems warranted.

## REFERENCES

1. Rosen, H.: Regression therapeutically induced as an emergency measure in a suicidal depressed patient. *J Clin Experim Hypnosis, 3*:58-70.
2. Margolin, S. G.: Psychotherapeutic principles in psychosomatic practice in Wittkower & Cleghorns's *Recent Developments in Psychosomatic Medicine*, Sir Isaac Pitman & Sons Ltd., London, pp. 134-156, 1954.
3. Azima, H.: Prolonged Sleep Treatment in Mental Disorders. *J Ment Sc., 101*:593-603, 1955.
4. Azima, H., and Wittkower, E.: Therapeutic effects of induced regression in prolonged sleep. unpublished data.
5. Gluck, C. Jr., and Reiss, H., and Bernard, L. E.: Regressive electroshock therapy. Presented at 111th Annual Meeting of American Psychiatric

Association, May, 1955.
6. Thompson, W. R., and Heron, W.: The effects of early restriction on activity in dogs. *J Com & Physiological Psychol.*, *47*:77-82, 1954.
7. Bexton, W. H., Heron, W., and Scott, T. H.: Effects of decreased variation in the sensory environment. *Canad J Psychol.*, *8*:70-76, 1954.
8. Scott, W. C. M.: Some embryological, neurological, psychiatric and psychoanalytic implications of the body-scheme. *Int J Psychoanal.*, *29*:141-155, 1948.
9. Azima, H., Cramer, Fern J., and Faure, H.: Le systeme reticule activateur central. Son role en psychopathologie. *Evol Psychiat.*, No. 1:121-144, 1955.
10. Jasper, H. H.: Diffuse projection system: the integrative action of the thalamic reticular system. *E.E.G. Clin Neurophysiol.*, *1*:405-419, 1949.
11. Penfield, W., and Jasper, H. H.: *Epilepsy and Functional Anatomy of the Human Brain*. Little, Brown and Co., Boston, 1954.
12. Penfield, W., and Erickson, T. C.: *Epilepsy and Cerebral Localization*. Thomas, Springfield, 1941.
13. Head, H.: *Aphasia and kindred disorders of speech*. McMillan, New York, 1926.
14. Schilder, P.: The image and appearance of the human body. International Univ Press, New York, 1950.
15. Lhermitte, J.: L'image de notre corps. *Nouvelle Revue Critique*, Paris, 1939.
16. Cameron, D. E.: Personal communication.
17. Sullivan, H. S.: *Conceptions of Modern Psychiatry*. The William Allanson White Psychiatric Foundation, Washington, D.C., 1947.
18. Angyal, A.: Foundations for a science of personality. *New York Commonwealth Fund*, 1941.
19. Cameron, D. E.: *General Psychotherapy*. Grune and Stratton, Inc., New York, pp. 2-8, 1950.
20. Heidegger, M.: *Existence and Being*. Regnery, Chicago, 1949.
21. Whitehead, A. N.: *Science and the Modern World*. Mentor Book, New York, pp. 66, 1949.
22. Scott, W. C. M.: Personal Communication.
23. Premier Congre Mondial de Psychiatrie, Section "Psychopathologie Generale," Chapter "Depersonalization." Paris, 1950.
24. Ackner, B.: Depersonalization, 1: Aetiology and phenomenology. *J Ment Sc*, *100*:838-853, 1954.
25. Fenichel, O.: *The Psychoanalytic Theory of Neuroses*. W. W. Norton & Company, Inc., New York, pp. 418, 1945.
26. Bergler, E., and Eidelberg, L.: Der mechanismus des Depersonalization. *Int Ztsch f Psychoanal*, *21*, 1935. (Cited by Bykowski.)
27. Feigenbaum, D.: Depersonalization as a defense mechanism. *Psychoanal Quart*, *6*:4-11.
28. Federn, P.: Narcissism in the structure of the ego. *Int J Psychoanal*, *9*:403-419, 1928.

29. Searl, N.: A note on depersonalization. *Int J Psychoanal, 13*:329-347, 1932.
30. Bykowski, G.: *Psychotherapy of Psychoses.* Grune and Stratton, New York, 1952.
31. Oberndorf, C. P.: The role of anxiety on depersonalization. *Int J Psychoanal, 31*:1-5, 1950.
32. Rosenfeld, H.: Analysis of a schizophrenic state with depersonalization. *Int J Psychoanal, 28*:130-139, 1947.
33. Flescher, J.: On neurotic disorders of sensibility and body-scheme. *Int J Psychoanal, 29*:156-162, 1948.
34. Cameron, D. E.: Psychic driving: Dynamic Implant. Presented at 111th annual meeting of American Psychiatric Association, May 1955.

# Chapter 2

# THERAPEUTIC CHANGES IN PSYCHIATRIC PATIENTS FOLLOWING PARTIAL SENSORY DEPRIVATION*
## A Pilot Study

ROBERT G. GIBBY, Ph.D.; HENRY B. ADAMS, Ph.D.,
AND RICHARD N. CARRERA, Ph.D.

$A$ NUMBER of reports have been published on the effects of drastic and prolonged reduction of normal environmental stimuli on human beings. Dramatic phenomena, such as depersonalization, hallucinations, thought disturbances, and other symptoms customarily associated with mental illness, have occurred under such conditions. Many investigators have regarded conditions of sensory deprivation as inherently stressful, and their published observations have placed great emphasis on the pathological consequences of prolonged sensory deprivation for normal subjects.

In a representative study, Wexler, Mendelson, Leiderman, and Solomon[1] (1958) subjected normal subjects to perceptual and sensory deprivation for periods up to thirty-six hours. They observed a variety of pathological events in these subjects, such as "pseudosomatic delusions, illusions, or hallucinations," and noted that "all subjects showed impaired ability to concentrate, distortions in time judgment, and degrees of anxiety." Further, they described sensory deprivation procedures as useful in inducing stress and in producing psychotic-like symptoms. In a recent survey of the literature, Solomon, Leiderman, Mendelson, and Wexler[2] (1957) reviewed autobiographical accounts of prolonged environmental isolation, reports of "brainwashing" of prisoners of war, and experimental laboratory studies, almost all of which stressed the disruptive effects of drastic, prolonged sen-

---

*Reprinted from the *Archives of General Psychiatry*, July 1960, Volume 3, pp. 33-42. Copyright 1960, American Medical Association.

sory deprivation on normal mental functioning. Such views have come to have widespread acceptance.

On the other hand, a few seemingly contradictory reports have also appeared, suggesting that under certain conditions sensory-deprivation procedures may have positive beneficial effects for some persons. Vernon and Hoffman[3] (1956) placed four college students in confined isolation for a period of forty-eight hours and tested their learning rate by means of a word list presented before, during, and after the sensory-deprivation experience. Comparing the performance of the four experimental subjects with a control group, they stated that "the ability to learn adjective lists improves with continued sensory deprivation." But it is noteworthy that the isolation and sensory deprivation had to be interrupted whenever the learning task was presented, so that the subjects were actually tested during periods when they were not undergoing the experience of sensory deprivation itself.

Azima and Cramer-Azima[4] (1956) exposed fourteen psychiatric patients representing four diagnostic categories to "partial sensory and expressive isolation" for periods averaging four days. They found two sets of changes occurring. First to be observed was a "disorganization of psychic structure which, according to the kind and quality of defenses, may lead to a psychotic state." In most cases the disorganization was followed by "reorganization of some aspects of a previously unsteady psychic state." This reorganization was accompanied by "constructive aggression" and an "increased tendency to socialization and relationship-undertaking." Following such reorganization, psychological testing showed "no significant impairment in concentration and efficiency." It was suggested that "the imposition of some action tendencies during the disorganization state may lead to reorganization according to planned patterns." This suggestion implies that sensory deprivation may produce positive therapeutic effects, as well as the negative phenomena reported by some other investigators.

In another investigation, Harris[5] (1959) placed schizophrenic patients under sensory deprivation for short periods, observing that they tolerated the experience much better than did normals and that in many patients the intensity of psychotic hallucinatory symptoms was reduced. Further, the constructive and therapeutic potential of sensory deprivation under certain conditions was suggested in a recent review by Lilly[6] (1956) of eighteen autobiographical accounts of survivors of prolonged social isolation. He commented that even though the persons involved had experienced some of the symptoms of mental illness, most of them also found "a new inner security and a new integration of themselves on a deep and basic level." The references cited above make it clear that isolation and sensory deprivation do not always have the same effects.

On the basis of the available evidence it appears reasonable to expect that a relatively short period of minimal social interaction, coupled with a reduction of environmental stimulation of less drastic degree than that reported in the majority of published studies, might produce a number of beneficial changes in psychiatric patients. If it could be shown that one comparatively short period of social isolation and reduced sensory stimulation could induce tendencies toward beneficial changes such as the increased socialization, the inner security, and the reorganization and integration of personality reported elsewhere, the therapeutic implications might have great theoretical and practical significance.

With the above considerations in mind, the present investigators initiated a long-range program of research to determine the differential effects of social isolation and partial sensory deprivation on psychiatric patients. The procedure used was first developed in a series of unpublished exploratory studies conducted by Gibby at Marion, Ind., in 1955. The procedure is characterized by (1) a reduction of stimuli with the use of ear plugs and eye coverings; (2) relatively brief temporal duration; (3) partial sensory deprivation, with vision and audition the only two sensory modalities being directly affected, and (4) minimal social stimulation, interaction, and feedback during the experiment.

This paper reports a pilot study of thirty psychiatric patients who were subjected to intensive study and observation before, during, and after exposure to the above procedure. It is concerned only with the changes in behavior observed in interviews conducted before and after the patients were exposed to the sensory-deprivation and social-isolation procedure. Other findings will be treated in further papers. This study deals with the primary question: "What differential changes occur in the behavior of a diagnostically heterogeneous group of psychiatric subjects following a single brief exposure to conditions of minimal social interaction and partial sensory deprivation?"

## Method

A total of thirty subjects were subjected to the experimental procedure. All were white male inpatients on the neuropsychiatric service of a VA general medical and surgical hospital. None of the patients had a known history or diagnosis of organic brain damage, and none was receiving any psychotherapy or psychiatric chemotherapy at the time he was placed in the experimental situation. All forms of shock therapy had been discontinued at least thirty days prior to the date the subject was to begin the scheduled sequence of experimental activities.

The age and educational characteristics of the subjects are set forth in detail in Table 2-I. Diagnostically, the patients formed a heterogeneous group, the primary psychiatric diagnoses of eight being classified as schizophrenic reactions, of thirteen as psychoneurotic disorders, of eight as personality disorders, and of one as a psychophysiologic autonomic and visceral disorder, the standard APA diagnostic classification (1956) being used.

Each subject chosen for the study was placed on a fifteen day

TABLE 2-I

AGE AND EDUCATIONAL CHARACTERISTICS
OF THE SUBJECTS

(N=30)

|  | Range | Median | Mean | S.D. |
|---|---|---|---|---|
| Age | 23-48 | 35 | 35.0 | 6.9 |
| Years of school* | 4-16 | 11 | 10.8 | 3.1 |

*Educational data for one subject were not available.

experimental schedule. On the first day all psychiatric chemo-therapy was discontinued. On the seventh day the subject was interviewed by a psychologist, and his interview behavior was rated on each of the twenty items of the Symptom Rating Scale developed for the VA Psychiatric Evaluation Project (Jenkins, Stauffacher, and Hester,[7] 1959). The subject was given a battery of psychological tests, and a psychiatric interview, and ratings were made of his ward behavior.

On the eighth day the subject was scheduled for the deprivation experience. He was placed in a quiet, air-conditioned observation room for a period not to exceed six hours. During this time he lay on a bed with his eyes covered by a ball of cotton underneath a plastic eyepiece, his ears plugged with glycerin-soaked cotton, and his head wrapped in a gauze bandage. The observer did not speak to the subject at any time until he was removed by the experimenter, or until he terminated the procedure himself. Before the ear, eye, and head coverings were applied, each subject was told that he could leave the deprivation situation at any time he wished, but was not told that there would be any time limit.

The subject received minimal auditory and visual cues to remind him of the observer's presence, since meaningfully patterned visual and auditory stimuli were reduced by head and eye coverings and cotton plugs. The air conditioner kept temperature and humidity at a constant level. Every subject was thus exposed to a relatively unvarying stimulus environment, with visual, auditory, and temperature stimulation held constantly at a low or moderate level, and with meaningfully patterned visual and auditory cues virtually eliminated. Moreover, no attempt was made to diminish tactual and kinesthetic cues. Each subject was free to move around while lying on the bed, his arms, legs, hands, and feet being free of restraints. During this period each subject was constantly observed, and his verbalizations were recorded on tape. Every fifteen minutes the observer made a rating of the degree of anxiety overtly manifested in the subject's movements and behavior.

On the ninth day the interviews, ratings, and psychological tests which had been given on the seventh day were repeated.

On the fifteenth day the subject was interviewed for a third time by a psychologist and his behavior rated once more on the Symptom Rating Scale, each subject being seen by the same interviewer for all three interviews. By the end of the fifteenth day all the scheduled procedures had been completed.

After each subject completed the fifteen-day schedule, three sets of interview behavioral ratings had been obtained. Ratings were made by four interviewers: two were Ph.D. staff members, and two were advanced doctoral trainees in clinical psychology. Numerical ratings, ranging from one to four, were given to the degree of overt pathology observed in the interview on each item of the Symptom Rating Scale.

The analysis of the rating scale data was concerned with changes which occurred after deprivation. Items on which the numerical ratings were the same on the first, second, and third interviews were classified as showing no changes. If the numerical ratings on a given item for the first and second interviews were different, the subject was considered to have shown a short-term change in the behavior pattern denoted by that item. If the numerical ratings on a given item for the first and third interviews were different, the subject was considered as having shown a long-term change. Direction of change was also taken into account. Changes on numerical ratings in the direction of less severity of symptoms were designated as positive, while those in the direction of increased severity were designated as negative.

## Results and Comment

Table 2-II summarizes the statistically significant changes (in both directions) on the individual items of the Symptom Rating Scale, indicating those items on which the percentage of subjects showing short-term or long-term changes in either direction was significantly different from zero. Not all the subjects exposed to deprivation were included in the data on which Table 2-II is based. Of the thirty subjects, two were not seen by the same interviewer the day following sensory deprivation, and hence the number of subjects for which short-term changes are reported is twenty-eight. For the same reason, the number of subjects for which long-term changes are listed is twenty-three.

TABLE 2-II

SYMPTOM RATING SCALE ITEMS ON WHICH THE PERCENTAGES
OF SUBJECTS SHOWING CHANGES IN EITHER DIRECTION
ATTAINED STATISTICAL SIGNIFICANCE

| | Short-Term Changes (N=28) | | Long-Term Changes (N=23) | |
| | Positive | Negative | Positive | Negative |
| Symptom Rating Scale Item | P | P | P | P |
|---|---|---|---|---|
| Withdrawn | 0.01 | 0.05 | 0.01 | n.s. |
| Evasive, guarded | 0.001 | 0.01 | 0.01 | n.s. |
| Uncooperative in interview | 0.05 | 0.01 | 0.001 | 0.05 |
| Lack of positive rapport | 0.05 | 0.05 | 0.01 | n.s. |
| Disoriented | n.s. | n.s. | n.s. | n.s. |
| Disorganized thinking | 0.05 | 0.05 | 0.01 | n.s. |
| Bizarre motor behavior | n.s. | n.s. | 0.05 | n.s. |
| Hallucinations | n.s. | n.s. | n.s. | n.s. |
| Suspiciousness | 0.05 | n.s. | 0.05 | n.s. |
| Manifest evidence of depression | 0.01 | 0.05 | 0.01 | 0.05 |
| Reported feelings of depression | 0.001 | n.s. | 0.01 | 0.05 |
| Apathy | 0.01 | n.s. | 0.01 | n.s. |
| Memory deficit | n.s. | n.s. | n.s. | n.s. |
| Manifest symptoms of anxiety | 0.001 | 0.05 | 0.01 | n.s. |
| Reported feelings of anxiety | 0.001 | n.s. | 0.01 | n.s. |
| Somatic complaints | 0.01 | n.s. | 0.02 | n.s. |
| Unmotivated toward life goals | n.s. | n.s. | 0.05 | 0.05 |
| Vagueness of posthospital goals | 0.05 | n.s. | 0.02 | 0.05 |
| Vagueness of goals of hospitalization | n.s. | 0.05 | 0.05 | 0.01 |
| Excessive hostility | n.s. | 0.01 | 0.05 | n.s. |

The number of items on which statistically significant percentages of subjects showed changes was far greater than would be expected by chance. Changes in the positive direction were more numerous, particularly long-term changes. Of the twenty scale items, there were thirteen in which the percentage of subjects showing short-term positive changes was significant, and seventeen in which the percentage showing a long-term positive change attained significance. By contrast, the percentage of subjects making short-term negative changes was significant for only nine items, and the percentage having long-term negative changes was significant on only six of the items.

The results presented in Table 2-II indicate that the effects of sensory deprivation on individual subjects varied, inasmuch as statistically significant percentages of subjects showed changes in both positive and negative directions on several of the items. However, the results in Table 2-II indicate that the positive changes, as far as the group as a whole was concerned, were in general more lasting than the negative changes. To verify this impression, a separate tabulation was made of all the items on which the percentage of subjects changing in a given direction was statistically significant for both short-term and long-term intervals. Items meeting this criterion (which are regarded as representative of more enduring changes) are listed in Table 2-III.

Table 2-III lists sixteen items which met the above criterion, and on thirteen of these the change was in the direction of less pathology. There are two scale items which showed enduring

TABLE 2-III

SYMPTOM RATING SCALE ITEMS ON WHICH PATIENTS
SHOWED ENDURING CHANGES OVER BOTH SHORT-TERM AND
LONG-TERM INTERVALS WHICH WERE STATISTICALLY
SIGNIFICANT AND IN SAME DIRECTION

| Symptom Rating Scale Item | Direction | Short-Term Changes (N=28) $P$ | Long-Term Changes (N=23) $P$ |
|---|---|---|---|
| Withdrawn | Less | 0.01 | 0.01 |
| Evasive, guarded | Less | 0.001 | 0.01 |
| Uncooperative in interview | Less | 0.05 | 0.001 |
| Uncooperative in interview | More | 0.01 | 0.05 |
| Lack of positive rapport | Less | 0.05 | 0.01 |
| Disorganized thinking | Less | 0.05 | 0.01 |
| Suspiciousness | Less | 0.05 | 0.05 |
| Manifest evidence of depression | Less | 0.01 | 0.01 |
| Manifest evidence of depression | More | 0.05 | 0.05 |
| Reported feelings of depression | Less | 0.001 | 0.01 |
| Apathy | Less | 0.01 | 0.01 |
| Manifest symptoms of anxiety | Less | 0.001 | 0.01 |
| Reported feelings of anxiety | Less | 0.001 | 0.01 |
| Somatic complaints | Less | 0.01 | 0.02 |
| Vagueness of posthospital goals | Less | 0.05 | 0.02 |
| Vagueness of goals of hospitalization | More | 0.05 | 0.01 |

changes in both directions: The percentages of subjects becoming
less cooperative in the interview and the percentages becoming
more cooperative were both significant, as were the percentages of
those showing evidence of both less depression and more depression. A significant percentage of the subjects also changed in the
direction of more vagueness when asked about immediate hospital goals. But, with these exceptions, exposure to the experimental conditions resulted in enduring changes for the better,
which were reflected in a wide variety of measures of overt behavior.

TABLE 2-IV

NUMBERS OF SUBJECTS CHANGING IN POSITIVE AND
NEGATIVE DIRECTIONS PER ITEM OF THE SYMPTOM RATING SCALE

| | Range | Median | Mean | Difference | S.D. | $t$ | $P$ |
|---|---|---|---|---|---|---|---|
| Short-term changes (N=28) | | | | | | | |
| Positive direction | 0-14 | 5.0 | 5.6 | | 3.8* | | |
| | | | | 2.6 | | 3.06 | 0.01 |
| Negative direction | 0-7 | 3.0 | 3.0 | | 2.3* | | |
| Long-term changes (N=23) | | | | | | | |
| Positive direction | 0-9 | 5.5 | 5.1 | | 2.6* | | |
| | | | | 3.3 | | 4.96 | 0.001 |
| Negative direction | 0-6 | 1.5 | 1.8 | | 1.7* | | |

*Differences between the sample standard deviations for both the short-term and the long-
term changes were significant at the 0.05 level.

Table 2-IV, showing numbers of subjects changing in both
directions per item of the Symptom Rating Scale, reveals that,
while there were a few items on which no subjects showed
changes, some subjects shifted on most of the items. In addition,
subjects changing positively outnumbered those changing negatively. The significance of differences between mean numbers of
subjects shifting in positive and negative directions was evaluated
for both short-term and long-term changes. In both cases the
mean number of subjects changing positively was significantly
greater, especially in the case of long-term changes. Positive shifters were about the same for both short-term and long-term intervals, but the number of negative shifters dropped appreciably

over the longer time interval. The data indicate that the negative changes were less enduring than positive changes and that subjects changing in the positive direction clearly outnumbered those shifting in the opposite direction on both post-deprivation interviews.

While the group as a whole showed amelioration of pathological symptoms following exposure to the experimental conditions, it is equally important to note the wide range of individual differences. Table 2-V shows the numbers of scale items per individual subject on which positive and negative changes were observed. The extensive range of individual differences is readily apparent.

Some subjects showed no changes on any items. At the other extreme, there were individual subjects who changed for the better on thirteen out of the twenty items, suggesting that for them the experience of sensory deprivation had led to broad, generalized improvement involving many facets of behavior. Conversely, there were subjects who showed evidence of extensive exacerbation of symptoms following the same experience, with

TABLE 2-V

NUMBER OF ITEMS PER SUBJECT SHOWING CHANGES IN
POSITIVE AND NEGATIVE DIRECTIONS ON SYMPTOM
RATING SCALE

(Total Number of Items=20)

| | Range | Median | Mean | Difference | S.D. | $t$ | $P$ |
|---|---|---|---|---|---|---|---|
| Short-term changes | | | | | | | |
| Positive changes | 0-13 | 3.8 | 3.9 | | 3.0 | | |
| | | | | 1.9 | | 2.50 | 0.02 |
| Negative changes | 0-10 | 2.2 | 2.0 | | 2.4 | | |
| Long-term changes | | | | | | | |
| Positive changes | 0-12 | 3.7 | 4.3 | | 3.3* | | |
| | | | | 2.9 | | 4.63 | 0.001 |
| Negative changes | 0- 5 | 1.8 | 1.4 | | 1.2* | | |

*The difference between the two sample standard deviations was significant at the 0.001 level.

short-term negative changes on as many as ten out of the twenty scale items.

Although there was a wide range of individual differences, it is nevertheless useful to know how the typical subject was affected by his experience. The means and medians given in Table 2-V indicate that the average subject showed positive changes on about four items and negative changes on about two. When the significance of differences between mean numbers of positive and negative item changes was evaluated, the number of positive changes was found to exceed significantly the number of negative changes over both short-term and long-term intervals.

The more enduring properties of the positive changes as contrasted with negative changes were assessed by correlational methods. It was inferred that if the positive changes were relatively long lasting, subjects making the greatest number of short-term positive changes on the scale items should also have the greatest number of long-term changes. Hence, positive short-term and long-term changes should be substantially correlated. Table 2-VI shows that this expectation was confirmed. Each subject was ranked according to the number of short-term and long-term positive changes, and the two sets of ranks were then intercorrelated.

TABLE 2-VI

INTERCORRELATIONS BETWEEN RANKINGS OF
SUBJECTS BY NUMBER OF ITEMS ON SYMPTOM
RATING SCALE SHOWING CHANGES FOLLOWING
EXPOSURE TO SENSORY DEPRIVATION

| Specific Types of Changes | No. of Subjects | $p$ | $P$ |
|---|---|---|---|
| Short-term and long-term changes | | | |
| Positive changes | 21 | 0.70 | 0.01 |
| Negative changes | 21 | 0.33 | n.s. |
| Positive changes and negative changes | | | |
| Short-term changes | 28 | 0.29 | n.s. |
| Long-term changes | 23 | -0.09 | n.s. |

A Spearman rank-difference correlation of 0.70 was obtained, which is significant at the 0.01 level. This indicates that subjects who were improved a day after the deprivation experience re-
· tained substantially the same degree of improvement over a one-week interval.

Using the same statistical procedures, the short-term and long-term negative changes were also intercorrelated, but the obtained correlation of 0.33 was not statistically significant. It would appear, then, that exposure to the experimental conditions did not result in enduring adverse changes comparable in extent to the positive changes. These two correlational findings are consistent with other observations suggesting that the beneficial therapeutic changes following sensory deprivation were relatively lasting, while the negative changes represented a more temporary upsurge of pathological symptoms.

A similar question, which was also dealt with by means of the correlational analysis shown in the lower half of Table 2-VI, was whether the occurrence of positive changes in individual subjects was associated in any definite way with the occurrence of negative changes. Short-term positive and negative changes were ranked and intercorrelated, using the procedures described in the preceding paragraph. The procedure was also repreated for the long-term positive and negative changes. As shown in Table 2-VI, both the resulting Spearman correlation coefficients were low, and neither was statistically significant. These two low correlations indicate that the appearance of overt positive changes was not related statistically to the appearance of negative changes. Thus, the enduring positive and therapeutic changes which followed exposure to the experimental conditions were independent (at least statistically) of the negative changes.

The tabulated results show clearly that the psychiatric subjects exposed to the deprivation conditions were altered by their experience, mainly for the better. But what was the nature of the underlying process which took place? Some additional observations are pertinent.

In general, the subjects demonstrated an increased desire for social contacts, and, in particular, for therapeutic relationships with the professional staff. After the deprivation experience, the subjects expressed in a variety of ways their increased awareness of inner conflicts and anxieties, and heightened perception of the fact that their difficulties stemmed from inner rather than from outer factors. The experimental conditions of minimal social interaction and reduced sensory input seem to have induced a social "stimulus hunger," manifested behaviorally by generalized efforts to relate and communicate with others. Presumably, they also induced distinct needs to discuss their new awareness of personal problems. These observations are consistent with those reported by other investigators, who noted that after sensory deprivation subjects of all types displayed a greatly increased need for contact with other persons and objects in the environment.

A second major change observed was a less rigid utilization of repressive and inhibitory defenses. The reduction of incoming stimulation led to recall and verbalization of previously forgotten experiences in many instances. For some subjects this recall was anxiety inducing, possibly accounting for the initial upsurge of behavioral manifestations of anxiety and emotional disturbance seen in certain persons. In others sensory deprivation brought about a decrease of inhibitory defenses, resulting in open expressions of hostility, which then subsided. In such cases the release of bottled-up negative affect was followed by a new inner tranquility. The blocking off of accustomed stimulation for a few hours may have facilitated a process of reassessment and reorganization of stimulus-response patterns carried over from earlier life experiences.

It is relevant to cite some observations made by Jenkins, Stauffacher, and Hester,[7] who developed the rating scale on which the results are based. They found that certain items were associated with favorable prognosis in hospitalized patients. These included cooperation in interview, positive emotional involvement in the interview, reported feelings of anxiety, and complaints about physical health. On all four of these items, enduring changes in the direction of improvement were observed in subjects in the present study. Jenkins et al. mentioned four other items which were indicative of an unfavorable prognosis, namely, withdrawal, disorganization of thinking, apathy, and lack of motivation toward significant life goals. Enduring positive changes in the direction of a decrease in these symptoms were found on all but one of these items in the present study. The authors cited observed that "the symptoms of favorable prognostic import relate to the patient's willingness or capacity to communicate with the interviewer, whereas those of unfavorable diagnostic import relate to lack of communication or to the patient's lack of motivation."[8] Positive changes on these scale items thus imply that exposure to the particular conditions used in the present investigation increased the motivation and effectiveness of a group of psychiatric patients in communicating and relating to other persons. Such changes also appear to have been associated with an improved prognosis for recovery from psychiatric disorder.

The findings reported in this paper may at first glance seem inconsistent with some other published reports of the effects of sensory deprivation. Although the present investigators found evidence of the arousal of social- and environmental-stimulus hunger in subjects after deprivation, the disruptive and pathological changes so often described by others were far less pronounced, and the beneficial therapeutic changes were more prominent. These seeming discrepancies may be of great significance and should be given careful consideration.

In an unpublished paper dealing with research on the effects of isolation, confinement, and sensory deprivation, Ruff, Levy, and Thaler outlined seven classes of variables which they consider important in planning such research. These include (1) the objective reality circumstances under which the isolation or sensory deprivation takes place, e.g. in a prison, a life raft, or a planned laboratory experiment; (2) characteristics of individual subjects, such as personality traits, background, motivation; (3) the extent to which the conditions create a sense of "aloneness" or of being separated, detached, or estranged from the real world; (4) the degree of communication or "feed-back" from other persons experienced by the subjects; (5) the degree of physical confinement; (6) the extent of constriction of the subjects' perceptual space, and (7) the modality, quantity, and pattern of sensory input. In addition to the seven they suggest, there appears to be one other variable of major importance in sensory-deprivation research, namely, the length or duration of the deprivation experience in time. For some of these variables the conditions set up in this investigation differed sufficiently from those employed in other studies to suggest that the differences in experimental conditions may have accounted for the differing results. One variable of particular importance is the temporal duration of the exposure to sensory deprivation. In the majority of published studies in which disruption of normal mental processes was reported, the disruptive phenomena did not begin to appear until after the reduction of sensory input had continued for prolonged periods of time. Delusions, hallucinations, and thought disturbances have rarely been observed except where conditions of reduced stimulation had been maintained for periods of several days. Perhaps the only major exception is set forth in Lilly's[9] account (1956), in which projection of visual imagery and hypnagogic-like phenomena were experienced by subjects during immersion in a tank for not more than three hours. But in his investigation, the conditions of physical confinement, constriction of perceptual space, and reduction in the modality, quantity, and pattern of sensory input were far more drastic than those in other studies. From comparison of the results presented in the present paper with those reported elsewhere, it seems reasonable to conclude that disruption of organized intellectual and perceptual processes does not occur until after a fairly drastic reduction of normal stimulation has continued without interruption over an extended period. It is also likely that beneficial and therapeutic types of changes take place *before* negative, disruptive tendencies begin to appear.

Lilly's account of his own experiments seems consistent with these suggestions. He reported that his subjects went through the following series of phenomenally experienced stages: (1) domination of consciousness by residues of recent experiences; (2) gradual restful relaxation; (3) onset of an acute stimulus-action hunger, with intense satisfaction resulting from self-stimulation; (4) gradual focusing of consciousness on whatever residual source of stimulation still remains; (5) shift to highly personalized, emotionally charged fantasies, and, finally, (6) the hypnagogic-like projection of visual imagery. Lilly did not continue his experiments beyond this stage to the point where severer forms of thought and perceptual disturbances were encountered, but it is noteworthy that the first perceptual anomalies described by him did not appear until after a number of other subjectively gratifying internal events had first transpired.

A second major difference between the present study and many of the others lies in the choice of subjects. It is quite possible that the effects of sensory deprivation on psychiatric patients may be quite different from effects on normals, with which most published studies have been concerned. But Harris stated that a group of schizophrenic patients exposed to sensory deprivation for short periods "were more tolerant than normal subjects of these conditions, which seemed to reduce the intensity of hallucinations" among the patients (1959).[10] He commented that "the hallucinations occurring in mental disease differ sharply from those produced by sensory deprivation in normal subjects in regard to the conditions which elicit or suppress them," and added that "normal sensory stimuli reinforce hallucinatory experiences in schizophrenia, in contrast to the effect of visual deprivation in mentally healthy individuals which can produce visual hallucinations." Although most of the patients used as subjects in the present study were not diagnosed as being schizophrenic, there is, nevertheless, reason for believing that Harris's observations may be applicable to other diagnostic categories.

The present study also differs from others as to when observations of the effects of deprivation were made. Most published studies have been concerned with effects which appeared during or immediately after exposure to the deprivation conditions. Few investigators have made any systematic comparisons of changes after deprivation, particularly over longer intervals of time. But in view of the findings reported in this paper, it would seem that the disruptive effects so frequently stressed in other publications are probably of a temporary nature. In the present study systematic observation of after-effects showed that positive changes were more numerous and more lasting than negative, disruptive changes. It is quite likely that other investigators might have reported similar findings had they observed their subjects over longer periods of time.

## Summary

Thirty white male VA neuropsychiatric patients, representing major categories of functional psychiatric disorders, were subjected to social isolation and deprivation of visual and auditory stimuli. They were placed in a quiet air-conditioned observation room, where they lay on a bed with their eyes covered and ears plugged for a period of not more than six hours. The subjects were free to terminate the experiment at any time they wished. Although they were observed continuously, the observer did not speak or reply to anything they said. Social interaction was minimized, and meaningfully patterned visual and auditory stimulus cues were virtually eliminated.

The subjects were interviewed a day before, a day after, and a week after the deprivation experience, and the interview behavior was rated numerically on a twenty-item Symptom Rating Scale. Changes on the scale items following the deprivation experience were then systematically tabulated and analyzed.

The number of subjects showing changes in both the positive (better) and the negative (worse) direction on the rating scale was much greater than chance, but positive changes for the group as a whole considerably outnumbered negative changes. Furthermore, positive changes were more enduring than negative changes. Positive changes apparently reflected more persisting internal modifications of a beneficial and therapeutic nature, while the negative changes appeared to be manifestations of a temporary upsurge or anxiety and emotional disturbance which later subsided.

A wide range of individual differences was found. Some subjects made extensive improvement; some showed no change, and some became much worse after the deprivation. For the average subject, positive changes occurred more than twice as often as negative changes. It was also found that individual subjects who did improve tended to hold virtually all their improvement. On the other hand, negative changes were not found to operate in any comparably consistent manner.

The results strongly suggested previously unsuspected psychotherapeutic possibilities of sensory deprivation methods, and appeared to be inconsistent with many other published investigations which stressed the disruptive effects of sensory deprivation on mental functioning. Three factors were suggested as possible explanations of the seeming inconsistencies: (1) The time of exposure and the reduction of total sensory input in the present study were less drastic and prolonged than in many other investigations; (2) whereas most other published studies have used normal subjects, we used psychiatric patients, on whom the effects of sensory deprivation may be different, and (3) systematic observations were made of changes over an extended period of time before and after deprivation, resulting in the finding of lasting positive changes which previous investigators may have overlooked.

## REFERENCES

1. Wexler, D., Mendelson, J., Leiderman, P.H., and Solomon, P.: Sensory Deprivation: A technique for studying psychiatric aspects of stress. *A.M.A. Arch. Neurol. & Psychiat., 79*:225-233, 1958, p. 233.
2. Solomon, P., Leiderman, P.H., Mendelson, J., and Wexler, D.: Sensory Deprivation. *Am. J. Psychiat., 114*:357-363, 1957.
3. Vernon, J., and Hoffman, J.: Effect of sensory deprivation on learning rate in human beings. *Science, 123*:1074-1075, 1956.
4. Azima, H., and Cramer-Azima, F.J.: Effects of partial perceptual isolation in mentally disturbed individuals. *Dis. Nerv. System, 17*:117-122, 1956.
5. Harris, A.: Sensory deprivation and schizophrenia. *J. Ment. Sc., 105*:235-237, 1959.
6. Lilly, J.: GAP Symposium No. 2. June, 1956, pp. 13-20.
7. Jenkins, R.F., Stauffacher, J., and Hester, R.: A symptom rating scale for use with psychotic patients. *A.M.A. Arch. Gen. Psychiat., 1*:197-204, 1959.
8. Jenkins, A symptom rating scale. p. 201.
9. Lilly, GAP Symposium.
10. Harris, Sensory deprivation. p. 237.

# Chapter 3

# REACTIONS TO PERCEPTUAL ISOLATION AND RORSCHACH MANIFESTATIONS OF THE PRIMARY PROCESS*

LEO GOLDBERGER, Ph.D.

THE phenomena produced in response to perceptual isolation in normal, human adults, have recently been of great interest to psychologists, psychiatrists, and the military services (Solomon et al., 1957 & Wheaton, 1959). These phenomena, consisting principally of thought disturbances of various kinds, and, in some instances, of hallucination-like imagery, have mainly been investigated within a neuropsychological framework, in which the problems of individual differences and their personality correlates are generally neglected. The present study represents a beginning attempt to study isolation effects within a psychoanalytic framework with particular attention to the problem of individual differences (see also Goldberger & Holt, 1958 and Holt & Goldberger, 1959).

The aim of this study was to predict some selected isolation effects from the knowledge of a person's ego structure. The characterological variable used as the predictor was a person's *mode of handling the primary process*, as gauged by the Rorschach test according to a scoring manual developed by Holt (1956 and Holt & Havel, 1960) for that purpose. The general hypothesis underlying the study was that the *manner in which a person* reacts to a situation permitting only limited contact with the structure of the external world (i.e. diminished "reality contact") would be predictably related to the management of the primary process in his enduring ego structure. A secondary aim was the exploration of

*From the *Journal of Projective Techniques*, 1961, 25:287-302, 1961. Courtesy of the Society of Projective Techniques, Inc.

relationships other than those explicitly hypothesized in order to stimulate future research in this area.

The over-all design was: (1) Ss were given the Rorschach, and the protocols were scored "blind" to assess the amount and mode of handling of primary-process manifestations. This measure was related, by a number of specific hypotheses, to a variety of selected isolation effects (the dependent variables); (2) Ss were isolated for a period of eight hours (under conditions of maximum homogeneity of external stimulation), during which time they were encouraged to talk freely about their thoughts and feelings; and (3) The predicted effects were assessed by administering a pre- and postisolation battery of cognitive tests, and by clinical ratings derived from the records kept of each S's isolation behavior, verbal productions and postisolation behavior.

## Theoretical Considerations

Two major theoretical formulations have been advanced to explain the isolation data. They derive from different levels of behavior analysis and should not be regarded as mutually exclusive.

The first formulation, employed in the McGill studies (Bexton, Heron & Scott, 1954; Hebb, 1955a; Hebb, 1955b; Heron, Doane & Scott, 1956), is based on recent neurophysiological evidence. Briefly, it states that environmental stimulation travels to the cortex via two routes. One is by way of the classical projection system through the thalamus to the cortex, the other is by way of the nonspecific, diffuse projection system of the reticular formation in the brainstem. The latter transmission is slow and devious, but is essential for the maintenance of *"arousal"* and organized cortical functioning and hence for adaptive behavior. With repetitive or homogeneous stimulation, the diffuse projection system rapidly becomes *"habituated"*; i.e. it loses its effectiveness in maintaining cortical "arousal." When this occurs, cortical functioning becomes disorganized and hypersynchronous firing of cells increasingly takes place. Psychologically, this may be reflected by such phenomena as hallucinations, thought-disturbances, and motivational drift. The isolation effects, in this view, are interpreted as reflections of a general *"habituation syndrome."* The problem of individual differences in isolation effects is neglected by this formulation.

The second formulation — the one employed in the present study — is based on psychoanalytic theory. The isolation situation, viewed from a psychoanalytic vantage point, is essentially one in which reality contact is diminished, taking the concept "reality contact" quite concretely to mean contact with the structure of the external world via the extereoceptors. The general isolation effects obtained by the previous investigators may readily be conceptualized as reflecting a reduction in secondary-process thinking and an increased tendency to engage in primary-process thinking*. Now, in relating the effects to the situation, we are led to the formulation, advanced by Holt (1953) that: "Secondary-process thinking depends on perceptual contact with the structure of the external world — " 'reality contact.' " Or, stating this conversely: *absence of reality contact facilitates the emergence of primary-process thinking.*

The hypothesized relationship between mode of thought and the presence or absence of reality contact is not a new one. It is particularly emphasized in the theory of ego development in which primary-process thinking is seen as arising during that

---

*The concepts of the "primary process" and the "secondary process" have a variety of controversial theoretical connotations attached to them, as a cursory review of the relevant psychoanalytic literature will show (Brenner, 1957; Fenichel, 1946; Fisher, 1957; Freud, 1925; Freud, 1933; Freud, 1954; Freud, 1955). In general, however, there is agreement that the "primary process" refers to a primitive, archaic, drive-dominated mode of psychic functioning, while the "secondary process" refers to a relatively drive-autonomous, adaptive, rational mode of psychic functioning. For the purpose of the present study, the concept of the "primary process" is conceived of as an intervening variable, following Holt (1965), referring to a mode of thought-operation that is inferred from and operationally defined by communicated thought exhibiting any one of the following characteristics: (1) inappropriate or unadaptive intrusion by libidinal or aggressive contents; (2) Condensation, symbolization, fragmentation, loose or fluid associations, syncretic or autistic logic, logical contradiction and impaired reality-testing. The "secondary process" is similarly conceived of as an intervening variable. It is inferred from and defined by thinking that is faithful to logic and to external reality thinking that is purposive and organized for efficient goal-directed activity, showing minimal drive-intrusion. These two contrasting modes of thought are conceived of as ideal extremes of a continuum, ranging from such behavioral phenomena as dreams, hallucinations and delusions, through wishful thinking and daydreams to purposeful, efficient reality-oriented thought, rather than constituting a simple dichotomy.

early period of life when the child has as yet not formed a conception of external reality, and secondary-process thinking is seen as
developing as a consequence of the establishment of reality-
contact. However, the hypothesis that there exists a continual
relationship between reality contact and secondary-process
thought, that is to say, that continual reality contact is required
for the *maintenance* of secondary-process thinking, is rather
novel. This formulation may seem paradoxical in view of the
extensive structuralization, stability and drive-autonomy with
which ego functions (including secondary-process thought) are
endowed in contemporary ego psychology.

In a recent paper on "Ego Autonomy" (1958) Rapaport takes
cognizance of this hypothesis by emphasizing that all the structures serving ego functions are only *relatively* autonomous, and
that they "depend upon stimulation for their stability, or to use
Piaget's terms, they require stimulation as nutriment for their
maintenance. When such stimulus nutriment is not available, the
effectiveness of these structures in controlling id impulses may be
impaired, and some of the ego's autonomy from the id may be
surrendered." (Rapaport, 1958, p. 13).

Specifically, then, with regard to the important ego function of
secondary-process thinking, this formulation holds that the psychic structures underlying the operation of logical, reality-
oriented thought require continual sensory contact with the order
and patterning of the real world, which the thought process is
epistemologically assumed to reflect. In the absence of such contact, the psychic structures lose their stability and drive-con-
trolling capacity, with the result that regression to the primitive,
archaic primary-process mode of functioning is facilitated.

How does this formulation account for the wide individual
differences reported in previous studies? It does so by assuming
that individuals differ significantly: (1) in their dependence on
reality contact for maintaining secondary-process thought; (2) in
the degree to which they can tolerate primary-process manifestations in consciousness; and (3) in the manner in which they
handle, control or use primary-process material once it is conscious.

## Modes of Handling the Primary Process

In the present study the principal concern is with predicting a number of selected isolation effects from the knowledge of the manner in which the primary process (which we assume is facilitated by the isolation situation) is generally handled in his enduring character structure.

Several modes of handling the primary process may be distinguished.

One mode available to the ego is to *prevent* its appearance into consciousness through a heavy expenditure of counter-cathectic energy, through defensive operations, repression, etc. Dynamically, this method of dealing with the primary process implies that a person's instinctual drives in the form of ideational derivatives (which is essentially what the primary process represents) are potentially threatening, disruptive, anxiety- or guilt-evoking to him.

Another mode of handling the primary process may be exemplified by a person who finds his instinctual impulse-derivatives threatening, disruptive, anxiety- or guilt-producing *but* whose ego strength does not measure up to the task of preventing their appearance into consciousness. Clinically, this type of individual is perhaps best exemplified by certain psychotic patients whose defenses have given way to the onslaught of the instinctual drives. A person of this type in the normal range characteristically experiences primary-process manifestations as ego-alien, as unpleasant, highly disruptive and foreign intrusions upon the ego.

Still another method of dealing with the primary process is to permit it into awareness in an ego-syntonic, modulated, controlled fashion without the creation of emotional havoc. The ego may even make adaptive use of primary-process elements.

The adaptive use of drive-directed, prelogical modes of experience has prompted the coinage of the term "regression in the service of the ego" by Kris (1952) who found such a concept to be centrally relevant in understanding the creative process. Dynamically, the capacity to regress in the service of the ego implies emotional maturity, flexibility and ego strength, as suggested by Schafer (1958, pp. 10-12) in his enumeration of the following list

of six overlapping factors fostering this capacity.
1.  ... the presence of a well-developed set of affective signals; the individual must be relatively secure in his sense of being in touch with his feelings.
2.  ... a secure sense of self or more broadly, a well-established ego identity.
3.  ... a relative mastery of early traumata so that the individual may feel free to re-experience in certain respects how it was once to have been a child and to have felt feminine, receptive, helpless and fluid in internal state and object relations.
4.  ... relatively moderate rather than archaic severe superego pressures and associated sets of relatively flexible rather than rigid defenses and controls.
5.  ... a history of adequate trust and mutuality in interpersonal relations.
6.  ... the meaningfulness to the larger community of this process that culminates in self-awareness and personal and effective communication.

This conception of the manner in which the ego may handle the primary process suggests that its manifestation in consciousness may occur either "because he (an individual) cannot help it, due to a temporary or permanent ego weakness; or because he *wants* to, for fun or for creative purposes, and is able to because he is not too threatened by his unconscious drives" (Holt, 1956, p. 16). It should be recognized that the three modes of handling the primary process described here are idealized conceptions. The three modes are conceived as points on a continuum ranging from uncontrolled, ego-alien "breakthrough" of primary-process elements into consciousness, through complete repression of primary-process manifestations, to controlled, modulated use of primary-process material in the service of the ego.

### The Rorschach Situation and the
### Emergence of the Primary Process

To formulate a rationale for the facilitative effect of the Rorschach situation in producing primary-process material, an analysis of the similarity between the Rorschach and the isolation situations may be helpful. First, what are the stimulus conditions confronting S in these two situations? In the isolation situation the external stimuli (in the present study consisting of "white noise," diffuse light and relatively homogeneous tactual stimuli) are essentially repetitive, patternless and non-representational. That is to say, the stimuli possess a low degree of reality-cue value. They afford only limited contact with the structure of the real world. The stimuli to which S is directed to attend in the Rorschach situation, the ink-blots, are similarly nonrepresentational, relatively unstructured; they, too, possess a relatively low reality-cue value and afford only limited contact with the structure of reality. In the light of the previous discussion on the relationship between reality contact and mode of thought, the Rorschach stimuli may be said to exert a pull towards primary-process responses.

A second and perhaps more salient similarity inheres in the type of instruction given S in the two situations. In both they are highly permissive, allowing S maximum freedom in his subjective definition of and approach to the respective situations. In both situations the instructions impart a directive set towards personalized, private responses. This is done explicitly in the isolation situation, where S is told to " ... talk about the thoughts that go through your mind, the feelings you are experiencing ...," while in the Rorschach situation this set is established more tacitly by the instruction " ... tell me what this looks like, what it reminds you of, what it might be ... there are no right or wrong answers ... what does it look like to you?" etc. In neither situation is there a definite directive to be logical and coherent, or to produce organized and connected narrative.

The Rorschach situation, as has been pointed out by Holt (1956), is characterized by certain unique features which favor the emergence of primary-process material. In taking the Rorschach test S is asked to produce visual images, which according to psychoanalytic theory, is a preferred mode of operation for the primary process. Furthermore, the presence of an external focus (in the form of the ink-blots) to some extent reduces the viewer's self-awareness and circumvents the generally encountered resistance to producing highly personalized responses. As Holt put it, the Rorschach stimuli offer S a "projective excuse" (1954, p. 544) for his responses. The complexity and variety of the stimulus configurations presented by the series of ink-blots afford varying degrees of external anchorage for almost any image the viewer may bring to bear on the situation. This feature of the Rorschach test enables us to discern individual differences in the ease or freedom with which an S can allow himself to abandon reality-anchored (secondary-process) thought, the degree to which he fails to prevent its abandonment, and the degree and manner of control exerted over primary-process products, once they (either due to ego strength or ego weakness) appear in consciousness.

### The Rorschach Manual for Scoring
### Primary-Process Manifestations

Holt recently developed a Rorschach scoring manual (1956 and Holt & Havel, 1960) designed to estimate the degree and mode of primary-process functioning in a given subject. The manual contains a large number of categories, referring both to the content and to the formal aspects of a response, presumed to embody indications of primary-process operations. The content of a response is scored as reflecting the primary process when it gives clear evidence of being an ideational or affective drive derivative. Examples taken from the manual of such responses and their category headings are:

| Category | Illustrative response |
|---|---|
| Oral | "Breast," "an open mouth" |
| Anal | "A pile of feces," "buttocks" |
| Exhibitionistic-Voyeuristic | "Human figure — nude" |
| Sexual | "Man — looks like his penis is erect" |
| Sexual-ambiguity | "Men with breasts" |
| Aggressive | "Witches tearing a woman apart" |
| Anxiety and Guilt | "Man tied, falling into space helplessly" |

The following are examples of formal aspects of a response scored as reflecting the primary process:

| Category | Illustrative response |
|---|---|
| Fusion of two separate percepts | "Vampire — the bat is the vampire — in action, |

|  | allure of the woman so to speak ... symbolic of the bat in action using the woman as bait" (V, bat is the whole card, woman the entire side area) |
|---|---|
| Arbitrary linkage of two percepts | "Women, sort of stuck together" |
| Fluid transformation of a percept | "Rats climbing a tree ... now the whole thing has turned into a flower." |
| Autistic logic | "Everything is so small it must be the insectual kind of thing." |
| Logical condensation | "Old maids, but they look very young." |
| Verbal contradiction | "Diaphragram" (Condensation of diagram and diaphragm) |
| Peculiar verbalization | "Part of a lady's vagina" |
| Self-reference | "My family," "insects crawling towards me" |

Each response containing some evidence of the primary process is further scored on a number of defense and control variables. These variables refer to the *way* S gives a particular response; they consider the demand implicit in a response for control, the types of control (remoteness, sequence, etc.) , and the effectiveness of these measures. The control and defense variables were developed with the aim of obtaining a measure of "the extent to which he (the subject) is master of or is mastered by the primary-process elements in his thinking" (Holt, 1956, p. 22). In the present study an over-all measure (based on the total Rorschach record and its scores) was assigned to each S along a continuum ranging from effective control of primary-process manifestations (assumed to characterize the mature ego) through an absence of primary-process material (found in rigidly defended persons), to poorly controlled manifestations of the primary process (exemplifying the person with a fragile defense system)*.

## General Predictions

The mature person with a well-developed ego theoretically should not be overwhelmed by the internal forces, since part of his maturity consists of being in close touch with his instinctual life. In the isolation experiment such a person might welcome drive

---

*A detailed description of the procedure used in arriving at the overall measure is available from the author.

tension (in the absence of any externally produced tension) and find discharge through the primary process; he might daydream, fantasize, etc. The important point is that he would maintain effective control over the primary process, which is to say that he would use it in the service of the ego. It would seem to follow that he would not be expected to show any serious disturbance in response to isolation. Although he might temporarily have abandoned secondary-process functioning, he may quickly and easily revert back to efficient, adaptive functioning when reality demands it. Thus, it is predicted that Ss with effective emotional control will show little if any impairment on the cognitive tests. It is further predicted that they will react to the isolation situation with less unpleasant affect than the type of persons to be described next. They may perhaps even react with some pleasurable affect in response to the opportunity of being temporarily removed from the demands of reality.

At the other extreme is the person with an immature ego — that is, having unstable, fragile defenses or an extremely rigid defense structure. To such a person the situational facilitation of primary-process operations would theoretically be extremely anxiety provoking. The overly rigid person would summon up all of his available defensive energy in order to prevent drive-domination. He would become progressively more restless, tense, bored and fatigued as a result of the defensive struggle. Upon being re-introduced to normal, external stimulation, he would still be somewhat disorganized and consequently would do poorer on the cognitive tests. He would, however, be less disorganized than the person with a fragile defense system, whose defensive battle against the primary-process influx is quickly lost and who becomes overwhelmed by unpleasant, anxiety- or guilt-arousing intrusions of the primary process. It is predicted that the latter type of person will not only show the greatest amount of cognitive impairment, but will attempt to terminate the experiment prior to its conclusion.

## Specific Hypotheses and Their Rationale

### *Hypothesis I*

Effective control of primary process manifestations in the

Rorschach is correlated positively with controlled primary-process thinking during isolation.

*Rationale:* This hypothesis is based on the fundamental assumption that the Rorschach measure of the primary process is not entirely specific to the Rorschach situation, but it is a measure of a person's general mode of dealing with primary-process manifestations, irrespective of the situation in which the primary process is evoked. A further reason for expecting a correlation between the two measures of primary process is that the criteria for the assessment of primary process in the respective situations parallel each other as much as possible.

### *Hypothesis II*

Effective control of primary-process manifestations in the Rorschach is correlated negatively with poorly controlled primary-process thinking during isolation.

*Rationale:* Since the isolation situation encompasses a much larger behavioral sample, extending as it does over an eight hour period, the possibility was recognized that an S may give evidence of both controlled and poorly controlled primary process at different points in time. Consequently, rather than measuring primary-process thinking on one dimension (i.e. controlled — poorly controlled), they were separated into two dependent variables, one being the dimension: "large amount — small amount of controlled primary process manifestations," the other being: "large amount — small amount of poorly controlled primary process manifestations." The rationale proper for Hypothesis II is the same as for Hypothesis I above.

### *Hypotheses III and IV*

Effective control of primary-process manifestations in the Rorschach is correlated positively with pleasant affect during isolation, and further, that it is correlated negatively with unpleasant affect during isolation.

*Rationale:* These two hypotheses are based on the assumption that the affective state of an S during isolation is related to the upsurge of drive tension. Pleasant affect is viewed as accompanying ego-syntonic discharge of drive tension into ideational drive derivatives, and, in part, as arising in response to the opportunity of being temporarily removed from the demands of external reality. Unpleasant affect is seen as accompanying repression or unsuccessful attempts at repression. The S who in the Rorschach displays an effective way of dealing with primary-process material, should likewise do so in the isolation situation, and he should consequently experience more pleasant affect than an S whose Rorschach rating is at the "poorly controlled primary process" pole. By the same token he should experience less unpleasant affect.

(*Note:* Pleasant and unpleasant affect are not treated here as extremes of one dimension, since both pleasant and unpleasant affect may occur during isolation in the same subject at different periods of time. The pleasant affect variable ranges from large amount to small amount of pleasant affect: similarly, unpleasant affect ranges from large amount to small amount of unpleasant affect.)

## Hypothesis V

Effective control of primary-process manifestations in the Rorschach is correlated negatively with actual termination or tendency to quit the isolation experiment prior to its conclusion.

Rationale: The rationale for this hypothesis is based on the assumption that actual quitting or tendency to quit constitutes an extreme indication of the extent to which S finds isolation threatening and intolerable. It follows, then, that the S who on the Rorschach gives evidence of being intolerant of the primary process or an S who becomes disturbed by its emergence in consciousness, will exhibit more "quitting" behavior than Ss for whom the primary process does not constitute an overwhelming threat.

## Hypothesis VI

Effective control of primary-process manifestations in the Rorschach is correlated negatively with cognitive test impairment in the isolation situation.

Rationale: It is assumed that the performance on a series of cognitive tests, administered towards the end of and immediately following the eight hour isolation period, reflects the accumulated effect of the total situation. It would seem to follow, then that the more threatening, disorganizing, and anxiety-producing the total isolation situation is to a given subject, the more his test performance will suffer, and the greater the test impairment will be. Assuming further that the threat and anxiety derives from the potential or actual emergence of the primary process, then, the S whose Rorschach reflects effective control of the primary process (implying that whatever threat inhered in the emergence of primary-process material was not disabling) should be least impaired in his test performance, while the S who in the Rorschach displays intolerance of or poor control of the primary process should be most impaired.

## Method

The detailed procedure has been reported elsewhere (Goldberger & Holt, 1958) and will be briefly summarized here. Fourteen first-year male undergraduates in the New York University School of Education were chosen from the class entering in September 1956. They agreed to participate in a program of interrelated researches and served as Ss in a number of experiments besides this one, which was referred to as "a day of doing nothing".*

About a week before the day of isolation, S was pretested on a battery of cognitive tests and on several other procedures not germane to the present paper†. Then on the appointed morning, he had half ping-pong balls attached to his eye sockets by rubber cement; a light flexible leather helmet containing earphones was fitted on his head; and his hands were encased in cotton work

---

*Only students with Ohio State Psychological Examination scores above the fortieth percentile of entering freshmen and nonpathological MMPI profiles were invited to participate; of those who responded, several were eliminated by further screening — interview and Rorschach — to eliminate those with too-precarious adjustment; fourteen remained.

†The cognitive tests (deductive and arithmetic reasoning, digit span and story recall) were a disappointment in that there was no generality of impairment, and indeed not even a mean decrement of performance on more than one (Watson-Glaser Critical Thinking logical deductions subtest, the reliability of which, unfortunately, is questionable). They will not be discussed here in detail (see Goldberger & Holt, 1958).

gloves inside cylinders of cardboard extending up to his elbows. He lay on a couch, his head in a deep, U-shaped foam rubber pillow, in a semi-soundproof room. Residual sounds from the street and the corridor were masked by a moderately loud "white noise" fed into the earphones. There was a two-way intercom between the experimental room and E's room, and a one-way mirror. S's lunch order was taken; he was told that he would be alone all day except for the lunch and for being taken to the toilet whenever he indicated the need, but the noise would not cease nor would the eye-cups be taken off until the end of the day. If he felt that he had to come out sooner, he might do so. He was asked to lie as quietly as possible, and to tell about his experience while it was going on when signalled by a rap on the microphone, and to cease talking when given another signal. E then took up his position on the other side of the one-way mirror, and gave the signal to talk. Thereafter, he recorded observations of S's behavior, noted (chiefly by variations in his breathing) when S slept and awakened, and started a tape recorder whenever S began to speak.

At the end of eight hours, E announced that there would be some tests, and turned off the "white noise." He readministered the battery of cognitive tests, released S from the apparatus and the room, had him fill out a questionnaire, gave a few more tests and interviewed him about his reactions to the situation (taking off from S's responses to the questionnaire). It was evening by the time S was finally through.

The dependent variables to be discussed here were derived from the protocol of the experiment: the transcribed tape, E's observations, and the final interview. Two judges (Dr. Holt and the author), neither of whom knew the S's ranks on the Rorschach measure, independently rated and ranked the protocols on the following pre-established qualitative variables*.

    I. *Affective states*
        *Unpleasant affect.* Amount of unpleasant affect in the form
        of anxiety, tension, boredom, restlessness, anger, depression
        and fatigue. (Inter-rater reliability, Rho = .99).
        *Pleasant affect.* Amount of pleasant affect in the form of
        relaxation, enjoyment and positive interest in the experi-

---

*The variables for which no explicit predictions were made are marked with an asterisk(*).

ment. (Rho = .93)

II. *Thought processes*

*"Stimulus-bound" thought.* Amount of thought devoted to the immediate experimental situation and relatively direct associations to the situation: e.g., thoughts pertaining to the room, the equipment, the purpose of the experiment, the experimenter. Also thoughts about footsteps, trucks and other adventitious noises heard (Rho = .91).

*Unimpaired secondary-process thought.* Amount of thought devoted to logical, relatively sustained and directed reflection pertaining to any topic other than the immediate experimental situation. The playing of familiar time-passing games was included here (Rho = .80).

*Inefficient secondary-process thought.* The degree to which the maintenance of logical, directed and relatively extended thought is impaired: e.g., verbalized complaints of difficulty in thinking and direct evidence of scatteredness, fragmentation, etc. (Rho = .88).

*Controlled primary-process thought.* Manifestations of the primary process, whether in content or form, without the accompaniment of anxiety or other unpleasant affect. To qualify as primary-process content the S's thinking had to show evidence of drive-domination: i.e., it must express libidinal or aggressive wishes, either blatantly or toned down in a more socially acceptable manner. To qualify as a formal indication of the primary process the S's thought process had to reveal one or more of the following features: condensation, symbolization, fragmentation, loose or fluid associations, autistic logic, contradiction, or impaired reality testing (Rho = .85).

*Poorly controlled primary-process thought.* Same as above, except that the primary-process appearance was accompanied by anxiety or other unpleasant affect (Rho = .96).

III. *Imagery*

Amount and vividness of spontaneous visual, auditory and other sensory imagery. Reports of imagery that were confused by S with reality received the highest rating. As a general rule, vividness took precedence over frequency (Rho = .89).

IV. *Self-stimulation*

The amount of singing, whistling, humming, tapping or

rocking. Stimulation received through exploration of the surroundings (e.g., exploring wall, table, microphone, etc., with cuffs or legs) is also included here (Rho = .84).

V. *Immobility*

The degree to which motor activity was inhibited as judged from E's recorded observations (Rho = .80).

VI. *Quitting*

This measure ranked Ss in terms of their expressed desire to quit, the highest rank being assigned Ss who actually did quit, and the lowest to those who remained and did not express any desire to quit. The time at which quitting or the desire to quit first occurred was taken into account in the rating (Rho = .92).

The judges considered each variable separately in ranking Ss. They used their clinical judgment freely in carrying out the ranking procedure, and used both direct and indirect evidence to support their inferences. The interrater reliability was excellent, ranging from a Rho of .99 to .80 with an average Rho of .89.*

The following variables did not require ratings since they were readily measurable by objective means:

*1. Verbal output.* Total number of lines, in the isolation transcription, per hour.

*2. Sleep.* The total time of sleep per hour.

*3. General disturbance.* This measure consists of the S's own ratings on items, in the first part of the self-administered questionnaire, interpreted as reflecting "general disturbance" in a broad sense. Each S's ratings on the different items were totaled, and the totals for all Ss were then ranked.

## Results

### Interrelation among the Isolation Effects

Table 3-I presents an intercorrelation matrix of the dependent variables on which Ss were ranked. The significant correlations obtained show a good deal of internal consistency and appear to be quite meaningful. Thus, we find that pleasant affect is nega-

---

*Disagreements between the judges' rankings were resolved through discussion.

TABLE 3-I

RANK-ORDER CORRELATIONS (RHO) BETWEEN MEASURES OF ISOLATION EFFECT

| | 1 | 2 | 3 | 4 | 5 | 6 | 7 | 8 | 9 | 10 | 11 | 12 | 13 |
|---|---|---|---|---|---|---|---|---|---|---|---|---|---|
| 1. Pleasant affect | | | | | | | | | | | | | |
| 2. Controlled primary process [a] | .84** | | | | | | | | | | | | |
| 3. Unimpaired secondary process | .67** | .67* | | | | | | | | | | | |
| 4. Self-stimulation | .45 | .71** | .37 | | | | | | | | | | |
| 5. Imagery [a] | .68* | .88** | .77** | .60* | | | | | | | | | |
| 6. Immobility | .36 | .60* | .32 | -.15 | .68* | | | | | | | | |
| 7. Verbal output | .72** | .70** | .95** | .29 | .87** | .41 | | | | | | | |
| 8. Unpleasant affect | -.67** | -.43 | -.52 | -.53* | -.56 | -.16 | -.56* | | | | | | |

| | | | | | | | | | | | | |
|---|---|---|---|---|---|---|---|---|---|---|---|---|
| 9. Poorly controlled primary process | -.09 | .33 | .13 | -.02 | .30 | .02 | .19 | .37 | | | | |
| 10. Inefficient secondary process b | -.58* | -.16 | -.44 | -.44 | -.22 | -.10 | -.42 | .53 | .75** | | | |
| 11. General disturbance a | -.46 | -.14 | -.29 | -.40 | -.19 | -.01 | -.34 | .52 | .58* | .64* | | |
| 12. Quitting | -.61* | -.26 | -.17 | -.18 | -.05 | -.26 | -.15 | .58* | .37 | .25 | .37 | |
| 13. Sleep | .18 | .22 | -.05 | .28 | .05 | .00 | -.13 | -.28 | -.10 | -.01 | -.22 | -.40 |
| 14. Stimulus-bound thought | .33 | -.01 | .40 | -.09 | .34 | .25 | .54* | -.42 | .17 | .01 | .21 | -.13 | -.22 |

*.05 level; **.01 level (two-tailed test) a N = 12, b N = 13, for the remaining variables N = 14

tively correlated with imagery, unpleasant affect,* quitting and inefficient secondary process, and positively correlated with controlled primary process and verbal output,† while unpleasant affect is positively correlated with quitting and negatively with verbal output. We find that immobility is positively correlated with imagery (and incidentally that both of these variables are significantly related to the absolute number of movement responses in the Rorschach‡ — a result that might have been predicted from either psychoanalytic or sensory-tonic theory (Singer, 1955). We also see that controlled primary process (which there was considerably more of than poorly controlled primary process in the present sample) is positively correlated with imagery — partly because these two variables overlap to a certain extent — and with immobility. The relationship found between primary process and immobility (relaxed supine position) has frequently been implied in the psychoanalytic literature, particularly in connection with the rationale for using the couch.

A syndrome analysis (Horn, 1944) of the significant correlation coefficients reveals two relatively pure clusters and several interrelated subclusters.

One cluster consists of the following positively correlated variables: pleasant affect, unimpaired secondary process, controlled primary process, imagery and verbal output. Related to this cluster are the following subclusters: (a) immobility, controlled primary process and imagery; (b) self-stimulation, controlled primary process and imagery; (c) pleasant affect negatively correlated with unpleasant affect and quitting; (d) pleasant affect negatively correlated with inefficient secondary process; and (e) pleasant affect and verbal output both negatively correlated with unpleasant affect.

The second relatively pure cluster consists of the following positively intercorrelated variables: poorly controlled primary

---

*It should be remembered that pleasant affect and unpleasant affect were rated independently.

†In this connection it should be pointed out that talking as a mode of defense against the experience of isolation was discouraged by the instructions.

‡Rorschach "M" vs. imagery with an N of 12, Rho = .60 (p < .50, with a two-tailed test); Rorschach "M" vs. immobility with an N of 12, Rho = .50 (p<.05, with a two-tailed test).

process, inefficient secondary process and general disturbance (as measured by the questionnaire).

These clusters may be interpreted as reflecting two general patterns in which Ss, to varying degrees, reacted to the particular situation in which they found themselves. One pattern consisted of engaging in a variety of behaviors, all within the limits set by the situation and the particular instructions. An idealized conception of the Ss responding in this manner is that they would avail themselves of the freedom to talk whenever they felt like talking, experienced pleasant affect and little unpleasant affect, thought about logical, rational matters (when and if they chose to do so), engaged in daydreaming, fantasying or playful thinking without the accompaniment of unpleasant affect, engaged in whatever self-stimulation (typically in the form of whistling or singing) was allowed them, welcomed and enjoyed the spontaneously appearing imagery, and since they had agreed to serve as subjects for the entire day were not too preoccupied with the option of quitting. The relatively small degree of restlessness experienced by these Ss, in addition to the instruction: "try not to move any part of your body," probably accounts for the fact that they were the most immobile. In summary, this pattern of reaction may be characterized as resourceful, flexible and, under the circumstances, quite adaptive.

The Ss fitting the second pattern found the isolation situation disturbing and anxiety provoking. They were neither able to maintain normal secondary-process thought, nor were they able to engage in primary-process thinking without its being accompanied by unpleasant affect. They were in a sense passive victims of the situation, lacking sufficient ego strength to modulate or control the mounting drive tension.

### The Hypothesized Relationship Between Rorschach Manifestations of the Primary Process and Isolation Effects

Hypothesis I predicted a positive correlation between the Rorschach measure of effectively controlled primary process and controlled primary-process thinking exhibited during isolation. This hypothesis was confirmed (p < .05; see Table 3-II).

TABLE 3-II

CORRELATIONS BETWEEN THE
RORSCHACH MEASURE OF PRIMARY
PROCESS AND ISOLATION EFFECTS

| Isolation effect | Rho | N |
|---|---|---|
| Unpleasant affect | -.50* | 14 |
| Pleasant affect | .47* | 14 |
| Controlled primary-process thought | .54* | 12 |
| Poorly controlled primary process thought | -.15 | 12 |
| Quitting | -.38 | 14 |
| Stimulus-bound thought | .13 | 14 |
| Sleep | .65** | 14 |
| General disturbance | -.30 | 12 |
| Verbal output | .33 | 14 |
| Immobility | .35 | 14 |
| Self-stimulation | .46* | 14 |
| Imagery | .45 | 12 |
| Unimpaired secondary-process thought | .45* | 14 |
| Inefficient secondary-process thought | -.36 | 13 |

*Significant at the .05 point for a one-tailed test
**Significant at the .02 level for a two-tailed test

Hypothesis II predicted a negative correlation between the Rorschach measure of effectively controlled primary process and the amount of poorly controlled primary-process thinking during isolation. Although the correlation was in the right direction this hypothesis was not confirmed. However, when poorly controlled primary-process thought was correlated with the Rorschach measure of *total amount* of primary process, the Rho was significant (-.60, p < .05, with a two-tailed test), indicating that an S who on the Rorschach gave few primary-process responses evidenced more poorly controlled primary-process thinking in the isolation situation than the S who on the Rorschach gave many primary-process responses, irrespective of the effectiveness with which they were handled. An *ad hoc* explanation for this finding is that a person potentially prone to primary-process intrusions and who is unable to modulate its expression successfully enough to make it a socially acceptable communication is likely to consciously guard against its emergence in the Rorschach situation, but is less able to do so in the isolation situation — presumably because of that situation's greater pull for the emergence of the primary process.

Hypotheses III and IV predicted a positive correlation between the Rorschach measure of effectively controlled primary process and pleasant affect generated during isolation, and a negative correlation between the Rorschach and unpleasant affect. Both of these expectations were confirmed (p < .05).

Hypothesis V predicted a negative correlation between the Rorschach measure of effectively controlled primary process and quitting. This hypothesis was not confirmed with the required degree of statistical confidence.

Hypothesis VI predicted a negative correlation between the Rorschach measure of effectively controlled primary process and cognitive test impairment. It was initially anticipated that a single impairment rank, based on all the separate test measures, could be assigned to Ss. In view of the meager findings on the cognitive test (presumably due, in part, to their lack of sensitivity) already referred to, and the generally low intercorrelations found among the impairment ranks on the various measures, each test measure was treated as a separate variable. Of the seven test impairment rankings only one turned out to be significantly related to the Rorschach measure, namely, Story Recall — total errors. The obtained Rho, in the hypothesized direction, indicated that Ss who showed effectively controlled primary process on the Rorschach test were less disabled in the task of faithfully reproducing a short, meaningful story paragraph.

### The Relationship Between the Rorschach Measure of Primary Process and the General Reaction Syndromes

Table 3-II also presents the correlation coefficients obtained between the Rorschach measure of effectively controlled primary process and the other dependent variables on which scores were available. These correlations were run in order to determine whether the Rorschach measure would differentiate between the two general reaction patterns mentioned above. Thus, it was hypothesized that the Rorschach measure of effectively controlled primary process would be positively correlated with unimpaired secondary-process thought, verbal output, imagery, self-stimulation and immobility and negatively with inefficient secondary-process thought and general disturbance. Two of these expectations were confirmed with statistical significance — namely, unimpaired secondary-process thought (p < .05) and self-stimulation (p < .05) while a third, imagery, came close to reaching statistical significance (.05 < p < .10). The remaining correlations were all in the expected direction, that is to say, verbal output and immobility were positive, while inefficient secondary-process thought and general disturbance were negative.*

Finally, composite ranks were computed for the two general syndromes comprising the following variables:

*Syndrome I*
> pleasant affect
> controlled primary-process thought
> unimpaired secondary-process thought
> self-stimulation
> imagery
> immobility
> verbal output

*Syndrome II*
> unpleasant affect
> poorly controlled primary-process thought
> quitting
> inefficient secondary-process thought
> general disturbance

---

*An unexpeted but theoretically consistent finding was the positive correlation beteen the Rorschach measure of effectively controlled primary process and sleep (p < .02 for a two-tailed test). This finding is viewed as lending support to the psychoanalytic theory of sleep, advanced by Hartmann (1951) and later Kris (1952), according to which sleep is conceptualized as a form of adaptive regression governed by the ego.

The composite ranks were correlated with the Rorschach measure on the hypothesis that it would correlate positively with Syndrome I and negatively with Syndrome II. This expectation received fair confirmation (Syndrome I, Rho = .50, p < .05; Syndrome II, Rho = -.46, .05 < p < .10).

## The Role of Intelligence

In order to determine the relevance of intelligence in the evaluation of the present data, correlations were run between scores on the Ohio State Psychological Examination and both the independent and dependent variables. Out of 24 correlation coefficients, only one reached the 5 percent level of statistical significance (Imagery; Rho = .59, p < .05 for a two-tailed test). On the basis of this finding it was concluded that intelligence plays an insignificant role and need not be partialled out for the proper evaluation of the data pertaining to the hypothesized relationships.*

## Discussion†

It may be recalled that the general hypothesis underlying this study was that the manner in which a person reacts to a situation permitting only limited contact with the structure of external world is related to the manner in which he generally deals with manifestations of the primary process in the normal waking state. This hypothesis was based on the theoretical assumption — which found empirical support in the reports of previous isolation studies that interference with reality contact leads to a decrease in the efficiency of secondary-process functioning, and to a facilitation of the primary process. Or to state this in Rapaport's terms, lack of adequate stimulus nutriment diminishes the ego's relative autonomy from the id (and to some extent also from the environment). It was further proposed that individual differences

---

*It should be remembered, however, that the restricted range of Ss' intelligence scores would tend to lower correlations with other scores.

†A more general discussion of phenomenological aspects of the data, specifically comparing the group findings, methodology and "hallucinatory" phenomena of the present study with those of other relevant investigations may be found elsewhere (Goldberger & Holt, 1958).

observed in the effects of isolation could theoretically be understood in terms of predispositional differences in ego-structure with respect to susceptibility to and modes of dealing with primary-process material. Thus it was hypothesized that the greater the amount of effectively controlled primary process in the normal waking state, as gauged by the Rorschach test, the greater would be the amount of controlled primary-process thinking during isolation. A number of corollary hypotheses were also offered concerning poorly controlled primary process, the affective state of the Ss, quitting, and secondary-process impairment (as measured by a battery of tests involving secondary-process functions) during isolation.

As the results have shown, the general hypothesis may on the whole be regarded as confirmed. It was shown that the Rorschach measure did correlate in the predicted direction with all the specified variables, except for impairments on most of the cognitive tests.

The correlation coefficients did not reach statistical significance on two of the specified variables: poorly controlled primary-process thought and quitting. For the first of these variables it was found that it correlated significantly, in a negative direction, with the Rorschach measure of *amount* of primary process. In other words, it was found that the more primary-process material (irrespective of the effectiveness with which it was handled) a person gave in the Rorschach, the less poorly controlled primary-process thinking he would reveal during isolation. As was briefly mentioned earlier, this finding may be interpreted in the following way: In the Rorschach situation a person whose ingrained defenses against the invasion of the primary process are poor or brittle, may give a highly controlled, constricted, guarded record in order to prevent primary-process elements in his private thinking from cropping up in his verbalized responses. In the isolation situation, however, the increased facilitation of the primary process may be too strong to be successfully warded off, leading to "breakthroughs" of poorly controlled primary-process stuff.

The lack of a significant correlation between the Rorschach measure and quitting may, in part, be attributed to the inhomogeneity of this variable. The variable consisted of *actual* quitting, on the one end of the dimension, and absence of a verbalized desire or preoccupation with quitting, on the other end. The three Ss who actually terminated the experiment did in fact obtain relatively low ranks (as predicted) on the Rorschach measure; however, for the remaining eleven Ss the ranks probably did not adequately reflect their desire to quit since the judges' assignment of ranks leaned heavily on the Ss' frankness in making what (in some Ss at least) would have been a painful admission of "weakness."

If we discard the data on secondary-process impairment as measured by the tests used in the present study, and look instead at our clinical ratings of inefficient secondary-process thought, we find that the expected relationship between the Rorschach measure and secondary-process impairment does hold, although not to a statistically significant degree (Rho = -.36; see Table 3-II). Subjects with effectively controlled primary process in the Rorschach tended slightly to be less impaired in their ability to engage in secondary-process thought during isolation. And conversely we see that the more effectively controlled primary-process material an S gave in the Rorschach, the more able he was to engage in unimpaired secondary-process thinking during isolation (Rho = .45, p < .05; see Table 3-II). From this we may conclude that the presence of well-controlled primary-process responses in the Rorschach does *not* necessarily indicate a lack of ability to maintain secondary-process thought, but rather (in a college population) indicates sufficient freedom to abandon secondary-process operations temporarily, especially in a situation that does not specifically call for logical, realistic thinking. This would appear to make tenable the equation of the concept "regression in the service of the ego" with what has here been referred to as "controlled use of the primary process."

The results of the present study attest to the predictive power of Holt's Rorschach manual (1956 and Holt & Havel, 1960). The manual was developed out of theoretical considerations stemming from the psychoanalytic theory of primary and secondary processes, and was up to fairly recently only applied to some exploratory research problems. The present findings of significant correlations between the Rorschach-derived measure of primary process and the clinical ratings of primary-process manifestations and other behavioral features in the isolation situation lend strong support to the usefulness of the primary-process concept in personality assessment.

In connection with the application of the Rorschach manual the present findings emphasize the importance of considering jointly the amount and effectiveness variables. Correlations run between each of these variables separately and each of the dependent variables used in the present study were mostly statistically nonsignificant. It is essentially the *manner* (in addition to amount and intensity) in which primary-process manifestations are handled that differentiates ego strength from ego weakness. Either strength or weakness may result in an abundance of primary-process material in the Rorschach; cf. the frequent clinical observation to the effect that it is the defenses and controls that distinguish the healthy from the sick.

## Conclusion

Conceptually, the data of the present study seem generally to support the psychoanalytically derived hypothesis that continued contact with the structure of reality is necessary for a person to maintain secondary-process thinking and to prevent the onslaught of drives, in the form of the primary process. The data further support the assumptions that individuals differ significantly in their dependence on reality contact for maintaining secondary-process thinking, in the degree to which they can tolerate primary-process manifestations in consciousness, and in the effectiveness with which they handle, control or use primary-process material once it is conscious. Specifically, it is concluded that a person who is generally able to handle primary-process intrusions effectively, is also able to deal more adaptively with a situation in which he is temporarily cut off from normal reality contact, than is a person who cannot tolerate or effectively handle the primary process.

## REFERENCES

Bexton, W. H., Heron, W. & Scott, T.: Effects of decreased variation in the sensory environment. *Canad. J. Psychol.*, *8*:70-76, 1954.

Brenner, C.: *An Elementary Textbook of Psychoanalysis.* New York, Doubleday, 1957.

Fenichel, O.: *The Psychoanalytic Theory of the Neuroses.* New York, W. W. Norton, 1946.

Fisher, C.: The concept of the primary process. Unpublished manuscript, 1957.

Freud, S.: The unconscious. In *Collected Papers,* Vol. IV. London, Hogart Press, 1925, pp. 98-135.

Freud, S.: *New Introductory Lectures on Psychoanalysis.* New York, W. W. Norton, 1933.

Freud, S.: Project for a scientific psychology. In M. Bonaparte, A. Freud & E. Kris (Eds), *The Origins of Psychoanalysis. Letters to Wilhelm Fliess, Drafts and Notes: 1887-1902.* Trans. by P. Mosbacher & J. Strachey. New York, Basic Books, 1954.

Freud, S.: *The Interpretation of Dreams.* Trans. by J. Strachey. New York, Basic Books, 1955.

Goldberger, L. & Holt, R. R.: Experimental interference with reality contact (perceptual isolation): Method and group results. *J. Nerv. Ment. Dis.*, *127*:99-112, 1958.

Hartmann, H.: Ego psychology and the problem of adaptation. In D. Rapaport (Ed.), *Organization and Pathology of Thought,* New York, Columbia Univer. Press, pp. 362-396, 1951.

Hebb, D. O.: Drives and the C.N.S. (Conceptual Nervous System). *Psychol. Rev.*, *62*:234-255, 1955. (a)

Hebb, D. O.: The mammal and his environment. *Amer. J. Psychiat.*, *111*:826-831, 1955. (b)

Heron, W., Doane, B. & Scott, T.: Visual disturbances after prolonged perceptual isolation. *Canad. J. Psychol.*, *10*:13-18, 1956.

Holt, R. R.: Unpublished memorandum, Res. Cen. Ment. Hlth., 1953.

Holt, R. R.: Implications of some contemporary personality theories for Rorschach rationale. In B. Klopfer, Mary Ainsworth, W. Klopfer & R. R. Holt, *Developments in the Rorschach Technique,* Vol. I. New York, World Book Co., 1954. pp. 501-560.

Holt, R. R.: Gauging primary and secondary processes in Rorschach responses. *J. Proj. Tech.*, *20*:14-25, 1956.

Holt, R. R. & Goldberger, L.: Personological correlates of reactions to perceptual isolation. *USAF WADC Tech. Rep.*, No. 59-735. 46 pp., 1959.

Holt, R. R. & Havel, Joan: A method for assessing primary and secondary process in the Rorschach. In Maria A. Rickers-Ovsiankina (Ed.), *Rorschach Psychology,* New York, Wiley, 1960.

Horn, D.: A study of personality syndromes. *Charact. and Pers., 12*:257-274, 1944.

Kris, E.: *Psychoanalytic Explorations in Art.* New York, Internat. Univer. Press, 1952.

Rapaport, D.: The theory of ego autonomy: A generalization. *Bull. Menninger Clin., 22*:13-35, 1958.

Schafer, R.: Regression in the service of the ego: The relevance of a psychoanalytic concept for personality assessment. In G. Lindzey (Ed.), *Assessment of Human Motives.* New York, Rinehart, 1958.

Singer, J.: Delayed gratification and ego development: Implications for clinical and experimental research. *J. Consult. Psychol., 19*:259-273, 1955.

Solomon, P., Leiderman, P. H., Mendelson, J. & Wexler, D.: Perceptual and sensory deprivation — A review. *Amer. J. Psychiat., 114*:357-363, 1957.

Wheaton, J. L.: Fact and fancy in sensory deprivation studies. *USAF Sch. Aviat. Med. Rev.,* No. 5-59. 60 pp., 1959.

# Chapter 4

# THERAPEUTIC EFFECTIVENESS OF SENSORY DEPRIVATION*
## Evaluation of Effectiveness

SIDNEY E. CLEVELAND, Ph.D., E. EDWARD REITMAN, Ph.D., AND CATHERINE BENTINCK, M.A.

RECENT years have seen a growing interest in an area of research commonly referred to as sensory deprivation (S-D). In these studies,[1-3, 10] persons are exposed to an environment altered in terms of the available stimulation. Subjects in most of these studies have been normal volunteers, and a common finding is that S-D produces some degree of disruption in behavior. Occasionally normal subjects report dramatic behavioral changes during S-D, with symptoms approximating pathological reactions such as hallucinations, delusions, and disorientation.

In a few studies subjects already experiencing behavior pathology, e.g., hospitalized psychiatric patients, have been subjected to a S-D situation. For example, Azima and Cramer,[1] Gibby et al.,[5] and Harris[6] placed schizophrenics and other types of psychiatric patients in S-D environments with the paradoxical finding that improvement in behavior occurred rather than a deepening of the pathology. However, only in the experiment by Gibby et al.[5] was any systematic and formal evaluation made of the subjects' behavior and mental status prior to and following S-D. Gibby and his associates carried out pre- and post-S-D behavioral ratings using a standardized psychiatric rating scale. In addition psychological tests were administered on a pre- and post-S-D basis. Changes in both the behavioral ratings and psychological test performance following S-D were interpreted by Gibby as indicating a lessening of the frequency and intensity of psychi-

*Reprinted from the *Archives of General Psychiatry*, May 1963, Volume 8, pp. 455-460. Copyright, 1963, American Medical Association.

atric symptoms and a constructive increment in cognitive and perceptual functioning. It should be noted, however, that in none of these studies claiming the therapeutic effectiveness of S-D were any control groups utilized to test whether the improvement in behavior could be due to some sort of placebo response.

Opportunity to test the therapeutic effectiveness of S-D was provided in an experiment carried out by us.[9] A schizophrenic and a nonpsychotic psychiatric group were subjected to a S-D experience. The focus of interest in this study was on the evaluation of body image in these groups and differential changes in body image following S-D. Advantage was also taken of the experimental situation to measure any behavioral or psychological test performance changes in both schizophrenic and nonpsychotic hospitalized groups concomitant with exposure to S-D.

## Method

### *Subjects*

A total of sixty subjects were utilized in this study. The sample was drawn from the inpatient population on the NP service of the Houston VA Hospital.* All subjects were volunteers who had been told that this was a new form of treatment, the nature of which involved lying on a soft bed in a quiet room. Subjects were not told the length of their stay, but were reassured that they could leave at any time, although the experimenter hoped they would remain until he indicated the period had ended.

Of the sixty subjects, forty were residents of a closed psychiatric ward who had a diagnosis of schizophrenia, confirmed by present hospital records, and a history of disturbance in thought processes, delusions, hallucinations, and/or inappropriate affect. These forty subjects made up two or the three experimental groups in this study. A third group comprised patients on open psychiatric wards, diagnosed as either anxiety reaction or character disorder, with no history of psychotic behavior. None of the subjects in this study had a known history or diagnosis of organic brain damage, mental retardation, or primary alcoholism, and

---

*Isham Kimbell, MD, was the psychiatrist medically responsible for these patients.

none were receiving shock treatment or psychotherapy at the time of the experimental condition. All schizophrenic subjects were on maintenance levels of tranquilizing drugs.

Of the three groups, one schizophrenic group and the nonpsychotic controls experienced the entire experimental procedure. The remaining schizophrenic group served as a second control group which was given all phases of the procedure with the exception of the S-D experience. In each group there were eighteen Caucasians, one Negro, and one Latin American. A comparison across groups of such variables as age, education, number of marriages, children, and socioeconomic status revealed no significant differences. The groups did differ, however, on two variables: length of present hospitalization and number of prior hospitalizations. Both were found to be significantly greater for the schizophrenic patients. However, these variables are characteristic of schizophrenic behavior, per se, and could, therefore, not have been avoided without the selection of a highly atypical schizophrenic population.

### Procedure

The experiment was conducted in a combined perception laboratory and sensory deprivation chamber which was established on a closed ward of the Houston VA Hospital. The availability of this one central facility enabled the experimenters to minimize the amount of extraneous stimuli and social contact encountered by subjects during the sensory deprivation and testing sessions. The perception laboratory consisted of one large room, fifteen feet by eighteen feet, which served as the testing room and an attached wing, seven feet by twenty-four feet, which served as the sensory deprivation chamber. The S-D chamber was bare with the exception of a hospital bed and a large white-noise generator and speaker system. The bed had a regulation hospital mattress which was covered by an additional four-inch foam rubber mattress to reduce both kinesthetic sensations and positional cues. Subjects were fitted with a pair of translucent eye goggles, loose cotton gloves, and arm-length cardboard gauntlets. Thus outfitted, subjects were then placed on the bed in a supine position and instructed to move as little as possible. During the S-D period, two overhead lights and the white-noise generator were turned on. The white noise, 76 db sound level intensity at the head of the subjects not only provided an unvarying, constant, auditory stimulus, but also served as an adequate masking tone for the minimal hospital sounds that might have otherwise penetrated the room. It can be seen that, although the patients were restricted in terms of visual, auditory, kinesthetic, and perceptual sensation, there was no reduction in the absolute level of stimuli intensity. Instead, subjects were exposed to an unvarying, repetitive stimulus environment in which meaningful patterned cues had been minimized.

All subjects were put on a two-day experimental schedule. On the first day, patients were interviewed by the clinical social worker* and the interview behavior rated on each of the twenty items of the Symptom Rating Scale (SRS) developed for the VA Psychiatric Evaluation Project (Jenkins, Stauffacher, and Hester[8]). The SRS is the same scale employed by Gibby et al.[5] in their S-D study. Later in the day they were taken to the laboratory and given a pretest psychological battery, the pertinent items of which included the Holtzman Inkblot Technique (HIT),[7] Draw-a-Person (DAP), and Bender-Gestalt tests.

The HIT is an inkblot test consisting of forty-five cards to which a subject gives one response per card. This test was used rather than the Rorschach because standardized alternate forms of the test are available and permit better control of practice effects on retesting. Information on the construction and standardization of the HIT is available elsewhere.[7] In the Draw-a-Person test a subject is required to make a free-hand drawing with paper and pencil of a human figure. The Bender-Gestalt test requires the copying of geometric figures. Both tests reflect degree of psychomotor control and are regarded as indirect indices of ego control and reality contact.

On the morning of the second day, the subject was once again brought to the laboratory where he was introduced to the S-D

---

Ms. Bentinck is a member of the VA Houston Psychiatric Evaluation Project team and thus well experienced in evaluating psychiatric patients and thoroughly familiar with the SRS.

experience. Questions raised by subjects regarding the duration of the experiment were disregarded in so far as possible. Patients were not informed of the predetermined maximum time of four hours in S-D. This four-hour period was established for a variety of practical reasons involving hospital routines of feeding and activity scheduling. Previous studies (Cohen et al.[3]; Ruff et al.[10]) demonstrated that a four-hour period was sufficiently long to produce the kind of behavior typically encountered in S-D situations.

Immediately on concluding the S-D experience, subjects were again administered the psychological test battery. On the day following S-D, they were reinterviewed by the social worker and rerated on the SRS. These interviews and ratings were conducted on a blind basis since the social worker was not informed as to which subject population a patient belonged.

## Results

### Symptom Rating Scale

The SRS contains twenty items covering various aspects of pathology such as the presence of hallucinations, disorientation, memory deficit, etc. A rating of one to four is made for each item, with the larger numbers indicating greater severity of pathology. For the purposes of the present analysis a total pathology score was calculated for each subject by adding the individual item

TABLE 4-I

PRE-S-D PSYCHIATRIC SYMPTOM RATINGS
FOR SCHIZOPHRENICS VERSUS NONPSYCHOTICS

|                | Low Pathol. | High Pathol. | $X^2$ |
|----------------|-------------|--------------|-------|
| Schizophrenics | 7           | 13           |       |
|                |             |              | 6.5*  |
| Nonpsychotics  | 15          | 5            |       |

*Significant between 0.02-0.01 level.

ratings. An over-all group median pathology score was then obtained and comparisons made between the subject groups using $\chi^2$ analysis. In Table 4-I is presented a tabulation of the low vs high pathology ratings received by schizophrenics and nonpsychotics prior to S-D. It will be noted that significantly more schizophrenics than nonpsychotics receive high pathology ratings. This finding is important since it indicates that these two subject groups do differ significantly in respect to clinical behavior. Also, this finding testifies to the validity of the ratings made on a blind basis.

TABLE 4-II

PRE-VERSUS POST-S-D PSYCHIATRIC
SYMPTOM RATINGS FOR SCHIZOPHRENICS

|          | Low Pathol. | High Pathol. | $X^2$ |
|----------|-------------|--------------|-------|
| Pre-S-D  | 7           | 13           |       |
|          |             |              | N.S.  |
| Post-S-D | 9           | 11           |       |

Turning next to Table 4-II a comparison is made of the pre- vs post-S-D ratings for schizophrenics. Following S-D, schizophrenics are seen as evidencing no significant change in behavior compared to pre-S-D ratings. A similar comparison for nonpsychotics appears in Table 4-III, and again no change in behavior is noted.

Item by item analysis of the SRS ratings also fails to reveal any consistent changes following S-D for either subject group. Moreover the schizophrenic control group which received no S-D failed to change from first to second evaluation.

## Psychological Tests

In the study by Gibby et al.,[4] the Rorschach was scored using the Klopfer Rorschach Prognostic Rating Scale (PRS). In this system responses to the inkblots are scored for movement, color, and form level. Gibby, et al.[4] interpreted increases in these scores

TABLE 4-III

PRE-VERSUS POST-S-D PSYCHIATRIC SYMPTOM
RATINGS FOR NONPSYCHOTICS

|  | Low Pathol. | High Pathol. | $X^2$ |
|---|---|---|---|
| Pre-S-D | 15 | 5 | |
| | | | N.S. |
| Post-S-D | 15 | 5 | |

following S-D as indicating increased ego strength. In the present study, the HIT records for the schizophrenics and nonpsychotic subjects were scored in a similar manner. Scoring was done by one of us (S. E. C.) on a blind basis. That is, the HIT records were arranged in such a way that the scorer was unaware as to whether a protocol belonged in the psychotic or nonpsychotic group or whether it was a pre- or post-S-D record. This point is important since by scoring the records blindly any examiner bias is eliminated. Response total on the HITS's was controlled by obtaining one response per card to each of twenty-five inkblots. Scoring for movement, color, and form level responses proceeded as described

TABLE 4-IV

PRE-VERSUS POST-S-D INKBLOT PROGNOSTIC SCORES
FOR SCHIZOPHRENICS AND NONPSYCHOTICS

| | Pre-S-D | | Post-S-D | | | |
|---|---|---|---|---|---|---|
| | Mean Score | Stand. Dev. | Mean Score | Stand. Dev. | $t$ | $P$ |
| Schizophrenics | | | | | | |
| Movement score | 10.8 | 7.3 | 9.7 | 5.9 | 0.71 | N.S. |
| Form level | 13.6 | 5.7 | 13.8 | 4.8 | 0.23 | N.S. |
| Color score | 6.2 | 3.2 | 6.6 | 2.8 | 0.60 | N.S. |
| Nonpsychotics | | | | | | |
| Movement score | 14.4 | 6.1 | 13.3 | 6.8 | 1.04 | N.S. |
| Form level | 16.3 | 4.1 | 17.4 | 3.4 | 1.31 | N.S. |
| Color score | 6.4 | 4.2 | 6.8 | 3.3 | 0.14 | N.S. |

by Holtzman et al.[7]

Table 4-IV presents the pre- and post-S-D PRS scores for the schizophrenic and nonpsychotic groups. In contrast to the findings by Gibby et al.,[4] none of the scores for either group demonstrates significant change following S-D. However, it will be noted that nonpsychotics significantly exceed schizophrenics on form level and movement scores, both before and after S-D, indicating greater ego strength in the nonpsychotic group, as would be anticipated.

Finally the DAP and the Bender-Gestalt drawings were scored and statistically compared. For the DAP, size of figure drawings was examined, including vertical height, shoulder width, and head diameter. In an earlier study, Azima and Cramer[1] observed an expansion in the size of figure drawings following S-D, which they interpreted as reflecting a release of hostility. In the present study no significant change in any size dimension of the figure drawings was observed following S-D. The DAP was also scored for articulation, a scoring system developed by Witkin[11] which takes into consideration the amount of definition and structure introduced into the drawings. Witkin considers a high degree of articulation in figure drawings as reflecting maturity and a well-defined self-concept. In the present study S-D produced no change in articulation scores for either subject group. Neither was there any shift in the size or degree of disorganization present in Bender-Gestalt drawings following S-D.

### Behavioral Observations

On emerging from S-D, all patients were questioned regarding any unusual experiences or perceptions occurring during their confinement. Since one of the common findings in S-D studies concerns reports of disturbed perceptual functioning, interest was focused on experiences of a hallucinatory nature. Two of the experiences most frequently reported were that the lights had been dimmed momentarily and that the door to the chamber had been opened and closed. Nineteen of the schizophrenics and all twenty of the nonpsychotics reported one or both of these phenomena. One schizophrenic became completely disoriented and thought he was back on his job. Experiencing vivid dreams difficult to distinguish from reality, seeing patterned light, hearing the rattling of keys were other commonly reported experiences. However, the groups did not differ either in frequency or intensity of these reported perceptual distortions. There is, of course, the possibility that these patients, especially the nonpsychotics, were reluctant to report strange or unusual sensations for fear of the effect such reports might have on their hospital treatment, i.e., that they might be placed on a locked ward or given electroconvulsive therapy, etc.

Prior to S-D five of the schizophrenics and none of the nonpsychotics admitted current hallucinatory experiences. S-D produced no change in these effects in contrast to the studies by Gibby et al.[5] and Harris,[6] where dramatic relief from hallucinatory experiences was reported. In fact, in the present study one schizophrenic with a long history of auditory hallucinations complained that S-D tended to make the voices louder and clearer.

Further analysis of the behavioral data reveals that the two subject groups differed in respect to the total time spent in S-D. It will be recalled that an arbitrary limit of four hours in S-D was set and that patients were encouraged to remain in S-D until told to leave. Patients were not informed of this four-hour limit. Of the forty subjects experiencing S-D, eight nonpsychotics and five schizophrenics remained for the total four-hour period. Schizophrenics averaged 163 minutes in S-D and nonpsychotics 185 minutes, a difference which is not statistically significant. The fact that schizophrenics spend somewhat less time in S-D than do nonpsychotics and that only five schizophrenics remained for the full experimental period tends to argue against the idea that S-D offers them a relaxing, therapeutic experience. At least the subjects in the present study were unlike the hebephrenics, observed by Harris, who were reluctant to leave the S-D room even on conclusion of his experiment.

## Comment

In the present study, schizophrenics and nonpsychotics demonstrate no significant change either in behavior or in personality structure following exposure to a period of sensory deprivation. This failure of S-D to effect change occurred despite a strong suggestion to each subject that the S-D situation constituted a new treatment approach. Failure to obtain S-D effects contrasts with the study by Gibby et al.,[4,5] who report both immediate and long-term behavioral changes as well as changes in psychological test performance following an S-D experience. On the other hand, the present findings are compatible with those of Harris[6] who found that only during the actual period of exposure to S-D did his schizophrenics report any alteration in symptoms. Following S-D Harris noted no significant change in behavior in any of his subjects.

It is not entirely clear why the results of the present study failed to replicate those of Gibby et al. Perhaps subjects in the Gibby study spent a somewhat longer period in S-D than did the present subjects, since in that experiment six hours of S-D was required. However, Gibby does not report how long his subjects actually remained in the experimental situation or how many remained for the full six hours.

The present investigators consider the introduction of a control group and the evaluation of all subjects on a blind basis to be of paramount importance in studying change effected by S-D. Only by utilizing a control schizophrenic group evaluated prior to and following S-D can placebo effect be eliminated. Unless such a control group is employed, any changes attributed to the effect of S-D may actually reflect nothing more than response to the research itself, with all of the attention it focuses on the subjects. And unless the investigators make their evaluations while remaining unaware of the type of treatment received by subjects, examiner bias may influence the ratings obtained.

It is hardly surprising that a few hours spent in an isolated situation, lying quietly on a bed, fails to interrupt what is often a life-long history of disturbed and deviant behavior. If this had proved otherwise, why would not a good night's sleep (an event approximating many of the conditions of S-D) alleviate the distressing symptoms of schizophrenia? Unfortunately the results of the present study offer little promise that simple exposure to a sensory deprivation situation constitutes a new therapeutic approach to the treatment of behavioral disorders.

## Summary

A group of twenty schizophrenic and twenty nonpsychotic hospitalized psychiatric patients was exposed to a period of sensory deprivation. Behavioral ratings were made and psychological tests administered prior to and following sensory deprivation in order to evaluate any resulting change in clinical condition or personality structure. A control group of twenty schizophrenics was evaluated in similar manner but without an intervening period of sensory deprivation. No consistent changes either in behavior or psychological test performance were observed following exposure to sensory deprivation.

## REFERENCES

1. Azima, H., and Cramer, F. J.: Effects of Partial Perceptual Isolation in Mentally Disturbed Individuals. *Dis. Nerv. Syst.*, *17*:117-122, 1956.
2. Bexton, W. H., Heron, W., and Scott, T. H.: Effects of decreased variation in the sensory environment. *Canad. J. Psychol.*, *8*:70-76, 1954.
3. Cohen, B. D., Rosenbaum, G., Dobie, S. I., and Gottlieb, J. S.: Sensory isolation: hallucinogenic effects of a brief procedure. *J. Nerv. Ment. Dis.*, *129*:486-491, 1959.
4. Cooper, G. D., Adams, H. B., and Gibby, R. G.: Ego strength changes following perceptual deprivation. *Arch. Gen. Psychiat.*, *7*:213-217, 1962.
5. Gibby, R. G., Adams, H. B., and Carrera, R. N.: Therapeutic changes in psychiatric patients following partial sensory deprivation. *Arch. Gen. Psychiat.*, *3*:33-42, 1960.
6. Harris, A.: Sensory deprivation and schizophrenia. *J. Ment. Sci.*, *105*:235-236, 1959.
7. Holtzman, W. H., Thorpe, J. S., Swartz, J. D., and Herron, B. W.: *Inkblot Perception and Personality.* Austin, University of Texas Press, 1961.
8. Jenkins, R. F., Stauffacher, J., and Hester, R.: A symptom rating scale for use with psychotic patients. *A.M.A. Arch. Gen. Psychiat.*, *1*:197-204, 1959.
9. Reitman, E. E., and Cleveland, S. E.: Changes in body image following sensory deprivation in schizophrenic and control groups. *J. Ab. & Soc. Psychol.*, to be published.
10. Ruff, G. E., Levy, E. Z., and Thaler, V. H.: Factors Influencing the Reaction to Reduced Sensory Input, in *Sensory Deprivation,* edited by P. Solomon et al, Cambridge, Harvard University Press, 1961.
11. Witkin, H. A.: Personal communication to the authors, 1961.

# PERSONALITY CHANGES AFTER
# SENSORY DEPRIVATION*

G. DAVID COOPER, Ph.D., HENRY B. ADAMS, Ph.D.,
AND LOUIS D. COHEN, Ph.D.

MOST sensory deprivation research has emphasized the disruptive effects on normal subjects, such as delusions, illusions, hallucinations, anxiety, impaired concentration and judgment.[35,38] Reports on "brainwashing" of prisoners of war have also emphasized the disruptive effects of prolonged social isolation and perceptual deprivation.[34]

In contrast, studies with psychiatric patients report more positive effects. Azima and Cramer[1] exposed fourteen psychiatric patients to continuous periods of partial sensory deprivation for an average period of four days. Initial signs of disorganization in these subjects were followed by "positive shifts in mood, release of constructive aggression and increased attempts at socialization." Cohen, Silverman, Bressler and Shmavonian[9] reported that out of four "normal" subjects, two who appeared to be schizoid personalities said that they liked isolation, while the other two reported they disliked the experience. Harris[16] placed twelve schizophrenic patients in conditions similar to those used by Bexton, Heron and Scott.[3] He found them more tolerant of deprivation than normal subjects; the patients showed fewer visual and auditory hallucinations than normals, or no hallucinations. His hebephrenic subjects especially liked being in the experimental situation, and were reluctant to leave.

Gibby, Adams and Carrera[12] investigated the effects of social isolation and relatively brief partial sensory deprivation on psychiatric symptoms. Their subjects were thirty white male psychiatric patients with various functional psychiatric disorders. Ss were interviewed a day before, a day after, and a week after deprivation, and their interview behavior rated on a twenty-item Symptom Rating Scale. Positive changes (less symptomatology) for the entire group were twice as frequent as negative changes, and the positive changes were relatively enduring while the negative changes were not.

Existing studies touch on important questions but leave many issues unresolved. Before attributing therapeutic effects to deprivation procedures it is necessary to rule out such variables as 1) spontaneous improvement in patients over time, 2) the supportive influence of increased attention, 3) adaptation to the testing or interview situation from which data for evaluation are derived. Even if therapeutic effects under controlled conditions could be attributed to deprivation, their practical utilization would still require understanding of relationships between personality functioning and reactions to deprivation.

This paper reports reactions of psychiatric Ss to brief, partial perceptual deprivation and social isolation. Two hypotheses were tested: 1) the psychological functioning of psychiatric patients will improve after exposure to a relatively brief period of social and perceptual deprivation, and 2) differences in responses to deprivation are related to individual differences in personality.

To test the first hypothesis it was necessary to select reliable, valid indices of generalized psychological functioning as measures of improvement. The indices used in previous research involved measures which are interpreted as indicators of socially effective, adaptive behavior, or ego strength. The concept of ego strength provides an inclusive set of criteria for assessing personality change and improvement. Operationally defined, ego strength includes 1) adequate reality testing, i.e., substantial correspondence between the consensually validated and subjectively perceived environment; 2) appropriate verbalized feelings of personal adequacy; 3) emotional integration, manifested by spontaneous yet appropriately controlled emotional responsivity; and 4) effectiveness in coping with reality situations, reflecting the efficiency with which goals are achieved.

The measures of ego strength used in the present study were psychological instruments considered to be appropriate indices of these functions. Each had an extensive research literature on which relatively unambiguous interpretation could be based. Each provided a quantifiable score which could be used in statistical tests of hypotheses.

Five measures of ego strength meeting these criteria were employed. The most important, the Rorschach Prognostic Rating Scale (RPRS), has been found a reliable, valid measure of the effectiveness of personality functioning. The RPRS consists of six component scores, derived by a process of differential weighting of Rorschach determinants according to a detailed set of criteria (Klopfer, pp. 690-695). These six component scores, Weighted *M*, Weighted *FM*, Weighted *m*, Shading, Color, and Form Level, are summed together into an overall Final Prognostic Score. This instrument is well suited for personality assessment and the prediction of individual response to traditional methods of psychotherapy. The RPRS has been used extensively in previous research on prognosis for therapy.[6,20] Butler and Fiske[4] reviewed the literature and concluded that "the Rorschach Prognostic Rating Scale appears to predict response to psychotherapy with a rather remarkable degree of accuracy." They found these results "surprising for two reasons: first, Prognostic Rating Scale relationships are in general considerably higher than those reported in many other Rorschach studies; secondly, they compare quite favorably with the best results established in psychometric testing."

A pilot study was carried out by the present writers to appraise the sensitivity of the RPRS to changes in ego functioning following deprivation.[10] A group of hospitalized white male psychiatric patients experienced several hours of social isolation and perceptual deprivation. The Rorschach was administered before and after deprivation and the protocols scored in accordance with Cartwright's modification of the RPRS.[6] The scores on this instrument showed significant changes in the "improved" direction, consistent with previous clinical impressions.

The present study has two parts. The first deals with the hypothesis of general improvement as shown in overall group trends on the RPRS and other measures of ego strength. The second part investigates individual differences and the prediction of differential responses after deprivation on the RPRS Final Prognostic Score.

## Procedures

### Subjects

Ss were inpatients in a Veterans Administration hospital, all diagnosed as having functional psychiatric disorders. All were white males between twenty and sixty, with no known history of organic brain damage or intracranial pathology. No S had received psychiatric chemotherapy for at least one week prior to deprivation. None had received any form of electroconvulsive or insulin shock therapy for at least three months prior to the experiment.

Two equivalent groups of twenty Ss each were formed. One served as an experimental group and received three hours of partial perceptual deprivation and social isolation. The other was a control group. The groups were equated for age, years of school, and mean pretest scores on five indices of ego strength. The RPRS Final Prognostic Score, the Barron Ego Strength (Es) scale of the MMPI, the Rotter Level of Aspiration Test, the Symptom Rating Scale, and the Leary Interpersonal Check List were the measures of ego strength employed. The means, standard deviations, and differences in pretest means between the two groups are given in Table 5-I, individual descriptive data are given in Table 5-II. None of the differences was significant.

### Experimenters

Two Es were involved in the study. *Experimenter 1* (E1) administered and scored all tests. *Experimenter 2* (E2) selected and ran Ss in deprivation, randomly assigning them to groups. Since E1 had no knowledge of the group to which Ss were assigned, experimenter bias could occur only when a patient spontaneously identified himself as an experimental S or a control on posttesting. Only four of the forty Ss tested actually did so. After testing of each S, the completed test protocol was given to E2, who removed the names and assigned a code number to each protocol. After a lapse of at least thirty days the protocols were returned to E1 for scoring.

### Experimental Group

Each S was tested on a three-day schedule. On the first day he underwent a diagnostic interview, after which a Rorschach, MMPI, self-ratings and ideal ratings on the Leary Interpersonal Check List, and scores on ten trials with the Rotter Board were obtained. The second day each S was scheduled for three hours of deprivation. On the third day he was again interviewed and re-tested with the same battery.

During the period of deprivation each S lay on a bed with eyes covered by cotton under a plastic eye piece. His ears were plugged with glycerin-soaked cotton, and his head wrapped in a gauze bandage. He was observed during the entire period. S remained three hours unless he spontaneously terminated early. The procedure was well tolerated; eighteen of the twenty Ss remained at least two hours.

In this situation meaningfully patterned visual and auditory stimuli were reduced to a minimum and social interaction virtually eliminated. Social isolation was pronounced but not complete, since S was aware that someone was within calling distance. Nevertheless, S received a minimum of sensory cues to remind him of the continued presence of others. No attempt was made to diminish tactile or kinesthetic cues. Requests by S for food, water, permission to smoke, and the like were ignored by the examiner. If an S complained repeatedly of the need to urinate, a urinal was silently placed in his hands. No other interaction was permitted.

Ss were retested a day later and told "We would like to see if there is any change in your condition on the ward from day to day." If an S wanted more explanation, the examiner said "Some people do change quite a bit from day to day on the ward, while others tend to be about the same. It is important to get a reliable picture of each person's condition, and this can best be done by getting two sets of tests spaced a little apart." No further explanation was given.

TABLE 5-I

PRE-TEST CHARACTERISTICS OF EXPERIMENTAL
AND CONTROL GROUPS

| Items | Group Means and Standard Deviations | | | | | |
|---|---|---|---|---|---|---|
| | Experimental group (N = 20) | | Control group (N = 20) | | Diff. | |
| | $\bar{X}_E$ | S.D. | $\bar{X}_C$ | S.D. | $\bar{X}_E - \bar{X}_C$ | $t^*$ |
| Age | 38.90 | 8.18 | 38.25 | 7.27 | -.65 | .27 |
| Years of school | 9.63 | 3.91 | 9.25 | 3.15 | -.38 | .38 |
| RPRS Prognostic Score | 1.14 | 2.64 | 1.84 | 2.65 | .65 | .76 |
| Barron Es Scale (Raw Score) | 28.76 | 9.50 | 36.15 | 9.63 | 2.61 | .83 |
| Symptom Rating Scale (Total Pathology Score) | 31.65 | 5.24 | 31.10 | 3.45 | -.55 | .39 |
| Leary Self-Ideal Discrepancy Score | 25.18 | 11.28† | 25.63 | 21.40† | .45 | .07 |
| Rotter Dp Score | .52 | 2.96 | .40 | 3.28 | -.12 | .12 |

*None of the differences between the two groups was statistically significant.
†F test indicates significantly greater variability in control group ($p < .01$).

## Control Group

Controls were interviewed and administered all the tests given to the experimental group. The only difference was that on Day 2 the controls continued their normal ward routine rather than receiving deprivation.

## Dependent Variables and Analysis of Data

### The First Hypothesis (Generalized Improvement)

Four other measures of personality functioning were used in addition to the RPRS. These measures and the experimental hypothesis associated with each are described below. The hypothesis of no change on retesting was made for the control group for each measure.

1) *The Symptom Rating Scale*: This adaptation of the Lorr Scale, developed for the VA Psychiatric Evaluation Project, has

TABLE 5-II

DESCRIPTIVE DATA FOR INDIVIDUAL SUBJECTS IN
EXPERIMENTAL AND CONTROL GROUPS

| Experimental Subjects | | | | Controls | | | |
|---|---|---|---|---|---|---|---|
| S | Age | Education | Admission diagnosis | S | Age | Education | Admission diagnosis |
| C1 | 40 | 18 yrs. | Manic depressive | C1A | 34 | NA* | Anxiety reaction |
| C2 | 44 | 12 yrs. | Dissociative reaction | C2A | 36 | NA* | Anxiety reaction |
| C3 | 39 | 3 yrs. | Schizophrenic reaction | C3A | 37 | 12 yrs. | NP unclassified |
| C4 | 41 | 5 yrs. | Pseudo-neurotic schizophrenic | C4A | 30 | NA* | |
| C5 | 28 | 13 yrs. | Personality pattern disturbance | C5A | 33 | 10 yrs. | Schizophrenic reaction |
| C6 | 56 | NA* | Paranoid personality | C6A | 50 | 12 yrs. | Neurotic depressive reaction |
| C7 | 54 | 4 yrs. | Conversion hysteria | C7A | 33 | 10 yrs. | Schizophrenic reaction |
| C8 | 28 | 6 yrs. | NP unclassified | C8A | 36 | 11 yrs. | Schizophrenic reaction |
| C9 | 38 | 10 yrs. | NP unclassified | C9A | 46 | 9 yrs. | Anxiety reaction |
| C10 | 46 | 16 yrs. | Depressive reaction | C10A | 44 | 3 yrs. | NP unclassified |
| C11 | 37 | 10 yrs. | Chronic gastritis | C11A | 38 | 9 yrs. | Psychoneurosis unclassified |

| | | | | | | | |
|---|---|---|---|---|---|---|---|
| C12 | 47 | 8 yrs. | Chronic schizophrenia | C12A | 30 | 8 yrs. | Inadequate personality |
| C13 | 40 | 12 yrs. | NP unclassified | C13A | 51 | 9 yrs. | NP unclassified |
| C14 | 28 | 7 yrs. | Conversion reaction | C14A | 39 | NA* | NP unclassified |
| C15 | 29 | 10 yrs. | Inadequate personality | C15A | 41 | 8 yrs. | Anxiety reaction |
| C16 | 39 | 10 yrs. | Anxiety reaction | C16A | 40 | 5 yrs. | Inadequate personality |
| C17 | 35 | 12 yrs. | Anxiety reaction | C17A | 53 | 10 yrs. | Depressive reaction moderate |
| C18 | 28 | 12 yrs. | Anxiety reaction | C18A | 33 | 7 yrs. | Psychological G.I. reaction |
| C19 | 42 | 7 yrs. | Paranoid schizophrenic | C19A | 33 | 12 yrs. | Schizophrenic reaction |
| C20 | 39 | 8 yrs. | Personality pattern disturbance | C20A | 28 | 16 yrs. | NP unclassified |

*Not available.

shown good reliability and validity.[18] The scale provides for assessment of overt behavior symptomatology in situations involving face-to-face interaction. Scoring is in a pathological direction only, higher scores indicating more severe symptoms. It was predicted that Ss would show a greater pre-post reduction of symptoms than the control group.

2) *The Interpersonal Check List* was used to obtain a report of S's conscious self-percept and his description of the ideal person. In accord with Leary's findings,[23] greater self-ideal discrepancies were considered to indicate less self-regard. It was predicted that the mean self-ideal discrepancy would decrease in the experimental group following deprivation, and that the experimental group would show a greater drop than the control group.

3) *The Barron Ego-Strength Scale* (Es) was included because it provides an index of S's feelings of personal adequacy and self-satisfaction.[2] It was predicted that the E's scores of the experimental group would increase after deprivation, and that the experimental group would show a greater positive change in ego strength than the control group.

4) *The Rotter Level of Aspiration Test* was included because previous research had indicated that goal-setting on this task is systematically related to self-regard and response to stress.[7,8,24,27] The Dp score measures shifts in predicted achievement following prior achievement. Excessively optimistic or pessimistic Dp scores indicate pathology. Since the present group of psychiatric patients gave uniformly constricted scores, an increase in the Dp scores following deprivation was predicted for the experimental group. A greater relative increase in Dp score was also predicted for the experimental group.

5) *The Rorschach Prognostic Rating Scale* (RPRS) was expected to show higher Final Prognostic Scores in the experimental group following deprivation. It was predicted that the pre-post increase would be greater than in the control group.

### The Second Hypothesis (Individual Differences)

The exploration of individual differences was concerned with changes in the Final Prognostic Score of the RPRS. Experimental

Ss were ranked in order from the most positive through the most negative change on this measure. Personality descriptions of Ss ranking in the top and bottom quartiles were then derived from a detailed examination of individual case protocols. These descriptions were based on all the information available on each S, including nursing notes, case histories, observations of behavior during deprivation, transcription of Ss' comments during deprivation, and the psychological measures of ego functioning.

The pretest personality descriptions indicated that Ss who later changed positively showed 1) poorly integrated and relatively unsuccessful psychological defense systems, 2) an overal lack of verbal productivity and general inability to relate verbally to others or deal symbolically with problems, 3) reliance on primary repression as a defense and a tendency to act out behaviorally when repressive defenses fail, 4) a tendency to regard themselves as helpless and dependent, and 5) an intrapunitive way of handling hostility. In contrast, the negative changers were characterized by 1) moderately well-integrated and effective defense systems, 2) comparatively adequate social skills and the ability to relate comfortably on a verbal level, 3) reliance on complex and elaborate defense systems utilizing isolation, intellectualization, reaction formation, and projection, and 4) a tendency to attribute responsibility for their difficulties to others.

Seven Rorschach indices were then selected to predict direction of change after deprivation on the RPRS Final Prognostic Score. Each index was intended to differentiate various aspects of the two personality constellations described above. Directional hypotheses for each index were made and cutting scores selected. The indices derived from extreme quartiles of the experimental group were tested by comparing predicted with actual changes for the entire experimental group. For this purpose, Ss with change scores on the RPRS Final Prognostic Score above the median constituted the positive-change group, while Ss falling below the median constituted the negative-change group. When predicted and actual changes coincided this was scored as a "correct" prediction. The statistical significance of "correct" versus "incorrect" assignments (predictions) was determined by the binominal expansion. (Siegel, 41). The indices were then cross-validated

against the Rorschach protocols used in the original pilot study.[10]
A description of these Rorschach indices and their expected relationship to changes on the RPRS Final Prognostic Score is given
below.

For each of the seven indices, Ss scoring above the pretest mean
are considered "high scorers" on that index while those below the
mean are considered "low scorers." Since change scores on the
RPRS Final Prognostic Score were ranked in order from the most
positive to the most negative change, the median RPRS change
score was used as the cutting point. Ss who scored above the
median showed high positive changes on the RPRS Final Prognostic Score; those below the median showed either negative or
low positive changes. On this basis they were categorized as "high
changers" and "low changers." The seven indices are:

1) *Hostility Index*: This index assigns weighted scores to
number of $C + CF$ responses, number of $m$ responses, skeletal and
soft anatomy, and $M$ and $FM$ responses with hostile content.
Since subjects whose RPRS Final Prognostic Scores changed
negatively following deprivation showed behavioral indications
of poorly controlled hostility, the Rorschach index of overt hostility developed by Schneider[31] was used. It was predicted that
high scorers on Schneider's Hostility Index would be low
changers on the RPRS following deprivation and that low scorers
on this index would be high changers on the RPRS.

2) *M plus Sum C*: The rationale for this index was proposed by
Gibby,[11] who stated that the traditional $M$: Sum $C$ ratio treated
statistically in the form $M$ + Sum $C$ can be regarded as a measure of
psychic energy. An absence of $M$ and $C$, reflecting low productivity, intellectual constriction and lack of intellectual responsiveness to the external world, was found in the individual
protocols of Ss who made greater positive changes after deprivation. It was predicted that Ss scoring low on this index of psychic
energy would be high changers on the RPRS and that high
scorers on this index would be the low changers on the RPRS.

3) *Number of Rorschach Content Categories*: This index reflects verbal facility and breadth of intellectual experience. It was
predicted that high scores on this index would be low changers on
the RPRS, and vice versa.

4) *Defensive Style:* This index is based on Schafer's[30] categorization of defenses into four syndromes: primary repression, projection, denial and isolation. These characteristic defensive patterns are of considerable interest. The patients who tended to rely mainly on primary repression as a defense came largely from three nosological groups: 1) the impulse neurotics, with rigid superego structures but weak ego controls; 2) sociopaths, who lack both adequate internal cues to evaluate their behavior in accord with social expectations and effective, socially approved techniques for achieving their goals; and 3) passive-dependent personalities who experienced affect with relative freedom and handled internal conflicts through repression or somatization. Ss relying on the other three defensive styles were more often diagnosed as psychoneurotics, and their case histories indicated that they functioned in socially more effective ways before hospitalization. The preliminary impression was that Ss who responded most positively to deprivation seldom manifested the elaborate psychological defenses generally thought to be characteristic of the classic psychoneurotic. It was therefore predicted that Ss who relied heavily on repression as a defense would be high changers on the RPRS, and that Ss in the other three categories would be low changers.

5) *Isolation Index (Klopfer K + k):* These determinants are traditionally interpreted as indicators of the use of isolation, withdrawal and intellectualization as defenses against free-floating anxiety. In accord with our observation that patients changing negatively on the RPRS had more rigid and complex defenses, it was predicted that high scorers on the Isolation Index would be low changers on the RPRS, and vice versa.

6) *Percent VIII through X:* Examination of case histories suggested that Ss showing the greatest positive change on the RPRS after deprivation responded to affectively-laden stimuli in characteristic ways. They tended either to deny the emotional implications of such stimuli entirely or, if their repressive defenses were overcome, to act out in childish, socially unacceptable ways. Their Rorschachs reflected the former defense. On the last three color cards they uniformly demonstrated repression and denial, manifested by card rejection. It was therefore predicted that Ss who gave more than 30 percent of their responses to cards VIII

through X would be low changers on the RPRS and that Ss giving less than 30 percent of their responses to these three cards would be high changers.

7) *Pretest RPRS Prognostic Score*: As noted above, the RPRS negative changers tended to have more elaborate and complex ego defenses. Although these defenses were used to a pathological degree, they nevertheless suggested more potential personality resources than were available to the inadequate, poorly socialized Ss who appeared to respond most positively to deprivation. Although persons with higher Final Prognostic Scores on the RPRS usually show greater gains on retest following traditional verbal psychotherapy, it was felt that an opposite relationship would hold for Ss in the present study. It was predicted that Ss who scored below the mean pre-test RPRS Final Prognostic Score would be above the median RPRS change score and that Ss above the mean pre-test RPRS Final Prognostic Score would fall below the median RPRS change score.

## Results and Discussion

The first hypothesis predicted positive changes in ego functioning following deprivation. The results summarized in Table 5-III generally bore out the expectations based on this hypothesis. Following exposure to deprivation, experimental Ss showed significantly greater positive shift on the RPRS than the controls, a significantly greater reduction in self-ideal discrepancy scores, and significantly more flexibility in predicting achievement on the Rotter. Differences in pre-post changes on the Barron Es scale and the Symptom Rating Scale Total Pathology Score were not significant.

Gibby, Adams and Carrera[12] broke down their data on changes in the Symptom Rating Scale into two separate indices. These were a Symptom Reduction Index, the total number of items on which Ss showed less severe symptomatology following deprivation, and a Symptom Increase Index, consisting of the total number of items on which the severity of symptoms was greater after deprivation. When the present data were similarly analyzed, it was found that the experimental Ss demonstrated significantly

TABLE 5-III

DIFFERENCES BETWEEN EXPERIMENTAL AND CONTROL GROUPS IN
PRE-TEST POST-TEST CHANGES ON FIVE MEASURES

| Instrument | Dependent Variable | Experimental Group (N = 20) | | Control Group (N = 19) | | t | p* |
|---|---|---|---|---|---|---|---|
| | | Mean change | S.D. | Mean change | S.D. | | |
| 1) Rorschach | RPRS Prognostic Score | .74 | 2.00 | -.13 | 1.56 | 1.56 | .07 |
| 2) SRS | Total Pathology Score | -1.75 | .77 | -1.35 | .50 | .44 | nsd |
| | a) Symptom Reduction Index | 4.05 | 2.55 | 2.95 | 1.83 | 2.17 | .03 |
| | b) Symptom Increase Index | 2.20 | 1.91 | 2.05 | 2.11 | .74 | nsd |
| 3) Leary | Self-Ideal Discrepancy | -6.65 | 3.46 | .06 | 4.67 | 2.03 | .025 |
| 4) MMPI | Barron Es Scale (Raw Score) | 2.35 | -.83 | .80 | 1.07 | 1.15 | nsd |
| 5) Rotter | Dp Score | .19 | 4.40 | -2.40 | 4.59 | 1.76 | .05 |

*One-tailed test.

more symptom reduction following deprivation than the controls.

Table 5-IV shows pre-post changes within each group. The experimental group changed in the direction of improved ego

TABLE 5-IV

WITHIN-GROUP CHANGES ON FIVE MEASURES IN
EXPERIMENTAL AND CONTROL GROUPS

| Measuring scale | Experimental Group (N = 20) | | | Control Group (N = 19) | | |
|---|---|---|---|---|---|---|
| | Mean change | t | p* | Mean change | t | p* |
| RPRS Prognostic Score | .74 | 1.58 | .10 | -.13 | .39 | nsd |
| Barron Es Scale (Raw Score) | 2.35 | 2.83 | .01 | .80 | .75 | nsd |
| Symptom Rating Scale (Total Pathology Score) | -1.75 | 2.27 | .025 | -1.35 | 2.68 | .02 |
| Leary Self-Ideal Discrepancy Score | -6.65 | 2.53 | .025 | .06 | .04 | nsd |
| Rotter Dp Score | .19 | .17 | nsd | -2.40 | 2.38 | .03 |

*One-tailed test.

functioning on all five measures, these changes approaching or attaining significance for every measure except the Rotter Dp Score. In the control group the only significant change clearly in the improved direction was on the Symptom Rating Scale Total Pathology Score. The mean Rotter Dp score for the control group did change significantly, but in a direction indicating increased emotional and behavioral constriction upon retesting.

The results show that exposure to deprivation produced significant positive changes, in many areas, in the adaptive functions of the ego. Overt symptomatology decreased and feelings of positive self-regard and self-acceptance increased.

The second hypothesis stated that direction of change on the RPRS Final Prognostic Score could be predicted from quantifiable aspects of individual differences in psychological functioning. The seven Rorschach indices derived from examination of Ss in the extreme quartiles of RPRS change scores were reapplied to the twenty Ss in the full experimental group. These results are summarized on the left side of Table 5-V. Since this group included Ss on whom the predictive indices were identified, this procedure could not be considered a convincing demonstration of the predictive utility of these indices. Consequently, the predictive indices were applied to two other groups which included no Ss whose test protocols had been reviewed for the original selection. These were the control group used in this study, and the experimental Ss used in the earlier pilot study. The criterion measure for improvement in each of these two groups was the median RPRS score for that particular group, a necessary modification, since the shorter Cartwright modification of the RPRS used in the earlier pilot study differs in scaling from the complete RPRS used in the later study. The results for the control group are given on the right side of Table 5-V and those for the pilot study Ss are given in Table 5-VI.

The results of these cross-validated procedures support the hypothesis that direction of change on the RPRS following deprivation can be predicted from pre-deprivation Rorschach protocols. For the pilot study group in Table 5-VI, three of the seven indices showed significant relationships in the predicted direction, two showed trends in the predicted direction and two showed no

TABLE 5-V

RELATIONSHIP OF RORSCHACH PREDICTIVE INDICES TO PRE-TEST POST-TEST CHANGES
ACTUALLY OCCURRING ON RPRS FINAL PROGNOSTIC SCORE:
EXPERIMENTAL AND CONTROL GROUPS

| Rorschach Index | Experimental Group (N = 20) | | | Control Group (N = 18) | | |
|---|---|---|---|---|---|---|
| | Correct assignments | Incorrect assignments | $p^*$ | Correct assignments | Incorrect assignments | $p^*$ |
| Hostility | 14 | 6 | .058 | 9 | 9 | nsd |
| M plus Sum C | 13 | 7 | .13 | 10 | 8 | nsd |
| Content Categories | 16 | 4 | .006 | 9 | 9 | nsd |
| Defensive Style | 14 | 6 | .058 | 6 | 12 | nsd |
| Isolation Index (K + k) | 18 | 2 | .001 | 8 | 10 | nsd |
| Percent VIII through X | 14 | 6 | .058 | 10 | 8 | nsd |
| Pre-test RPRS Prognostic Score | 13 | 7 | .13 | 9 | 9 | nsd |

*Binominal expansion (one-tailed test).

TABLE 5-VI

RELATIONSHIP BETWEEN RORSCHACH
PREDICTIVE INDICES AND ACTUAL CHANGES ON
CARTWRIGHT MODIFICATION OF RPRS AFTER
DEPRIVATION: CROSS-VALIDATION (PILOT STUDY)
GROUP (N = 28)

| Rorschach Index | Correct Assignments | Incorrect Assignments | $p^*$ |
|---|---|---|---|
| Hostility | 17 | 11 | .17 |
| *M* plus Sum *C* | 13 | 15 | *nsd* |
| Content categories | 17 | 11 | .17 |
| Defensive style | 22 | 6 | .0024 |
| Isolation Index ($K + k$) | 19 | 9 | .04 |
| Percent VIII through X | 16 | 12 | *nsd* |
| Pre-test RPRS Prognostic Score | 19 | 9 | .04 |
| Combined Index | 21 | 7 | .007 |
| Clinical prediction | 13† | 1† | .001 |

*Binominal expansion (one-tailed test).
†Only the fourteen protocols representing highest and lowest quartiles are included; see test for explanation.

significant relationship. It may therefore be concluded that the seven Rorschach indices of personality functioning and differential responses to deprivation are systematically related. As expected, no relationship was found in the control group between any predictive index and direction of change on retesting.

Two additional indices appear in Table 5-VI. One is a combined index, derived by assigning a score of one for each of the seven indices in which the score fell within the range predicting positive change. Ss above the mean on the combined index were predicted to fall above the median RPRS change score; those below the mean on this index were predicted to fall below the median RPRS change score. The combined index correctly assigned twenty-one of the twenty-eight Ss, the chance probability of which is only .007.

The other index is an independent clinical demonstration based on the pilot study protocols. For this E2 selected and coded the twenty-eight pre-test Rorschach protocols for which post-deprivation protocols were also available. Then El selected from the total group the seven protocols which in his clinical judgment were most consistent with the qualitative personality descriptions of the extreme positive-change Ss. Seven protocols were also selected which were judged to be most consistent with the personality descriptions of the extreme negative-change Ss. These selections were made from multiple clinical criteria. Only the fourteen protocols representing the highest and lowest quartiles were selected, since it was felt desirable to restrict this demonstration to Ss who could be unambiguously categorized into one of the two personality configurations. The selections by El were then compared with the distribution of RPRS change scores for the total group, ranked in order from most positive to most negative change. Ss judged as positive changers were considered correctly assigned if their change scores fell above the median of change scores for the total group. Those judged as negative changers were considered correctly assigned if their change scores fell below the median. By this rather liberal criterion thirteen of the fourteen clinical judgments were "correct." (The combined index described in the paragraph above assigned twelve of these fourteen Ss correctly.) Both of these special indices predicted direction of change at far better than change expectancy.

## Discussion

Previous research has suggested that psychiatric patients show improved psychological functioning following brief perceptual deprivation and social isolation, in contrast to "normals." The present findings are in agreement. After exposure to deprivation the present experimental group showed generalized improvement in psychological functioning, manifested by 1) reduction of overt symptoms, 2) increase in positive self-regard and self-acceptance, and 3) more effective utilization of defenses at the level of functioning tapped by the Rorschach.

What variables might have contributed to these changes in the experimental group? It seems logical to assume that whatever factors operated to produce changes in the controls also influenced the experimental subjects. It will be recalled that a significant reduction in overt symptoms was found in the control group. This change probably reflects the supportive effect (Hawthorne or placebo effect) of our extensive testing and interview procedures. It is also likely that the experimental Ss were better adapted to the interview situation on retesting. The increased cautiousness of prediction noted among our controls on the Rotter goal-setting task suggests that the controls were motivated to appear less disturbed when retested. The reduction in overt symptoms indicates that they were capable of making a better outward appearance on retesting.

Although these factors undoubtedly did influence the experimental group, the data indicate, nevertheless, that the overall changes in the experimental Ss represented much more than a placebo or test-retest effect. The significant changes in the experimental group included several covert and presumably stable functions, such as Rorschach responses, self-perception and self-acceptance. These personality changes were far more profound than any of those occurring in the control group, indicating alterations at deeper, more fundamental levels of functioning.[23]

Exploration of individual differences on the Rorschach permits even more confidence in concluding that the observed changes resulted from deprivation. Direction of change on the RPRS following deprivation could be predicted quite well from the pretest Rorschach protocols of both the experimental and the pilot study groups. Yet in the control group there was a complete lack of relationship between the same pretest Rorschach indices and direction of change on the RPRS. It must therefore be concluded that the improved functioning in the experimental and pilot study groups resulted from deprivation.

It is appropriate to ask how this simple procedure could produce such substantial personality changes. One explanation proposed by Heron[17] emphasizes the homeostatic functions of the reticular activating system in attention, motivation and perception. He considers the behavioral changes during and after deprivation to result from the disruption of these regulatory functions.

The findings [the McGill studies] are in line with the recent studies of the brain, especially the reticular formation in the mid-brain. . . . In some way the reticular formation regulates the brain activity. The recent studies indicate that normal functioning of the brain depends on a continuing arousal reaction generated in the reticular system, which in turn depends on constant sensory bombardment. It appears that aside from their specific functions, sensory stimuli have the general function of maintaining the arousal, and they rapidly lose their power to do so if they are restricted to the monotonously repeated stimulation of an unchanging environment. Under these circumstances the activity of the cortex may be impaired so that the brain behaves abnormally (Heron, p. 96).

The present results suggest that Heron's explanation is a gross oversimplification. If the changes after deprivation were due solely to impaired cortical activity, a uniform deprivation response should have occurred, with relatively small individual differences. Yet the widely differing changes seen in Ss in the present study could be predicted in advance from Rorschach indices of the coping mechanisms and defense styles characteristic of each individual. Heron's explanation would seem applicable only if one can assume a direct relationship between individual differences in ego defenses and activity in the reticular formation of the midbrain.

An alternative approach considers the effect upon ego functions of deprivation of the environmental context in which these functions were initially differentiated and in which they are maintained. Rapaport[26] speaks of "stimulus nutriment" as necessary for the maintenance of ego defenses. Similarly, Ruff, Levy and Thaler [28] mention a diffusion of ego boundaries when orientation in space and time is lost. Within a phenomenological framework Snygg and Coombs[33] have discussed the differentiation of the self from the environment. Cambareri[5] maintains that certain ego structures, including the self, undergo gradual dedifferentiation during sensory deprivation.

Despite differences in terminology, there is considerable convergence among these explanations, which employ purely psychological constructs. All assume that during deprivation organized psychological functions undergo a dedifferentiation which modifies and impairs their operation. They offer a rationale for the markedly different responses of "normals" Ss and psychiatric patients. In "normals," where ego functions are used adaptively to permit the organization and interpretation of experience as a basis for effective interaction with the environment, the dedifferentiation would manifest itself by a disruption of organized functioning. Such disruption has been reported in the majority of deprivation studies using normal individuals. On the other hand, ego functions are essentially maladaptive in psychiatric patients. A breakdown of pathological ego defenses might well permit constructive personality reorganization.

Ruff, Levy and Thaler [28] identified three characteristic phases in the reactions of their "normal" Ss during deprivation: 1) an increase in anxiety level; 2) an enhancement and exaggeration of characteristic defenses; and 3) a breakdown of ego defenses. Mendelson et al.[25] noted the same response patterns in two Ss. Their first S, an anxiety neurotic who relied primarily upon represssive defenses, exhibited an extremely rapid response, tolerated the procedure fairly well, and showed no negative after-effects. Their second S, characterized by rigid, paranoid defenses, showed a delayed reaction followed by a paranoid break of some severity.

Goldberger and Holt[13,14,15,18] reported the response to deprivation of a group of normal college Ss and a group of unemployed New York actors. Although the two groups were different in many respects, the authors were able to identify common factors in personality organization which seemed to determine response to the deprivation situation. Two syndromes were distinguished: 1) an adaptive syndrome consisting of controlled primary process thought, free secondary process thought, self-stimulation and imagery; and 2) a maladaptive syndrome consisting of unpleasant affect, poorly controlled or anxiety-laden intrusions of the primary process, quitting or strong preoccupation with the idea of termination, impaired efficiency in secondary process thinking and general disturbance. In both groups the maladaptive syndrome was associated with deficiencies in ego structuralization, whether it be the rigid, precarious pose of tough masculinity assumed by the college students who responded maladaptively or the diffusion of self-concept exhibited by the unemployed actors (promiscuous homosexuality and the "beatnik syndrome").

The undergraduates who responded adaptively differed in their personality orientation from both the actors and undergraduates who responded maladaptively. For this group, although some regressive phenomena were noted, the release of primary process material occurred in a controlled and adaptive manner without strongly unpleasant affect and without disruption. The authors point out the relevance of Hartmann and Kris's concept of regression in service of the ego to understanding of the psychological mechanisms determining the adaptive syndrome. Those Ss who were able to experience a controlled, comfortable and adaptive dedifferentiation of ego defenses indicated, prior to deprivation, a personality configuration consisting of acceptance of their passive, feminine side, and intellectual flexibility, breadth and richness, and emotional freedom versus emotional construction or ungenuineness. Further analysis of the projective data indicated that response to deprivation was correlated with responses to primary process material on the Rorschach. Two points emerge from Goldberger and Holt's work which are entirely consistent with the present findings. First, it is possible to distinguish between effects due to specific sensory alterations and effects due to the psychological response to the general deprivation situation. Second, psychologically determined responses to deprivation involve a person's characteristic configuration of ego defenses, which can be assessed separately from the deprivation situation by other techniques such as the Rorschach.

Although the investigators cited utilized non-psychiatric Ss, their observations may shed some light upon the nature of the deprivation response in the present negative change subgroup. Among the experimental Ss, those with more rigid and elaborate defenses tended either to show little response to deprivation or else to manifest a pathological exaggeration of their characteristic defenses.

These findings are not surprising if it is remembered that ego functions include acquired perceptual processes. Ego functions and defenses are learned as a result of environmental interaction, and exercised in response to environmental cues. The environmental cues providing the context in which ego defenses are differentiated also appear to provide the context which sustains these defenses. One would therefore expect that Ss who have considerable investment in their external environment in terms of elaborate defense systems would react negatively to perceptual deprivation.

As applied to our positive-change experimental Ss, the preceding explanation seems appropriate if their psychological defenses are thought of as undergoing partial dedifferentiation during deprivation. A majority of these Ss carried diagnoses of personality disorders, such as passive dependent personality, immaturity reaction, and similar diagnoses. Unlike patients with rigid and well-established defense systems, those diagnosed as personality disorders had few delay and detour functions. Often their symptoms were not due to any internal conflicts, but instead were behavioral responses to the negative reactions of others to their own inappropriate conduct. When placed in deprivation, these Ss tended to use defenses of primary repression and withdrawal. These poorly organized defenses were readily abandoned during deprivation. Then they were able to respond to the generally supportive effect of the total experimental procedure, becoming emotionally more open to social relationships.

In seeking further explanations for differences between the positive and negative change subgroups, it was noted that Ss showing the most improvement on the RPRS impressed as rather childish and immature. They tended to assume a passive-dependent role in relations with other adults. For these Ss, a friendly, supportive examiner putting them to bed with the injunction that "it is sometimes helpful for a person to get away by himself so that he can think quietly" might well represent fulfillment of passive wishes to be cared for and nurtured. But to the negative changers, struggling to hold their feelings and impulses in check through rigid intellectual defenses, the same situation might be interpreted as a threat to their personal integrity and self-esteem.

Subjects with more rigid and elaborate defenses thus showed little response to brief periods of deprivation. The limited responses that did occur represented an enhancement or exaggeration of characteristic defenses. However, a breakdown of these organized defenses might have occurred eventually, if deprivation had been prolonged. Other investigators have reported that such breakdowns are usually accompanied by reduced effectiveness of psychological functioning, and that recovery is slow.

In contrast, those Ss with less complex defense systems tended to respond rapidly to deprivation. Their defenses dedifferentiated quickly without marked behavioral disorganization. Their affect was either neutral or mildly positive. They seemed more open to new social influences after deprivation and showed no lasting negative effects.

It is inaccurate to speak of a unitary "deprivation effect" as though there were one general response or class of responses entirely or even substantially determined by the reduction of patterned stimulation. On the contrary, reactions to perceptual deprivation apparently reflect lifelong developmental processes, which produce the psychological defenses characteristic of the individual's personality. These reactions are not fundamentally different from reactions following prolonged exposure to any strange environment. There is an increase in anxiety, mobilization of ego defenses, and eventual breakdown of ego defenses. Unlike most such situations, perceptual deprivation is a completely novel setting in which the activated defenses can elicit no response. The elimination of feedback from the environment may be largely responsible for whatever unique qualities deprivation procedures possess.

Kubie[22] has taken a similar approach in comparing deprivation to the state of normal sleep. He points out that virtually all the regressive therapies, including traditional psychoanalysis, involve afferent isolation, and that one possible response to such isolation is "normal" sleep. He further suggests that a number of phenomena reported in deprivation experiments are not uncommonly experienced during sleep or in the states immediately preceding or following sleep. The initial response to the deprivation experience in many of the present Ss was a brief period of sleep, even though deprivation was deliberately scheduled for the morning hours immediately after breakfast. At this time of day, Ss were unable to sleep for more than a few minutes. Awakening to a condition of continued perceptual deprivation and unable to retreat again into sleep, they were forced to utilize alternative defenses. The effectiveness of the relatively brief deprivation procedures may thus have been partly due to the time of day.

The results of this study suggest that future investigations of response to deprivation must consider Ss' characteristic defenses to a far greater extent than has been done. The generally positive effects observed here seem largely a function of the personality characteristics of the psychiatric inpatients used. A group of college students or well-integrated psychiatric outpatients might have shown very different results.

Perhaps a more interesting possibility is the therapeutic use of perceptual deprivation. Although Klopfer describes the RPRS Final Prognostic Score as a measure of generalized ego functioning, most studies have investigated its validity for predicting response to conventional verbal psychotherapies. The increased RPRS scores suggest that the majority of the present psychiatric Ss were more able to respond positively to conventional techniques of psychotherapy after exposure to deprivation, and that their overall functioning improved. Thus, deprivation as a therapeutic technique may have properties quite different from orthodox verbal psychotherapies.

The Rorschach indices characterized Ss who improved the most after deprivation as showing 1) poorly integrated and relatively unsuccessful defense systems, 2) low verbal productivity and limited ability to relate verbally to others or deal symbolically with problems, 3) reliance on primary repression as a defense and tendencies to act out behaviorally when repression fails, 4) a tendency to regard themselves as helpless and dependent, and 5) intrapunitive ways of handling hostility. These traits are not typical of patients with the best prognosis for traditional verbal psychotherapy. The negative changers, by contrast, were characterized by 1) moderately well-integrated and effective defense systems, 2) comparatively adept social skills and the ability to relate comfortably on a verbal level, 3) reliance on complex and elaborate defense systems utilizing isolation, intellectualization, reaction-formation and projection, and 4) a tendency to attribute to others the responsibility for their own difficulties. Thus, the negative changers resembled patients usually selected for traditional verbal psychotherapy far more than the positive changers.

## Summary

Previous experimentation by the writers suggested that relatively brief periods of partial sensory deprivation and social isolation may have positive beneficial effects on the personality changes assessed by several measures of ego strength and ego functioning.

Two hypotheses are tested: 1) that the psychological functioning of hospitalized psychiatric patients will improve after exposure to a relatively brief period of social isolation and partial perceptual deprivation; and 2) that significant relationships may be demonstrated between personality characteristics and differential responses to deprivation.

Subjects were forty white male psychiatric inpatients. Half received three hours of deprivation and half were controls. The two groups were equated for age, education, and scores on five measures of ego strength.

Both hypotheses were supported. On three of the five measures the experimental (deprivation) group showed significantly more improvement than the controls. Several indices based on pre-deprivation Rorschach protocols predicted much better than chance individual differences in direction of change following deprivation on Klopfer's Rorschach Prognostic Rating Scale.

The possibility of using these indices to select patients who might respond favorably to deprivation as a therapeutic technique but be poor risks in verbal therapy was considered. It was suggested that positive changes observed in the group exposed to deprivation were related to the personality structure typical of the hospitalized patients used as Ss. Differing responses to deprivation seem to be determined largely by each individual's characteristic pattern of ego functioning.

## References

1. Azima, H. and Cramer, F.: Effects of partial perceptual isolation in mentally disturbed individuals. *Dis. Nerv. Syst.*, *17*:117-122, 1956.
2. Barron, F.: An ego-strength scale which predicts response to psychotherapy.

In Welsh, G. S. and Dahlstrom, W. G., eds. *Basic Readings on the MMPI in Psychology and Medicine,* Univ. of Minnesota Press, Minneapolis, 1956, pp. 226-234.

3. Bexton, W. H., Heron, W. and Scott, T. H.: Effects of decreased variation in the sensory environment. *Canad. J. Psychol., 8:*70-76, 1954.

4. Butler, J. and Fiske, D.: Theory and techniques of assessment. *Ann. Rev. Psychol., 6:*327-356, 1955.

5. Cambareri, J. D.: The effects of sensory isolation on suggestible and non-suggestible psychology graduate students. Unpublished doctoral dissertation, Univ. of Utah, Salt Lake City, 1958.

6. Cartwright, R. D.: Predicting response to client-centered therapy with the Rorschach Prognostic Rating Scale. *J. Counsel. Psychol, 5:*11-15, 1958.

7. Cohen, L. D.: Patterns of response in Level of Aspiration Tests. *Educ. Psychol. Measurement 10:*664-668, 1950.

8. Cohen, L. D.: Level-of-Aspiration behavior and feelings of adequacy and self-acceptance. *J. Abnorm. Soc. Psychol., 49:*84-86, 1954.

9. Cohen, S. I., Silverman, A. J., Bressler, G. and Shmavonian, B.: Problems in isolation studies. In Solomon, P., Kubzansky, P. E. , Leiderman, P. H. *et al.,* eds. *Sensory Deprivation,* Harvard Univ. Press, Cambridge, 1961, pp. 114-129.

10. Cooper, G. D., Adams, H. G. and Gibby, R. G.: Ego strength changes following perceptual deprivation. *A.M.A. Arch. Gen. Psychiat., 7:*213-217, 1962.

11. Gibby, R. G.: The stability of certain Rorschach variables under conditions of experimentally induced sets: 1. The intellectual variables. *J Project Techn., 15:*3-26, 1951.

12. Gibby, R. G., Adams, H. B., and Carrera, R. N.: Therapeutic changes in psychiatric patients following partial sensory deprivation. *A.M.A. Arch. Gen. Psychiat., 3:*33-42, 1960.

13. Goldberger, L.: Reactions to perceptual isolation and Rorschach manifestations of the primary process. *J. Project. Tech., 25:*287-302, 1961.

14. Goldberger, L.: The isolation situation and personality. In Coopersmith, S., ed. *Proceedings of the XIV International Congress of Applied Psychology, Vo. 2: Personality Research.* Munksgaard, Copenhagen, 1962.

15. Goldberger, L. and Holt, R.: Experimental interference with reality contact (perceptual isolation): Method and group results. *J. Nerv. Ment. Dis., 127:*99-112, 1958.

16. Harris, A.: Sensory deprivation and schizophrenia. *J. Ment. Sci., 105:*235-236, 1959.

17. Heron, W.: The pathology of boredom. *Sci. Amer., 196:*52-56, 1957.

18. Holt, R. L. and Goldberger, L.: Personological correlates of reactions to perceptual deprivation. W.A.D.C. Tech. Rept 59-735. Aerospace Medical Lab, Wright Air Development Center, Wright-Patterson Air Force Base, Ohio, November, 1959.

19. Jenkins, R. L., Stauffacher, J. and Hester, R.: A symptom rating scale for use with psychotic patients. *A.M.A. Arch. Gen. Psychiat., 2*:197-204, 1959.
20. Kirkner, F., Wisham, W. and Giedt, H.: A report on the validity of the Rorschach Prognostic Rating Scale. *J. Project. Techn., 17*:320-326, 1953.
21. Klopfer, B., Ainsworth, M., Klopfer, W. and Holt, R. G.: *Developments in the Rorschach technique*, Vol. I. World Book Company, Yonkers-on-Hudson, New York, 1954.
22. Kubie, L. S.: Theoretical aspects of sensory deprivation. In Solomon, P., Kubzansky, P. E., Leiderman, P. H. *et al.*, eds. *Sensory Deprivation*, Harvard Univ. Press, Cambridge, 1961, pp. 208-220.
23. Leary, T.: *The Interpersonal Diagnosis of Personality*. Ronald Press, New York, 1957.
24. Lewin, K., Dembo, T., Festinger, L. and Sears, P. S.: Level of Aspiration. In Hunt, J. McV. ed., *Personality and the Behavior Disorders*. Ronald Press, New York, 1944.
25. Mendelson, J., Kubzansky, P. E., Leiderman, P. H. *et al.*: Physiological aspects of sensory deprivation: A case analysis. In Solomon, P., Kubzansky, P. E., Leiderman, P. H. *et al.*, eds. *Sensory Deprivation*, Harvard Univ. Press, Cambridge, 1961, pp. 91-113.
26. Rapaport, D.: The theory of ego autonomy: A generalization. Bull. Menninger Clin., *22*:13-15, 1958.
27. Rotter, J.: Level of aspiration as a method of studying personality: II. Development and evaluation of a controlled method. *J. Exp. Psychol, 31*:410-422, 1942.
28. Ruff, G. E., Levy, E. Z. and Thaler, V. H.: Factors influencing reaction to reduced sensory input. In Solomon, P., Kubzansky, P. E., Leiderman, P. H. *et al*, eds. *Sensory Deprivation,* Harvard Univ. Press, Cambridge, 1961, pp. 72-90.
29. Schafer, R.: *The Clinical Application of Psychological Tests.* International Universities Press, New York, 1948.
30. Schafer, R.: *Psychoanalytic Interpretation of Rorschach Testing.* Grune & Stratton, New York, 1954.
31. Schneider, S.: The prediction of certain aspects of the psychotherapeutic relationship from Rorschach's test: An empirical and exploratory study. Unpublished doctoral dissertation, Univ. of Michigan, Ann Arbor, 1953.
32. Siegel, S.: *Nonparametric Statistics for the Behavioral Sciences.* McGraw-Hill, New York, 1956.
33. Snygg, D. and Coombs, A. W.: *Individual Behavior: A New Frame of Reference for Psychology.* Harper, New York, 1949.
34. Solomon, P., Leiderman, P. H., Mendelson, J. and Wexler, D.: Sensory deprivation. *Amer. J. Psychiat., 114*:357-363, 1957.
35. Solomon, P., Kubzansky, P. E., Leiderman, P. H. *et al*, eds.: *Sensory Deprivation.* Harvard Univ. Press, Cambridge, 1961.
36. Walker, H. M. and Lev, J.: *Statistical Inference.* Holt, New York, 1953.
37. Weiss, B. A.: Relationship between developmental experience and choice of

defensive behavior: Study 1, Male. Unpublished doctoral dissertation, Univ. of Houston, Houston, 1956.

38. Wexler, D., Mendelson, J., Leiderman, P. H. and Solomon, P.: Sensory deprivation: A technique for studying psychiatric aspects of stress. *A.M.A. Arch. Neurol. Psychiat.*, *79*:225-233, 1958.

# Chapter 6

# INDIVIDUAL DIFFERENCES IN BEHAVIORAL REACTIONS OF PSYCHIATRIC PATIENTS TO BRIEF PARTIAL SENSORY DEPRIVATION*

HENRY B. ADAMS, G. DAVID COOPER,
AND RICHARD N. CARRERA

*Summary:* Thirty hospitalized psychiatric in-patients exposed to a few hours of partial sensory deprivation (SD) showed a wide range of individual differences in their reactions. Reduced symptoms and improved intellectual functioning after SD were the predominant group trends, but some individuals showed substantial changes in opposite directions. Individual differences in behavioral reactions during and after SD were significantly related to MMPI personality characteristics. Symptom reduction after SD was a function of characteristics quite different from those usually associated with prognosis for conventional verbal psychotherapy. The results suggested that many persons unlikely to benefit from traditional therapeutic procedures might show improved personality and intellectual functioning after a brief exposure to SD. There were many other complex relationships between personality variables and reactions to SD.

IN recent years there has been a growing recognition of the potential therapeutic applications of sensory deprivation (SD) techniques in the treatment of psychiatric patients and other emotionally disturbed individuals. These therapeutic potentialities have been discussed in several recent reviews, notably those by

*Reprinted with permission of author and publisher from: Adams, H.B., Cooper, G.D., and Carrera, R.N. Individual differences in behavioral reactions of psychiatric patients to brief partial sensory deprivation. *Perceptual and Motor Skills*, 1972, 34: 119-217.

116

Brownfield (1965), Schultz (1965), Gaines and Vetter (1968), and Suedfeld (1969). Brownfield observed that the earliest research reports suggested that sensory deprivation procedures inevitably led to deterioration in organized mental functioning, whereas more recent empirical studies had demonstrated that exposure to sensory and/or perceptual deprivation can produce definite beneficial effects under some conditions for some Ss. Brownfield's survey cited nineteen publications reporting positive, beneficial, or therapeutic results, but only one reporting negative or inconclusive results. Since the publication of Brownfield's book numerous additional reports of beneficial effects have appeared.

The writers have been involved in an extensive, systematic program of research involving therapeutic uses of SD techniques, with primary emphasis on practical applications in the treatment of hospitalized psychiatric patients (Adams, 1964, 1965; Adams, Carrera, Cooper, Gibby, & Tobey, 1960; Adams, Robertson, & Cooper, 1964, 1966; Cooper, 1962; Cooper, Adams, & Cohen, 1965; Cooper, Adams, Dickinson, & York, in press; Cooper, Adams, & Gibby, 1962; Gibby & Adams, 1961; Gibby, Adams, & Carrera, 1960). It was observed that a few hours of relatively mild conditions of sensory deprivation and social isolation led to reduced overt symptomatology and improved mental functioning in these patients. Studies using control groups demonstrated conclusively that the observed improvement was due to the experimental conditions of sensory deprivation and social isolation. While the predominant group tendency among psychiatric patients was toward positive, "improved" changes after SD, there was a wide range of individual differences. Some patients showed little or no reduction in symptoms of personality disorder, while others showed increased overt symptomatology and evidence of impaired mental functioning after their SD experiences.

Many investigators have reported average group reactions to SD as though these reactions were entirely contingent upon experimentally-induced objective-stimulus conditions. They have directed their primary attention more to external kinds of variables and to generalized group effects. There have been relatively few investigations of the range of differences in responses between individual subjects placed in objectively identical SD experimental conditions. For purposes of theoretical understanding and practical application it is just as important to investigate these individual differences and their correlates as it is to study average group trends.

The research literature on sensory deprivation is filled with many seemingly contradictory findings. We believe that many of these seeming inconsistencies may stem in part from a lack of systematic attention to individual differences. Only if these differences between individual Ss are systematically investigated can the basic parameters and causal factors underlying differing personal reactions to SD be reliably assessed.

There is now considerable research evidence for the therapeutic potentials of sensory deprivation, but there are also indications that these procedures are not equally suitable for all individuals or even for all psychiatric patients. In determining when and how SD might be optimally utilized for therapeutic purposes it is necessary to determine empirically what kinds of individuals derive the most benefit, compared with those who show little or no positive change and those who change negatively. The resulting empirical data can be used to provide indications and guidelines for practical applications in clinical settings. These are essentially the same considerations that would be involved in determining indications and contraindications for other treatment procedures.

The present study is an investigation of individual differences in a single group of psychiatric patients, all of whom were exposed to the same SD conditions. The specific aims were to determine (1) the nature and extent of variations in overt symptoms and behavioral reactions before, during, and after sensory deprivation, (2) other factors related to or correlated with those behavioral reactions, and (3) changes in intellectual functioning after sensory deprivation and their relation to other SD behavioral phenomena.

### Method

#### Subjects

Ss were thirty white male in-patients on the neuropsychiatric service of a Veterans General Medical and Surgical Hospital. Data on age, educational, intellectual, and diagnostic characteristics are set forth in Table 6-I. No S had a history or diagnosis of organic brain damage, and none was receiving any psychotherapy. None had received any form of shock therapy for at least thirty days prior to his being placed in SD.

TABLE 6-I

AGE, EDUCATIONAL, INTELLECTUAL, AND DIAGNOSTIC
CHARACTERISTICS OF Ss (N = 30)

| | Range | Mdn | M | SD |
|---|---|---|---|---|
| Age | 23- 48 | 35 | 35.0 | 6.9 |
| Years of School | 4- 16 | 11 | 10.8 | 3.1 |
| IQ Scores (Pretest) | 69-128 | 96 | 96.8 | 14.7 |
| Diagnostic Classification | | n | | |
| Schizophrenic Reactions | | 8 | | |
| Psychoneurotic Disorders | | 13 | | |
| Psychophysiologic Visceral and Autonomic Disorders | | 1 | | |
| Personality Pattern Disturbances | | 4 | | |
| Personality Trait Disturbances | | 4 | | |
| Σ | | 30 | | |

## Treatment Conditions

Each S chosen for the study was assigned to a fifteen-day schedule. On the first day, psychiatric chemotherapy, if employed, was discontinued. On the seventh day S was interviewed by a psychologist and his interview behavior rated on each of the twenty items of the Symptom Rating Scale (SRS) developed by Jenkins, Stauffacher, and Hester (1959). After the interview each S was administered the MMPI and five subtests of the Wechsler Adult Intelligence Scale, namely, Information, Arithmetic, Similarities, Digit Symbol, and Block Design.

On the eighth day S was placed in SD, during which he lay on a bed in a quiet, air-conditioned room for a period of not more than six hours. Immediately before SD he was told that he could leave any time he wished, but he was not informed that there would be any time limit. His eyes were then covered, his ears plugged with cotton, and his head wrapped in a gauze bandage. All Ss were free to leave at any time, but those still in SD at the end of six hours were removed by E. Full descriptions of the experimental conditions, facilities, rooms used, and procedural details have been published elsewhere (Gibby, et al., 1960; Cooper, et al., 1962). These conditions provided for exposure to relatively brief partial sensory deprivation and social isolation.

On the ninth experimental day, i.e. the day immediately after SD, the interviews, ratings, and subtests of the WAIS administered the day before SD were repeated. On the fifteenth day, one week after SD, S was interviewed for the third time by the same psychologist who had conducted the previous two interviews, and his interview behavior rated once more on the same twenty-item rating scale. Each S was seen by the same interviewer for all three interviews. On completion of the third interview (scheduled for the fifteenth experimental day) all of the procedures were completed, and chemotherapy, if indicated, was then resumed.

### Measures Used

Four behavioral rating indices were developed. These indices were derived from ratings of interview behavior before and after SD and from ratings of observable behavior during the SD experience.

(1) *Behavioral Anxiety.* This score was based on ratings of the degree of anxiety overtly manifested in the behavior of Ss while undergoing exposure to the SD conditions. A rating was made by an observer every fifteen minutes as long as S remained in SD. Ratings were made on a scale which ranged from zero, indicating no visible signs of anxiety, to a high of seven, which indicated a panic state. After SD all numerical ratings for each S were summed and a mean rating computed. The resulting mean was the S's Behavioral Anxiety score. As a check on reliability, the first twenty Ss to be run in sensory deprivation were observed simul-

taneously but rated independently by two observers. Substantial agreement in their Behavioral Anxiety ratings was found ($r = .81, p < .001$).

(2) *Gross Symptomatology.* The Gross Symptomatology index was a global score reflecting the severity of overt symptomatology manifested at the time of the pre-deprivation interview. Each S's interview behavior was rated using the twenty-item Symptom Rating Scale (SRS). Each of the twenty SRS items was assigned a numerical score of 1 if a given symptom was absent or fell within normal limits. Scores above 1 indicated the presence of the symptom in some degree, the highest scores reflecting the most severe symptoms. Numerical scores for the twenty separate items were then summed, and the resulting total score was the Gross Symptomatology index. The lowest possible score was twenty, which would indicate a complete absence of overt symptoms, while the highest possible score was seventy-six, obtainable only by an individual presenting the maximum degree of symptomatology on every single item. The highest score actually obtained by any S was 44.

(3) *Symptom Reduction.* This index was also a global score which reflected the degree of reduction in overt symptomatology after SD. It was based on a comparison of the pre-deprivation interview ratings on each of the twenty SRS items with corresponding SRS-item ratings derived from the two post-deprivation interviews. Both "short-term" positive changes, from the pre-deprivation interview to the first post-deprivation interview, and "long-term" positive changes, from the pre-deprivation interview to the second post-deprivation interview, were taken into account in computing this index. "Positive" pre-post changes were those in the direction of less severe symptoms after SD. The total number of SRS items on which each S showed *both* short-term and long-term positive changes was his Symptom Reduction index score. (Items showing short-term or long-term changes only were not included when Symptom Reduction scores were computed.) This method of analysis was adopted because previous research (Gibby et al., 1960) had shown that for each S the short-term and long-term positive changes were highly correlated ($rho = .70$, $p < .01$) and hence that reduc-

tions in symptomatology after SD tended to be relatively enduring. Combined change scores were considered more reliable as over-all indicators of symptom reduction than the short-term or long-term changes taken separately. It was also found that changes on the SRS in the direction of reduced symptomatology after SD were not significantly correlated with changes in the opposite direction. For this reason, the data on symptom reduction were combined into a single index and analyzed separately from the data on symptom increases.

(4) *Symptom Increase.* This index was a measure of negative changes in the direction of increased symptomatology following deprivation. Each S's index score was simply the number of SRS items on which he showed short-term negative changes after sensory deprivation. Long-term changes were not taken into account in computing the Symptom Increase index, since previous investigation had shown that increases in symptomatology after exposure to sensory deprivation of this kind were temporary in nature and tended to disappear relatively quickly. Short-term and long-term negative changes after SD were not significantly correlated (Gibby et al., 1960).

(5) *MMPI.* The group form of the Minnesota Multiphasic Personality Inventory was employed. In addition to the standard ten clinical scales and four validity scales, three special scales were also scored: the Welsh *A* (anxiety) and *R* (repression), and the Barron *ES* (ego-strength) scales. In the statistical analysis raw scores with the *K* correction were used.

(6) *WAIS.* Five subtests of the Wechsler Adult Intelligence Scale (WAIS), namely, Information, Arithmetic, Similarities, Digit Symbol, and Block Design, were administered to all Ss the day before and the day after SD. Full-scale IQ scores were estimated from these subtest scores by prorating. Pre-post changes on each of the five subtest scores, and on the estimated Full-scale IQ scores were then computed.

## Results

### Over-all Trends

Table 6-II shows the highest and lowest possible scores on each of the four behavioral rating indices, as well as the medians, means, and standard deviations of the scores actually obtained from the thirty Ss. The Behavioral Anxiety scores indicate that these Ss as a group displayed marked anxiety while undergoing SD. The Gross Symptomatology scores pointed up the presence of marked degrees of overt symptomatology in the pre-deprivation interview behavior of most Ss. Scores on the Symptom Reduction and Symptom Increase indices showed simultaneous increases and decreases in symptomatology after SD, with the average S making some changes in both directions. However, reductions in overt symptoms after SD outnumbered changes in the opposite direction. There were substantial individual differences, which are reflected in the standard deviations of scores on the four indices.

TABLE 6-II

LOWEST AND HIGHEST POSSIBLE SCORES, AND OBTAINED MEDIANS, MEANS AND STANDARD DEVIATIONS ON FOUR BEHAVIORAL INDICES

| Index | Possible Score | | Obtained Scores ($N$ = 30) | | |
|---|---|---|---|---|---|
| | Highest | Lowest | *Mdn* | *M* | *SD* |
| Behavioral Anxiety | 7 | 0 | 3.9 | 3.8 | 1.3 |
| Gross Symptomatology | 76 | 20 | 35.0 | 33.4 | 5.8 |
| Symptom Reduction | 20 | 0 | 7.5 | 7.8 | 5.7 |
| Symptom Increase | 20 | 0 | 1.7 | 2.1 | 2.3 |

## Relationships Between Indices

Intercorrelations among the four behavioral rating indices were computed using the Pearson product-moment correlation coefficient. Of the nine resulting correlations, eight were too low to be statistically significant. There was a significant positive correlation of .71 ($p < .001$) between Gross Symptomatology and Symptom Reduction, which indicated that Ss display more severe symptoms before SD tended to show the most "improvement" or symptom reduction afterward. The greater the over-all symptomatology before SD, the greater the subsequent general improvement. These results imply that SD procedures may be especially beneficial among psychiatric patients who present more severe overt symptomatology.

The statistically insignificant correlation of -.15 between Symptom Reduction and Symptom Increase indicated that the degree of symptom reduction in individual Ss following SD was not related in any consistent way to changes in the opposite direction. As noted above, many Ss showed a reduction in some symptoms along with an increase in others.

The absence of significant correlations between Behavioral Anxiety and the other three indices deserves comment. These results mean that the degree of anxiety manifested by Ss during the SD experience was not a function of the degree of overt symptomatology before deprivation nor of the direction or extent of change in symptoms afterward.

### Psychiatric Diagnosis

In order to determine if there were relationships between psychiatric diagnosis and the four behavioral rating indices, diagnostic categories were combined for purposes of statistical analysis into three groups: (1) Group S consisted of eight patient Ss with the diagnosis of schizophrenic reaction; (2) Group N included fourteen Ss diagnostically classified under various psychoneurotic categories or as psychophysiologic visceral and autonomic disorders; and (3) Group P contained eight Ss with diagnoses of personality pattern disturbances and personality trait disturbances. Differences between these three groups in mean index scores were evaluated using the analysis of variance. There were no significant F ratios, and hence the small differences between group means on the four behavioral rating indices were not statistically significant. From these negative results, it may be concluded that major psychiatric diagnostic categories did not differentiate with respect to degrees of symptomatology prior to SD, anxiety during SD, or the directions or extent of change in symptomatology afterward.

## Age, Education, and Intelligence

Data on the S's ages, education (years in school), and estimated Full-scale WAIS IQ scores prior to SD are given in Table 6-I. These three subject variables were correlated with the four behavioral indices. None of the four indices correlated significantly with age or IQ. However, there was a significant positive correlation ($r = .37$, $p < .05$) between years of school and Behavioral Anxiety, the more educated Ss displaying more anxiety during SD. Since IQ and education also had a significant positive correlation, a partial correlation was computed to determine whether educational level was related to Behavioral Anxiety with differences in IQ held constant statistically. A partial correlation of .55 ($p < .01$) was found, suggesting an even more clear-cut relationship between educational level and anxiety during SD. This unexpected relationship is not easy to interpret. A possible explanation may be that the more educated individuals had stronger needs for environmental and social stimulation of all kinds, needs which were also reflected in the greater number of years they had previously spent in school. The absence of meaningfully patterned environmental stimulation and social interaction during SD may have been most disconcerting for Ss with more education, contrasted with those having less education and presumably less curiosity and interest in their environment.

## "Terminators" Versus "Stayers"

Before being placed in SD all Ss were told that they could leave whenever they wished. None was informed in advance that *E* had set a six-hour time limit. Those who remained for the full six hours were designated "stayers" and those who voluntarily discontinued early were called "terminators." Of the thirty Ss twelve were stayers and eighteen were terminators. The mean scores of the terminators and stayers on the four indices were compared and differences between means evaluated using the *t* test. Differences in Overt Symptomatology, Symptom Reduction, and Symptom Increase were not statistically significant. However, there was a significant difference on Behavioral Anxiety ($t = 4.09$, $p < .001$), the terminators scoring much higher than the stayers. Detailed examination of individual scores showed virtually no overlap between the two groups. Nearly every S with a low Behavioral Anxiety score was a stayer and almost every S with a high score was a terminator. It seems that the terminators were motivated to leave early as a result of the relatively high levels of anxiety they experienced during SD.

The absence of significant differences between terminators and stayers on the other three indices also merits comment. These negative results mean that individual choices whether to terminate early or to remain for the full six hours were not a function of the severity of symptoms prior to deprivation, nor were they significantly related to the degree or direction of change in overt symptomatology afterward.

### *MMPI Scores**

Valid MMPI protocols were obtained from twenty of the Ss prior to SD. MMPI raw scores without the $K$ correction were then correlated with the four behavioral indices. The analysis included seventeen MMPI scales: the ten standard clinical scales, the four validity scales, the Welsh $A$ (anxiety) and $R$ (repression) scales, and the Barron $Es$ (ego strength) scale. As Table 6-III shows, the number of statistically significant correlations with all four indices was well beyond chance expectancy.

Six of the seventeen MMPI scales correlated significantly with Behavioral Anxiety, and four others showed correlations which approached significance ($p = .10$). Of these ten, $D$, $Hy$, $Mf$, $Pa$, $Pt$, $Sc$, $Si$, and $A$ were positively correlated with Behavioral Anxiety, while $K$ and $Es$ were negatively correlated. This pattern of correlations suggests that greater anxiety during SD was associated with relatively limited ego strength, generalized feelings of ineffectiveness, depression, dysphoria, subjectively felt personal inadequacy, and lack of self-confidence. Relatively low anxiety levels

---

*The authors are indebted to Dr. Grant Dahlstrom and Dr. G. S. Welsh for their helpful suggestions on the clinical interpretations of the MMPI data. Drs. Dahlstrom and Welsh served as consultants to the Richmond VA Hospital while this research was in progress.

TABLE 6-III

CORRELATIONS OF MMPI SCALES (RAW SCORES) WITH
FOUR BEHAVIORAL RATING INDICES ($N$ = 20)

| MMPI Scale | Behavioral Anxiety | | Gross Symptomatology | | Symptom Reduction† | | Symptom Increase | |
|---|---|---|---|---|---|---|---|---|
| | $r$ | $p$ | $r$ | $p$ | $r$ | $p$ | $r$ | $p$ |
| Hs* | .26 | | -.01 | | -.05 | | .12 | |
| D | .53 | .02 | .33 | | .09 | | .24 | |
| Hy | .41 | .10 | .02 | | .44 | .05 | .02 | |
| Pd* | .13 | | .37 | .10 | .24 | | .65 | .01 |
| Mf | .54 | .02 | -.19 | | .12 | | .33 | |
| Pa | .45 | .05 | .19 | | .04 | | .48 | .05 |
| Pt* | .44 | .05 | .43 | .10 | .21 | | .35 | |
| Sc* | .42 | .10 | .39 | .10 | .17 | | .59 | .01 |
| Ma* | -.12 | | .53 | .02 | .61 | .01 | .27 | |
| Si | .37 | .10 | .23 | | -.01 | | .15 | |
| ? | .30 | | .22 | | .32 | | .21 | |
| L | .18 | | .11 | | .08 | | .26 | |
| F | .30 | | .42 | .10 | .29 | | .49 | .05 |
| K | -.40 | .10 | .17 | | -.13 | | -.53 | .02 |
| A | .47 | .05 | .31 | | .07 | | .42 | .10 |
| R | .19 | | -.21 | | -.37 | .10 | -.20 | |
| Es | -.66 | .01 | -.17 | | .00 | | -.25 | |

†Multiple correlation of Symptom Reduction Index with the combination of (1) Gross Symptomatology Index, (2) $Hy$, (3) $Ma$, and (4) $R$ Scales: Multiple $R$ = .82, $p <$ .001.
*$Hs$, $Pd$, $Pt$, $Sc$, and $Ma$ scales not $K$-corrected.

were associated with greater degrees of emotional security, self-confidence, consciously masculine attitudes, openness, self-assertion, and directness in interpersonal relationships. Ss who manifested less anxiety during SD apparently had greater tendencies to deny psychiatric symptoms, to present an outward facade of personal adequacy, to meet new situations in a confident, constructive manner, and to be less prone toward social withdrawal. Statements regarding the Ss of low anxiety must of course be considered in relation to the population from which they were drawn. All were psychiatric in-patients and none could be regarded as making a truly adequate social adjustment.

The Gross Symptomatology index showed correlations with four scales (*Pd, Pt, Sc,* and*F*), which approached significance (*p* =

.10) and one (*Ma*) which was clearly significant. All five correlations were positive and they represented much better than chance expectancy. The correlational pattern suggests that Ss with more severe initial symptoms prior to SD tended to give MMPI responses typical of psychotic reactions. The five MMPI scales are often elevated among psychotics. Such results are not inconsistent with the fact that all our Ss were hospitalized psychiatric inpatients.

The Symptom Reduction index correlated significantly and positively with two MMPI scales, *Hy* and *Ma*, while the negative correlation with *R* approached significance ($p = .10$). As noted in the second section of the Results, there was also a significant positive correlation between the Symptom Reduction index and the Gross Symptomatology index. The latter index was combined with the *Hy*, *Ma* and *R* scales and a multiple correlation computed to determine the joint relationship between Symptom Reduction and the combination of these four measures. A very high joint relationship was found (Multiple $R = .82$, $p < .001$).

This combined relationship seems to imply that greater symptom reduction occurred in Ss who were more inclined to act out and express their feelings openly, more readily revealed negative aspects of themselves in their overt behavior, and were more spontaneous and uninhibited. These Ss also displayed less blocking of thought and verbalization, were prone to meet new situations by direct action (either appropriate or inappropriate), seemed more responsive to external environmental cues, and tended to be more open to new social influences. In addition, Ss who showed the most symptom reduction after SD displayed more severe overt symptoms initially. At the other end of the scale, those scoring lowest on Symptom Reduction had less severe overt symptomatology before SD; and apparently had less energy, more rigidity, less susceptibility to external stimulation and social influence, and a greater inclination to utilize repression as a defense.

A very different pattern was seen in the correlations between MMPI scales and Symptom Increase. This index had significant positive correlations with *Pd, Pa, Sc,* and *F,* a significant negative correlation with *K,* and a positive correlation with *A* which approached significance. This pattern suggests that Ss showing the greatest increases in symptomatology following SD had responded to the MMPI in ways suggesting the presence of severe, deep-seated personality disturbances. The MMPI results imply that they had a precarious adjustment prior to deprivation, felt generally hypersensitive and resentful toward the world around them, and could be precipitated into clear-cut but relatively transitory disturbances as a consequence of relatively mild stresses. The absence of familiar stimulus cues during SD appears to have been especially disturbing for them because of their limited tolerance for stress and uncertainty. Conversely, the better-integrated, better-adjusted Ss tended to show correspondingly smaller scores on the Symptom Increase index after SD, reflecting less personality disturbance and disruption of functioning.

## Intellectual Functioning

Five WAIS subtests were administered the day before and the day after SD. Full-scale IQs were estimated by prorating the subtest scores. Pre-post changes on the five subtests and on the estimated Full-scale IQ scores were then computed. The statistical significance of these changes was evaluated by means of the $t$ test of repeated measures. As Table 6-IV shows, there were significant increases on the estimated Full scale IQs and on all five of the

TABLE 6-IV

CHANGES IN WEIGHTED SCORES ON FIVE WAIS SUBTESTS
AND PRORATED FULL-SCALE WAIS IQ SCORES BEFORE AND AFTER
EXPOSURE TO SENSORY DEPRIVATION ($N$ = 28)

| WAIS Subtest | Pre-deprivation | | Post-deprivation | | $M$ Increase | $t$ | $p$ |
|---|---|---|---|---|---|---|---|
| | $M$ | $SD$ | $M$ | $SD$ | | | |
| Information | 10.5 | 1.5 | 11.5 | 3.3 | 1.0 | 2.81 | .01 |
| Arithmetic | 10.8 | 2.9 | 12.8 | 3.4 | 2.0 | 4.42 | .001 |
| Similarities | 9.6 | 3.4 | 10.4 | 3.8 | .8 | 1.72 | .10 |
| Digit Symbol | 7.8 | 2.4 | 8.6 | 2.8 | .8 | 2.79 | .05 |
| Block Design | 8.5 | 2.5 | 9.8 | 3.1 | 1.1 | 2.18 | .10 |
| Estimated IQ | 97.2 | 15.0 | 103.9 | 15.0 | 6.7 | 6.43 | .001 |

subtests, indicating generalized improvement in intellectual functioning after SD.

While the mean IQ score for the group as a whole increased from 97.2 on pretesting to 103.9 on post-testing, there were wide individual differences. Some Ss showed substantial increases, some little or no change, and a few showed sizable declines. In order to determine whether IQ changes after SD were related to other behavior variables, the pre-post changes in estimated Full-scale IQs were correlated with the four behavioral indices. The results in Table 6-V show some significant relationships.

There was a significant positive correlation between Behavioral Anxiety and IQ change, Ss who were more anxious during SD showing greater IQ increases afterward. It appears that the presence of anxiety during SD in some way facilitated later improvement in organized intellectual functioning. Likewise, Ss who experienced less anxiety during SD tended to show relatively little improvement in intellectual functioning afterward. (It is pertinent here to remember that Behavioral Anxiety was also correlated positively with educational level.)

TABLE 6-V

CORRELATIONS BETWEEN CHANGES IN ESTIMATED
WAIS IQ SCORES AND FOUR BEHAVIORAL
RATING INDICES* ($N = 28$)

| Behavioral Index | $r$ | $p$ |
|---|---|---|
| Behavioral Anxiety | .42 | .05 |
| Gross Symptomatology | -.06 | |
| Symptom Reduction | .29 | |
| Symptom Increase | -.48 | .01 |

*Correlation of IQ change with combination of all four behavior rating indices: Multiple $R = .80$, $p < .001$.

There was a significant negative correlation between IQ change and Symptom Increase. Ss with the greatest increases in overt symptomatology after SD were those whose IQ scores tended to decline the most, presumably reflecting diminished intellectual efficiency on post-testing. The MMPI data discussed above suggested that Ss scoring higher on Symptom Increase had little stress tolerance and very precarious, marginal patterns of adjustment before being placed in SD. Their limited tolerance of stress seems to have been reflected both in reduced intellectual efficiency and intensified overt symptomatology after exposure to SD. Reduced IQ scores and Symptom Increase thus constitute two measurable aspects of the transient personality disturbances which some Ss displayed after SD. Conversely, Ss whose IQ scores improved most after SD also showed the smallest increases (or none) in overt symptomatology. The Symptom Reduction index, however, did not correlate with IQ change, reflecting the effects of sources of variation statistically unrelated to Symptom Increase.

When the combined association of the four behavioral rating indices with IQ change was determined by multiple correlation, the joint relationship was much greater than the zero-order correlation with any single index (Multiple $R = .80, p < .001$). The high multiple correlation suggests that most of the variance in the IQ-change scores was due to the same constellation of factors which were reflected in the joint effects of the four behavioral indices. The severity of symptomatology before SD, the degree of anxiety experienced during SD, and the extent and direction of change in symptomatology afterward were variables whose combined effects were also manifest in changed intellectual efficiency after deprivation.

## Discussion

In summary, the major findings were that our psychiatric patient Ss began their participation presenting substantial degrees of overt symptomatology before being placed in SD. They became markedly anxious during the SD experience and showed both increases and decreases in symptoms afterward. Decreases were more numerous and more lasting than increases, but there were wide individual differences. Parallel changes were observed in scores on the WAIS, indicating generally improved intellectual functioning after SD for the group as a whole, but once again there was a range of individual differences. These individual differences and their correlates are the major focus of this paper.

Four indices were developed: (1) Overt Symptomatology prior to SD, (2) Behavioral Anxiety during SD, (3) Symptom Reduction after SD, and (4) Symptom Increase after SD. The four indices were not significantly correlated except for the Gross Symptomatology and Symptom Reduction indices, which were significantly and positively correlated. Ss showing most symptom reduction or "improvement" after SD had more severe symptoms initially. This relationship implies that SD procedures may be most beneficial for patients presenting more severe personality disorders. The lack of significant correlations between Symptom Reduction and the other two indices means that the degree of reduction in overt symptoms after SD bore no relationship to (1) the level of anxiety during SD or (2) increases in symptoms afterward. None of the four indices showed significant relationships with psychiatric diagnosis, age, IQ scores, or education, except that Behavioral Anxiety was positively correlated with educational level.

Significant differences in levels of anxiety during SD were found in comparing "terminators", who left voluntarily before the six hour time limit, and "stayers", who remained for the full time. The terminators manifested much more anxiety and apparently left early because SD generated more anxiety than they could tolerate. Terminators did not differ significantly from stayers on severity of symptoms before SD or symptomatic changes afterward. Thus, the length of time Ss spent in SD was not related to the severity of their initial symptoms or to subsequent changes in their symptoms, either positive or negative.

The MMPI was administered to some Ss prior to SD. Each of the four indices showed a distinctive pattern of correlations with the MMPI, reflecting four different constellations of personality traits. Ss scoring highest on Symptom Reduction tended to be (1) more impulsive and open to new experiences, (2) more spontaneous and less inhibited in their interpersonal relationships, (3) emotionally less rigid and repressed, and (4) had more severe symptoms to begin with. Those scoring lowest on Symptom Reduction were seen as (1) relatively impervious to new experiences and novel environmental influences, (2) guarded, rigid, and overcontrolled in their personal relationships, (3) emotionally defensive, repressed, and inhibited, and (4) displayed relatively little overt symptomatology before SD.

The Symptom Reduction index was associated with personality characteristics apparently quite different from those affecting prognosis for conventional types of psychotherapy. The Barron *Es* (ego strength) scale, originally devised as an indicator of prognosis for verbal psychotherapy, showed a zero correlation with Symptom Reduction, indicating that the likelihood of symptomatic improvement after SD could not have been predicted any better than chance from scores on the *Es* scale. This unexpected finding suggests that the personality traits which make for improvement after conventional verbal therapy are not the same as those which made for symptom reduction after SD. It is obvious that SD differs substantially from traditional verbal therapy. In addition to the complete absence of verbal interchange, normal social interaction is eliminated. Under the conditions of this experiment, there could be no therapist-patient or counselor-client relationship during SD. Compared with other types of individual and group psychotherapy, SD procedures fall into a unique category. The objective situation is different, the symptomatic changes are distinctive, and the individuals most likely to benefit from the use of SD techniques may not necessarily be good candidates for conventional kinds of therapy.

In its correlations with other measures, Behavioral Anxiety showed some interesting but unexpected relationships. Behavioral Anxiety had a high negative correlation with *Es*, which meant that Ss with more ego strength, who would have been considered better candidates for verbal psychotherapy, became less anxious in SD, while those low in ego strength showed high anxiety. The other MMPI data suggested that Ss made most anxious during SD were typically ineffective, depressed individuals, troubled by subjective feelings of personal inadequacy. Behavioral Anxiety and Symptom Reduction did not correlate significantly. This finding takes on special importance when it is remembered that Behavioral Anxiety and *Es* were negatively related. Low ego strength, which made for more anxiety during SD, was not related to reduction of symptoms after SD. Similarly, high ego strength, which would suggest a favorable prognosis for verbal therapy, and which was associated with low anxiety during

SD, did not make for greater symptom reduction after the experience of SD.

Although the Gross Symptomatology index showed a high positive correlation with Symptom Reduction, its pattern of correlations with MMPI scales suggested that more severe overt symptoms reflected a generalized tendency to respond to environmental stimuli in a psychotic-like fashion. However, Gross Symptomatology was unrelated to the official psychiatric diagnoses recorded in the patients' charts. The traits associated with Gross Symptomatology differed in several respects from those associated with Symptom Reduction.

The correlations between the MMPI and the Symptom Increase index made it apparent that the greatest increase of overt symptoms after deprivation was most likely to occur in poorly integrated, resentful, hypersensitive individuals who had previously achieved only a precarious, marginal adjustment. Lacking tolerance for ambiguous situations and emotional stresses, these poorly equipped Ss were precipitated into a transient state of acute distress and personality disruption when the novel SD experience eliminated familiar stimulus cues from the surrounding environment.

The lack of relationship between Symptom Increase and Symptom Reduction demonstrates that transient increases in symptomatology after SD are not contraindications for the use of SD. Some individuals had high scores on both indices. Increases in symptoms were a function of personality characteristics distinctly different from those making for reduced symptoms. Not one of the MMPI scales which correlated significantly with Symptom Increase had a significant correlation with Symptom Reduction.

Another important aspect of change after SD was an improvement in intellectual functioning, as shown in higher scores on the WAIS measures following SD. There were substantial individual differences here as well. Some Ss showed little change in WAIS IQs after deprivation, and a few showed decreases. These were analogous to the observation that some individuals showed little change in symptoms while others showed increased symptomatology after SD. Measures of change in intellectual functioning on the WAIS gave a range of individual differences comparable to those found on the four behavioral indices.

IQ scores increased most in Ss who became most anxious during deprivation. IQ change and Behavioral Anxiety were positively and significantly correlated, which would imply that anxiety during SD had some kind of facilitating effect on intellectual functioning. This facilitation was apparently a function of personality variables quite different from those making for reduced symptomatology, since Symptom Reduction did not correlate significantly with IQ change. (However, Symptom Increase correlated *negatively* and significantly with IQ change.) Ss more anxious during SD had more formal education but less ego strength, personal adequacy, or self-confidence. One possible interpretation of these relationships is that the greater anxiety experienced by those individuals during SD resulted in their becoming more alert and better organized after the experience. It is also possible that their enhanced intellectual efficiency reflected tendencies to utilize intellectual defenses previously acquired as a byproduct of greater formal education and higher intelligence. (Pre-deprivation WAIS IQs were positively correlated with educational level.)

The negative relation of Behavioral Anxiety to *Es* indicated that Ss rendered more anxious during SD were those considered to have the poorest prognosis for conventional verbal therapy. Yet those most anxious during SD were the same individuals whose IQ scores tended to improve most afterward. In this instance, intellectual functioning tended to improve more after SD in individuals who would have been considered less promising candidates for conventional verbal therapy, on the basis of their *Es* scores.

Although IQ change was unrelated to Symptom Reduction, it had a significant negative correlation with Symptom Increase. Ss displaying the greatest exacerbation of overt symptoms after SD also gave evidence of the greatest impairment in intellectual functioning after the experience. Their IQ scores either dropped or else failed to show any substantial increase. Their transient generalized disturbances were manifested simultaneously in increased overt symptomatology and decreased intellectual efficiency. By contrast, those with the most improvement in IQ scores after SD had the least (if any) increase in symptoms.

The complex interrelationships affecting changes after sensory deprivation are pointed up by an additional finding which is highly significant statistically but difficult to interpret in psychological terms. The multiple correlation of IQ change with the combination of all four behavioral indices (Multiple $R = .80, p < .001$) was much higher than the simple zero-order correlation of IQ change with any one of the four indices (see Table 6-V). The combined relationship accounted for nearly two-thirds of the variance in IQ change scores.

This summary of results makes it obvious that brief statements and facile generalizations cannot adequately summarize the real complexities which emerged from analysis of these data. Every S was exposed to essentially the same conditions of sensory deprivation, but there was a wide range of varied individual reactions. These differing reactions to the same conditions were contingent upon many interacting variables which proved complicated and difficult to interpret. In our first tentative steps at interpretation, the results compelled us to set aside many of our own initial hypotheses and earlier theoretical preconceptions. It is hoped that future research might assess more fully the validity and generality of the preliminary interpretive statements which we have offered.

The greatest number of statistically significant relationships emerged from the correlations between overt behavioral reactions and personality measures. Taking these relationships as the starting point, it may be meaningful to draw parallels between reactions to SD and responses to projective techniques such as the Rorschach, TAT, etc. In both instances there are wide individual differences in modes of responding and in the possible dimensions of variation involved in any objective analysis. When projective techniques are used the individual S is presented with some kind of ambiguous or unstructured stimulus material and invited to respond in his own idiosyncratic way. His responses are then interpreted as indicators of underlying predispositions and personality traits. These interpretations are based on some integrated combination of personality theory, clinical experience, and empirical research. The problems and difficulties of research in projective techniques are well known, but extensive research relating responses on projective techniques to personality variables has nevertheless been completed. Little if any comparable research now exists in the field of SD.

In SD, Ss are not presented with ambiguous stimuli as would be the case in administering projective techniques. Instead, they are placed in a novel environment where all meaningfully structured patterned stimuli are greatly reduced, and if possible, totally eliminated. The elimination of structured stimulus patterns during SD represents a more extreme ambiguity in the total environment than would be the case, for instance, in the administration of the Rorschach ink blot test. Differences between SD and the familiar projective tests are essentially differences in the over-all degree of stimulus ambiguity or structure as presented to individual Ss. In both instances, individual reactions reflect established behavioral propensities and predispositions, i.e., personality traits.

Our data supplied numerous indications that the individuals most likely to benefit therapeutically from SD differ in several respects from those who would usually be considered the best prospects for conventional verbal types of psychotherapy. Similar suggestions have appeared in two of our earlier publications (Cooper et al., 1962; Cooper et al., 1965).

The first (1962) reported on changes in ego strength after SD, using the Cartwright modification of Klopfer's Rorschach Prognostic Rating Scale as a measure of ego strength. Statistically significant group changes in the direction of enhanced ego strength were found, with notable individual differences. Psychiatric Ss with lowest ego strength scores prior to SD tended to show the greatest increases afterward. It was concluded that "subjects who initially functioned least effectively were those who derived the most benefit from exposure to deprivation."

This conclusion led to the observation that

> Cartwright's scale and Klopfer's original Rorschach Prognostic Rating Scale, from which Cartwright's modified scale was derived, have been employed with great success in predicting the degree of improvement resulting from conventional verbal types of psychotherapy with these patients. Higher scores on these Rorschach measures indicate a greater likelihood of

improvement following conventional verbal psychotherapy. If exposure to sensory deprivation produced essentially the same types of changes as those resulting from orthodox verbal psychotherapy, there would have been significant positive relationships between initial scores on the Rorschach measures and changes on these measures following deprivation. But exactly the opposite relationship was found. This suggests that subjects who have relatively low scores on the Rorschach measures of ego strength, which means that they would be relatively poor candidates for traditional verbal psychotherapy, are the ones who derive the greatest positive benefit from exposure to sensory deprivation procedures. The results imply that sensory deprivation techniques may thus prove therapeutically most useful in patients for whom orthodox techniques of verbal psychotherapy are relatively unfruitful (Cooper et al., 1962, p. 216).

These issues were explored more extensively in a later published report on individual differences in personality changes after sensory deprivation, using a variety of Rorschach measures (Cooper et al., 1965). They showed that a majority of the hospitalized psychiatric patients evaluated in that study "were more able to respond positively to conventional techniques of psychotherapy after exposure to deprivation, and that their over-all functioning improved." When comparisons were made between those who showed the most improvement and those who showed the least, as measured by Klopfer's Rorschach Prognostic Rating Scale, some important personality differences were found.

The Rorschach indices characterized subjects who improved the most after deprivation as showing (1) poorly integrated and relatively unsuccessful defense systems, (2) low verbal productivity and limited ability to relate verbally to others or deal symbolically with problems, (3) reliance on primary repression as a defense and tendencies to act out behaviorally when repression fails, (4) a tendency to regard themselves as helpless and dependent, and (5) intrapunitive ways of handling hostility. These traits are not typical of patients with the best prognosis for traditional verbal psychotherapy. The negative changers, by contrast, were characterized by (1) moderately well-integrated and effective defense systems, (2) comparatively adept social skills and the ability to relate comfortably on a verbal level, (3) reliance on complex and elaborate defense systems utilizing isolation, intellectualization, reaction-formation, and projection, and (4) a tendency to attribute to others the responsibility for their own difficulties. Thus, the negative changers resembled patients usually selected for traditional verbal psychotherapy far more than the positive changers (pp. 116-117).

The Rorschach was not included in this paper but the data obtained with other measures were generally consistent with earlier Rorschach results. Ss with more severe initial symptoms, more openness to new environmental influences, and stronger tendencies toward impulsive acting out were most likely to have shown symptomatic improvement following SD. Ss with reduced symptoms after SD were not necessarily those patients who would have been selected for verbal types of therapy.

One major implication is that SD techniques might ultimately render possible significant therapeutic benefits among formerly unreachable segments of the population, who might have been written off previously as unpromising candidates for older conventional procedures. This would be particularly true for those whose lack of verbal fluency, social naivete, impulsive acting out, and severe overt symptomatology render them relatively poor prospects for the verbal (and often rather intellectualized) types of psychotherapy now in widest use.

SD techniques also have other desirable features. These include simplicity, low cost, and the fact that routine applications do not require the direct services of highly trained professional personnel. The only facilities required are a quiet, comfortable, sound-proof room, a bed, suitable coverings for the head, eyes and ears, and one person (who can be a non-professional assistant working under professional supervision) to prepare Ss and place them in deprivation.

An additional advantage, in which SD contrasts favorably with drug, LSD, and shock treatment, is the absence of significant risks, medical hazards, or adverse side effects, at least where conditions of mild deprivation and relatively short duration are maintained. (These statements may not hold true for drastic or prolonged conditions of deprivation. We did not explore these extremes in our own research, since our major focus was on beneficial therapeutic applications.)

There are still many unanswered questions concerning the therapeutic application of mild SD techniques. An extensive research program would be needed to answer the unresolved questions which have already arisen from our own work. When the first reports of SD experiments appeared it was widely but prematurely concluded that SD procedures produced only harmful, stressful, disruptive, and disorganizing effects. Early reports of beneficial results achieved with psychiatric patients and emotionally disturbed individuals were often met with skepticism. But continued research has repeatedly demonstrated real benefits among selected psychiatric patients. The task for future investigation is to determine more fully how these promising new techniques can best be utilized for desirable therapeutic purposes.

## REFERENCES

Adams, H. B.: Therapeutic potentialities of sensory deprivation procedures. *International Mental Health Research Newsletter, 6*(4):7-9, 1964.

Adams, H. B.: A case utilizing sensory deprivation procedures. In L. Krasner & L. Ullmann (Eds.), *Case Studies in Behavior Modification.* New York, Holt, Rinehart & Winston, 1965, pp, 164-170.

Adams, H. B., Carrera, R. N., Cooper, G. D., Gibby, R. G., & Tobey, H. R.: *Personality and Intellectual Changes in Psychiatric Patients Following Brief Partial Sensory Deprivation.* Cleveland, Convention Reports Duplication Service, 1960.

Adams, H. B., Robertson, M. H., & Cooper, G. D.: Facilitating therapeutic personality changes in psychiatric patients by sensory deprivation methods. In *Proceedings of 17th International Congress of Psychology.* Amsterdam, North Holland Publishing, 1964, pp. 108-109.

Adams, H. B., Robertson, M. H., & Cooper, G. D.: Sensory deprivation and personality change. *Journal of Nervous and Mental Disease, 143*:256-265, 1966.

Brownfield, C. A.: *Isolation.* New York, Random House, 1965.

Cooper, G. D.: Changes in ego strength following brief perceptual and social deprivation. Unpublished doctoral dissertation, Duke Univer., Durham, 1962.

Cooper, G. D., Adams, H. B., & Cohen, L. D.: Changes in personality after sensory deprivation. *Journal of Nervous and Mental Diseases, 140*:103-118, 1965.

Cooper, G. D., Adams, H. B., Dickinson, J. R., & York, M. W.: Experimenter role playing and responses to sensory deprivation. *Journal of Personality,* in press.

Cooper, G. D., Adams, H. G., & Gibby, R. G.: Ego strength changes following perceptual deprivation. *Archives of General Psychiatry*, 7:213-217, 1962.

Gaines, L. S. & Vetter, H. J.: Sensory deprivation and psychotherapy. *Psychotherapy: Theory, Research and Practice*, 5:7-12, 1968.

Gibby, R. G., & Adams, H. B.: Receptiveness of psychiatric patients to verbal communication. *Archives of General Psychiatry*, 5:366-370, 1961.

Gibby, R. G., Adams, H. B., & Carrera, R. N.: Therapeutic changes in psychiatric patients following partial sensory deprivation. *Archives of General Psychiatry*, 3:33-42, 1960.

Jenkins, R. F., Stauffacher, J., & Hester, R.: A symptom rating scale for use with psychotic patients. *Archives of General Psychiatry*, 1:197-204, 1959.

Schultz, D. P.: *Sensory Restriction*. New York, Academic Press, 1965.

Suedfeld, P.: Changes in intellectual performance and in susceptibility to influence. In J. P. Zubek (Ed.), *Sensory Deprivation: Fifteen Years of Research*. New York, Appleton-Century, Crofts, 1969, pp. 126-166.

# Chapter 7

# INTERVIEWER'S ROLE-PLAYING AND RESPONSES TO SENSORY DEPRIVATION: A CLINICAL DEMONSTRATION*

G. David Cooper, Henry B. Adams,
Joe R. Dickinson, and Michael W. York

*Summary:* Ten Ss with a history of intransigent hypochon-driacal personality disorder were subjected to two and one-half hours of sensory deprivation preceded and followed by planned interviewing procedures. Each interview was designed to pre-structure the interpersonal meaning of the experience of sensory deprivation and selectively reinforce social roles antithetical to S's characteristic, maladaptive interpersonal behavior. As pre-dicted, Ss showed a significant ($p < .01$) shift from passively hostile to an actively warm social role. The changes in social role were also reflected in a significant ($p < .01$) reduction in number of medical clinic visits. These effects were still operative thirty days following the procedure, whereas an equated base-line group of ten Ss showed no significant change in behavior over the same period of time.

A NUMBER of recent research studies have reported positive, beneficial, or therapeutic effects in psychiatric pa-tients exposed to sensory deprivation procedures. These positive changes have involved a variety of psychological functions at many levels, ranging from overt interpersonal behavior through conscious self-descriptions to the covert attitudes reflected in re-sponses to projective tests (Brownfield, 1965; Gaines & Vetter,

---

*Reprinted with permission of author and publisher from: Cooper, G.D., Adams, H.B., Dickenson, J.R., and York, M.W. Interviewer's role-playing and responses to sensory deprivation: a clinical demonstration. *Perceptual and Motor Skills, 40*:291-303, 1975.

1968; Suedfeld, 1969). In addition, wide individual differences have been found, along with evidence that the most beneficial effects occur in psychiatric patients who would be considered relatively poor candidates for traditional types of verbal psychotherapy (Adams, 1964b; Adams, Cooper, & Carrera, 1972; Cooper, 1962; Cooper, Adams, & Cohen, 1965; Cooper, Adams, & Gibby, 1962). These promising initial findings led the writers to further study of therapeutic potentialities and techniques for the practical application of sensory deprivation.

This paper reports a clinical demonstration using an approach combining sensory deprivation with systematically planned role-playing by an interviewer. The theoretical rationale for the combined procedures grew out of a reassessment of the factor which the present writers and other researchers found most relevant to therapeutic change in psychiatric patients. Our own earlier publications reported that a majority of the psychiatric patients who were exposed to relatively mild conditions of sensory deprivation of short duration (three to six hours maximum) showed generally positive responses following the procedure. However, there were wide individual differences, with a minority of patients showing no significant improvement and a few individuals experiencing negative responses or impairment of functioning after exposure to deprivation.

As Brownfield's (1965) review of the literature stated, a majority of the published research studies on therapeutic applications of sensory deprivation have reported positive results with psychiatric patients. But it is significant that a minority of investigators failed to replicate those positive results, despite the fact that they used experimental procedures that were quite similar to the physical and temporal conditions of reduced sensory input which, in other settings, brought about beneficial effects for psychiatric patients. Such glaring discrepancies pointed up the need for critical reappraisal as a first step toward determining the variables responsible for these divergent research findings.

Our own reappraisal made us realize the necessity for closer consideration of the interpersonal aspects of our earlier research. There is now general agreement that experience in sensory deprivation characteristically brings about a state of "stimulus hunger" in Ss, which generally enhances their general receptivity to all environmental influences. Rosenthal (1966) and many other recent writers have observed that interpersonal communication between Es and Ss constitutes a potent influence on the results of all psychological experiments. It appears that these interpersonal influences are maximized in experiments on sensory deprivation as a consequence of the increased receptivity of Ss. For this reason, patients placed in deprivation should be expected to become much more open to all interpersonal influences. Any expression of attitudes, expectations, psychological sets, or other verbal and nonverbal communications from E should have a subtle but persuasive impact on each S during and after the experience. Moreover, recent studies suggest that manipulation of nonverbal role defining behavior may be more important than verbal content in establishing role expectancies (Abramson & Cooper, 1970; Cooper, 1970; Rice, 1969).

It follows that any discussion of sensory deprivation which regards psychological changes as reflecting the effects of deprivation alone would be incomplete and misleading. The interpersonal context of the experimenter-subject relationship is crucially important and cannot be ignored in any meaningful analysis of effects of the deprivation.

Nevertheless, few, if any, published reports of experiments on sensory deprivation contain accounts of the personal interaction between Ss and Es. While there have often been lengthy, elaborate descriptions of the physical conditions, apparatus, and other noninterpersonal variables, few of these publications mention any of the possible interpersonal cues which might profoundly influence the reactions of Ss in the total sensory deprivation.

Awareness of the importance of interpersonal variables is only a first step toward fruitful analysis and understanding of the phenomena. One recurring difficulty in all discussions of interpersonal behavior has been the lack of a suitable language system and conceptual framework for categorizing and interrelating observations of interpersonal interaction within a single comprehensive system. Such a conceptual system must necessarily encompass the full range of both adaptive ("normal," "healthy," "adjusted," etc.) and maladaptive ("abnormal," "sick," "disturbed," etc.) interpersonal behaviors. A major step in overcoming this deficiency is the Interpersonal System originally developed by Leary (1957), and later elaborated by Foa (1961) and Carson (1969). This system provides a comprehensive descriptive model, a means for classifying and modifying behavior, and a meaningful basis for the systematic manipulation of both Es' and Ss' roles in interpersonal exchanges. The empirical basis for this conceptual system, which employs the two dimensional "circumplex" as its fundamental model, has been set forth elsewhere by Foa (1961), Adams (1964a), and Carson (1969).

Personal recollections and written records provided insightful data on the interpersonal interactions between Ss and the team of investigators who had participated in the series of studies of sensory deprivation conducted at the Richmond VA Hospital (Adams, 1964b, 1965; Adams, Carrera, Cooper, Gibby, & Tobey, 1960; Adams, Cooper, & Carrera, 1972; Adams, Robertson, & Cooper, 1964, 1966; Cooper, 1962; Cooper et al., 1962, 1965; Gibby & Adams, 1961; Gibby, Adams, & Carrera, 1960). These interpersonal interactions were categorized using the conceptual framework and language system of Leary, Foa, and Carson.

Most of the patients who served as Ss in the Richmond studies presented personality disorders which would be classified according to the Leary-Foa-Carson Interpersonal System as "Self-effacing Masochistic" or "Skeptical-distrustful" forms of maladaptive interpersonal behavior. In their face-to-face contacts these patients tended to be passive, inert, sullen, and hostile. Their typical interpersonal "message," i.e., the generalized covert attitudes they implicitly communicated to others in their interpersonal exchanges, centered around feelings of weakness, inadequacy, and querulous resentment. These generalized interpersonal communications tended to elicit active, assertive, but somewhat patronizing attempts to help from members of the Richmond VA Hospital staff. A pattern of mutually reciprocal roles thus developed. In their interpersonal transactions the patients tended to present a somewhat inflexible over-commitment to a role of passive hostility, which would in turn elicit from staff members mildly hostile and dominant reactions. Once established, these mutual reaction patterns often became self-perpetuating. Reactions of hospital personnel to the patients' stereotyped, inflexible interpersonal roles served inadvertently to confirm the patient's implicit sense of personal inadequacy and inferiority. The patterns of staff-patient interactions which had unwittingly been established prior to the experience of sensory deprivation appeared to reinforce the same long-standing maladaptive behavior patterns which had originally led to the admission of those patients to the Richmond VA Hospital.

The interpersonal messages transmitted to those patient-subjects by the Richmond Es were in decided contrast to the prior negative staff-patient interactions. Despite conscious, deliberate efforts to minimize biases and suggestion effects through the use of matched controls and other conventionally accepted formal procedural methods, Es came to the realization that they had in fact manifested a definitely positive, actively assured manner in the presence of their Ss. The unspoken expectations and attitudes conveyed from Es to Ss had apparently served to induce a positive set, implicitly encouraging Ss to perceive and interpret their experiences in sensory deprivation as benign, supportive, and therapeutic in nature. These positive interpersonal influences, appearing in the context of increased stimulus hunger and heightened receptiveness following deprivation served to modify Ss' interpersonal roles and social perceptions in a selective fashion. In turn, those modified roles and perceptions produced lasting aftereffects on overt behavior for post-deprivation periods as long as a week after a single relatively brief period of sensory deprivation. There were suggestions that patients' behavior may have modified the perceptions and responses of ward personnel, producing a more positive interaction.

If we regard sensory deprivation as catalytic and increasing the perceptual saliency of a confirming or disconfirming social message, we are forced to consider the impact on S of E's interpersonal role. According to the rationale of the Interpersonal System, positive, friendly behavior tends to elicit warm, friendly reactions, hostile behavior elicits hostile reactions, dominant behavior draws passive, submissive responses, while passive behavior in turn tends to engender dominant, assertive reactions from others. Various combinations of these reciprocal patterns of interpersonal interactions constitute the basic conceptual framework of interrelationships used for determining the behavior most appropriate for E confronted with the actions of a patient whose maladaptive patterns require modification. These reciprocal role interactions have been observed to hold up in a great variety of social situations.

Assuming that the reciprocites identified in the Leary-Foa model related to the behavior of the Richmond VA patients, then the dominant and warm behavior of Es confirmed the submissive Ss' behavior but *disconfirmed* hostile Ss' behavior. The increased openness and comfort of Ss following deprivation would then allow the supportive interview, enhanced by the stimulus hunger which deprivation tended to produce, to exercise an additional reinforcing effect. Since the purpose of the terminal interview was to elicit reactions to the experience in sensory deprivation from S, the interviewer in this situation was maintaining a warm and positive approach but was reducing the dominance of his own behavior in order to permit maximally informative responses of Ss. According to Leary (1957) this passive, warm behavior of E would tend to reinforce active warmth in Ss, thereby encouraging those behavioral roles which were most characteristically and maladaptively absent in Ss' role repertoire before they were placed in sensory deprivation.

## Procedures

The primary emphasis of our study was to predict shifts in interpersonal role of Ss experiencing a combination of an interviewer's role-playing and sensory deprivation. A secondary purpose involved a demonstration that nonessential clinic visits to air hypochondriacal complaints would be reduced following the induced change in interpersonal roles. The Richmond findings suggested that a two-step social disconfirmation procedure involving social role-structuring in interviews conducted immediately before and after the deprivation could produce self-enforcing behavioral changes in the passive-dependent, hypochondriacal and schizoid Ss most often encountered in VA hospitals and domiciliaries. To test the two-step role-disconfirmation model suggested by the Leary-Foa-Carson schema, systematic training of the interviewers was required to assume the role appropriate in dealing with passive-dependent or schizoid personality disorders. Adjectives from the interpersonal checklist were used to describe interpersonal characteristics which defined interviewer roles. The methods of training and of rating accuracy of role modeling are described elsewhere (Rice, 1969). It was expected that any interviewer or therapist could learn to take the appropriate roles and thereby achieve a controlled enhancement of the effect of sensory deprivation. The interviewer was required to assume a role of active warmth prior to the deprivation to allow for an increase in warmth after deprivation. With schizoid Ss, the interviewer also emphasized frank, matter-of-fact handling of content to reduce Ss' suspicion and skepticism. During the post-deprivation interview, the interviewer was gradually to assume a role of passive warmth to allow the patient to become more dominant. From these general expectations a series of more specific hypotheses was generated.

It was hypothesized that following deprivation and the post-deprivation interview domiciliary members would show increases in both warmth and dominance compared with their pre-deprivation interpersonal behavior. Since (1) an increase in warmth would tend to produce a more positive response on the part of clinic personnel, and (2) an increase in activity or dominance in the member would tend to reduce the number of inappropriate clinic visits, it was hypothesized that the number of clinic visits by members would be significantly less during a thirty-day period immediately after the sensory deprivation than in the comparable thirty-day period immediately before the experience. Finally, it was expected that the subjective impressions of these patients by the medical personnel would change in positive directions.

Ss were twenty male veterans ranging in age from forty-three to seventy-five years, divided into two groups of ten Ss each. All came from a lower socio-economic background, were vocationally and socially disabled, and resided in a VA domiciliary. Medical histories showed extensive attempts at rehabilitation and therapy had been uniformly unsuccessful. Final selection was made by the Domiciliary Physician and Nurse Supervisor using the following criteria: (1) all Ss consistently exhibited behavior which was both passive and mildly antagonistic, (2) all Ss made frequent, inappropriate medical clinic visits during which they ventilated largely hypochondriacal complaints, and (3) all Ss regarded themselves as more disabled than their physical condition would justify. Ss were independently rated as exhibiting all three criteria by both physician and nurse.

After twenty Ss had been selected, the psychologist assigned them randomly to either the baseline or the demonstration group. Ss assigned to the baseline group were not seen personally by the psychologist or in any way informed that their behavior during clinic visits was being rated in order to avoid partial "treatment" effects. The baseline Ss had been given a routine light work assignment by their section leader and performed these details at the same time experimental Ss were undergoing interviews and sensory deprivation.

Ss in the group chosen for the demonstration procedures were not told in advance of the planned procedures. Each was summoned individually from the Domiciliary to the interviewer's office. On arrival, he was informed that he had been referred by the Domiciliary Physician because he seemed to have many problems. The interviewer then urged S to sit and make himself comfortable. He was informed that the conversation would be recorded on tape and then asked "How have you been getting along lately?"

S responded to the interviewer's opening question in a variety of ways, usually listing numerous physical complaints. On the basis of S's behavior during this early phase of the interview, the interviewer made a quick assessment to determine if S was in fact playing one of the two roles used as a criterion for preselection. If S's behavior fell into the Leary categories (Self-effacing Masochistic or Skeptical-distrustful), the interviewer continued through the procedure. If S appeared to be playing any other role, the interviewer had the option of terminating the interview at that point. All ten Ss preselected by the Domiciliary Physician were judged to fall within the appropriate categories. A warmly supportive role was then used with Ss whose social role emphasized Self-effacing Masochistic behaviors; a matter-of-fact approach was used with Ss whose social role emphasized Skeptical-distrustful behaviors. It was predicted that these pre-deprivation interviewer's roles would reduce Ss' maladaptive behavior and prepare them psychologically for the disconfirmation of orienting social hypotheses.

After the interview, each S was instructed to lie down on a bed in an air-conditioned room. Cotton was placed over his eyes and held in place by gauze to shut out the light. Earphones were placed over his ears to help reduce auditory stimulation. A microphone was placed beside the bed. S was instructed that he could say anything he wanted although the interviewer would not answer him. Plantar electrodes were attached to the soles of his feet to monitor skin conductance. S was told that the session would last for two hours and that the interviewer would be in the adjoining room monitoring the equipment.

After two hours in sensory deprivation, S was removed by the interviewer, who then returned him to the interview room next door for the post-deprivation interview. During the post-deprivation interview the interviewer initially assumed the role of active warmth, shifting to a role of passive warmth during the final fifteen minutes. After the post-deprivation interview, all the procedures for each S were completed.

The interviewer then edited the tape recording of the pre-deprivation and post-deprivation interviews. In editing the tapes two five minute segments were selected from (1) the initial free-response segment of the pre-deprivation interview, i.e., the initial first portion of the pre-deprivation interview, before the interviewer had made his assessment of the patient's interpersonal role and assumed the interviewer role considered theoretically appropriate, and (2) the last fifteen minutes of the post-deprivation interview, during which the interviewer had assumed the role of passive warmth. These segments were edited so as to delete any references to the sensory-deprivation procedure and any indication as to which interview was to be rated.

A total of twenty 5-minute taped interview segments were to be rated by judges. Two judges analyzed and rated the twenty taped segments. The interviewer played each of the twenty 5-minute segments to the two judges, who made independent ratings of the

Ss' role during the 5-minute recorded interaction, using the Leary Interpersonal Check List. In the subsequent analysis of the data, the means of the two judges' raw-score ratings on the Interpersonal Check List for each S in the demonstration group were transformed into scores on the Dominance-Submission dimension and the Love-Hostility dimension, according to the procedures in Leary's manual (1956). For purpose of statistical analysis, each of the ten S's Dominance and Love scores for the pre-sensory-deprivation interview segment was contrasted with the same two scores for the post-sensory-deprivation interview segment. This analysis involved pre-post changes on two sets of ten measures each.

In addition to ratings of Ss' interpersonal roles during the two interview segments, records of clinic visits on the thirty days before treatment and the thirty days immediately after treatment were obtained. All clinic visits made by Ss in the baseline group during a sixty-day period were tabulated for comparison. Finally, the physician involved in treating these Ss was also asked informally how he would describe every patient he had referred, including all those in both the demonstration group and the baseline group and was asked to indicate presence or absence of the three criteria originally used for selection.

### Results

It was predicted that Ss in the demonstration group receiving sensory deprivation, coupled with appropriate interviewer role playing, would become more warm and more dominant afterward. Statistical analysis of the judges' mean checklist ratings on Dominance and Love indicated that the predicted role shifts occurred in seventeen out of the twenty sets of ratings. These results are significant at the .01 level, using the sign test. One S increased in warmth but not in dominance as reflected in the Dominance ratings. This S was initially judged as Skeptical-Distrustful. Another S did not change in the predicted direction on either Leary dimension. This S was rated by the judges as Competitive-Narcissistic prior to deprivation, although the interviewer had rated him as Self-effacing-Masochistic before completing the procedure.

Another prediction was that the number of clinic visits for the demonstration group would be greatly reduced after deprivation but that there would be no corresponding change in the baseline group. To test this prediction, two sign tests for paired data were computed, one for the demonstration group and one for the baseline group. Chi squares comparing frequency of the visits in the two groups during similar thirty-day time intervals also were computed.

In the thrity days following treatment, the total number of clinic visits by the ten Ss in the demonstration group was nine, contrasted with forty-nine visits in the thirty days before. For purposes of comparing the two thirty-day time intervals in the baseline group, the median date, when half the Ss in the demonstration group had gone through the treatment procedure, was used as a mid-point. The baseline group made fifty visits during the thirty days prior to this mid-point date and fifty-three visits in the thirty days after the mid-point date. The reduction of frequency of clinic visits by Ss in the demonstration group was significant at the .01 level by the sign test. There was no significant change in frequency of clinic visits by Ss in the baseline group.

To compare differences between the two groups, the mean number of clinic visits was used. For both groups the mean number of clinic visits per S during the first thirty-day period was five. Of the ten Ss in the demonstration group, five made fewer than five clinic visits while another five made more than five visits during the thirty days before they received the sensory-deprivation experience. The figures on clinic visits were identical for the ten Ss in the baseline group.

During the second thirty-day period, six Ss in the baseline group made more than five visits and four made fewer. In the demonstration group, no S made as many as five visits in the comparable thirty-day post-treatment period. This difference was significant ($P = .001$) by Fisher's exact probability statistic. Subjective impressions of clinic personnel were more positive for demonstration group members but not for baseline Ss. Physician's ratings of the demonstration group Ss on the three selection criteria showed nine of ten Ss judged as exhibiting fewer negative traits.* Ratings of baseline group Ss were unchanged. The difference in rated change between the two groups was significant ($p = .005$) using Fisher's exact probability statistic.

All clinical records of the ten Ss in the demonstration group were reviewed six months after the date they had received sensory deprivation. Seven of the ten Ss had continued visiting the clinic at a greatly reduced rate, i.e., one or two clinic visits per month. Their relatively few visits were judged by the physician to represent appropriate medical complaints rather than hypochondriacal maneuvers. Every demonstration S went to the clinic less often after sensory deprivation than had been the case during the thirty-day pre-deprivation period. The physician expressed the opinion that these Ss were generally more active and more friendly than they had been prior to sensory deprivation. Ratings for selection criteria showed seven of ten demonstration group members judged as exhibiting fewer negative traits compared to original ratings. Nine baseline group members showed no change. The remaining baseline S was not available for rating. The difference between demonstration and baseline group was significant ($p = .01$) using Fisher's exact probability statistic.

## Discussion

Our results strongly support the feasibility of producing predictable corrective changes in role-playing for Ss with established, maladaptive social roles through the combined use of interviewer role-playing and sensory deprivation. There was also support for the hypothesis that role shifts would be attended by a reduction of inappropriate behaviors incompatible with the new role. Data for the stability of the effect were suggestive rather than conclusive, but pointed to the possibility that shifts in role-playing might set up self-reinforcing contingencies stabilizing improved behavior over surprisingly extended periods. The minimal investment of time and extent of improvement in Ss with established high resistance to conventional therapies recommend the procedure for continued consideration as a therapeutic modality.

---

*The nurse involved in the original ratings was unfortunately unavailable for post-deprivation ratings.

The global, qualitative clinical impressions and the objective statistical data agreed in indicating two major points. First, successful predictions of results obtained from short-term sensory deprivation were determined primarily by the *interpersonal context* in which sensory deprivation occurred. Second, the reinforcement contingencies which served to modify Ss' interpersonal behavior after deprivation were a function of the confirmation and/or disconfirmation of their implicit hypotheses about their behavior and the reactions of other persons. These processes of confirmation and disconfirmation appeared to lend themselves readily to an analysis in terms of cognitive learning theory (Tolman, 1932; Heider, 1958).

Our results suggest that changes in behavior and personality were lawfully determined by principles which apply equally well to ordinary social environments and to novel environments in which social feedback has been artificially limited. In both situations a person will seek from the environment discriminable social data which confirm or disconfirm his expectations with regard to the behavior of other significant persons. In normal everyday situations, continued social feedback can be readily elicited from other persons. Through such feedback, a constant mutual shaping of behavior occurs. In sensory deprivation the environment fails to provide this continual source of corrective data, requiring S to make use of internal sources of information to maintain a secure perception of himself. The interpersonal set induced just prior to a deprivation experience is critical in determining the interpersonal meaning of such an experience for individual Ss. By eliminating competing stimuli and the possibility of self-initiated correction of incoming data, sensory deprivation makes any social data acquired immediately beforehand far more significant for determining consequent behavior than would otherwise be the case. The interviewer's role prior to and immediately following sensory deprivation then becomes an extremely potent reinforcer, allowing relatively decisive confirmation and disconfirmation of S's orienting social hypotheses and producing marked change in his social behavior.

The changes toward passive warmth in most Ss receiving sensory deprivation suggested that those Ss modified their interpersonal roles in order to reestablish reciprocities with the interviewer. The effects of sensory deprivation appeared to be a kind of catalyst, increasing the impact of disconfirming interpersonal messages. The procedures also seemed to increase the perceptual cognitive impact of disconfirming interpersonal roles in the interviewer immediately after sensory deprivation. Our data indicate that Ss not only shifted to a role of passive warmth in response to the initial interpersonal contacts but readily shifted to a role of active warmth immediately after sensory deprivation in lawful, consistent ways which were a function of the role adopted by the interviewer.

It is significant that Ss' behavior with regard to clinic visits showed marked changes for an extended period of time after sensory deprivation. The cognitive model assumes that the reinforcer of our Ss' behavior was not praise or censure, reward or punishment, but rather the confirmation or disconfirmation of hypotheses concerning the reaction of other persons to self-generated behavior. The Leary model identifies two major dimensions of social behavior: (1) the dimension of dominance vs submission and (2) the dimension of love vs hate. It also assumes that discriminable interpersonal roles, described as an intersect function of the two dimensions, could be ordered along a further dimension of intensity. Reexamining Ss' behavior in terms of their orienting social hypotheses, we would say that each person unwittingly organized his own behavior in ways that served to confirm his expectations of intensity, dominance and hostility. The passive, hostile S would then expect others to be hostile and dominant toward him. If this expectation were confirmed, the passive, hostile S would continue to maintain his characteristic interpersonal role in spite of its maladaptive implications.

This theoretical description corresponds to the observations of our Ss' pre-sensory-deprivation behavior, as described by clinic personnel and the examining physician. Each S typically gave an interpersonal impression of extreme passivity, inertia, and mild hostility, in effect saying, "I am weak, worthless and resentful." They elicited behavior from others which was dominant and supportive but mildly rejecting. Most persons responded with behavior which in effect communicated the interpersonal message, "We will attempt to help you, but we can neither respect nor like you." These patronizing attitudes only confirmed the hypochondriacal and passive-dependent Ss' feelings of worthlessness, thereby sustaining the very behavior which efforts at assistance attempted to relieve. Even where the initial approach by clinic personnel was warm and supportive, Ss often misperceived it as emphasizing their weakness and unworthiness. They tended to reject, in a variety of subtle ways, the positive concern of the hospital personnel, acting as though such "undeserved" help increased their guilty sense of obligation and self-contempt.

The procedures used in the demonstration allowed a successive series of partial disconfirmations of Ss' orienting hypotheses. Disconfirmation in a series of partial steps was based on the empirical observation that dramatic total disconfirmations of a person's expectations often produce intense anxiety. Under such conditions perceptual constriction so limits behavior that veridical hypothesis testing becomes difficult and alternative roles may not be available for reestablishing social reciprocities.

The initial interview disconfirmed the implicit, generalized hypothesis of hostility in the other, allowing a shift to a warmer and more affiliative posture prior to sensory deprivation. During the deprivation Ss appeared to perceive and interpret the procedure in terms of these more positive expectations, describing it as a benign, helpful, supportive experience in the post-deprivation interview. Their increased comfort and enhanced willingness to communicate seemed to facilitate disconfirmation of the previous implicit hypothesis of weakness and passivity, allowing them to move toward a role of active warmth. Since it was judged that Ss' most entrenched role-hypothesis concerned their posture of helplessness and weakness, the disconfirmation of this dimension of personal expectations followed sensory deprivation, when "stimulus hunger" and receptiveness were maximized. This shift in Ss' roles reestablished the reciprocities which the interviewer had disrupted by his role playing. Although measures were not made of the intensity of Ss' behaviors, the impression of the judges was that in the predeprivation interviews the intensity of Ss' submissiveness and hostility diminished rapidly prior to the shift toward more affiliation.

Previous research has indicated that sensory deprivation may permit therapeutic change in Ss who do not respond well to traditional verbal therapies (Cooper et al., 1962, 1965). These results support these prior findings, since the ten Ss in the demonstration group represented a type of personality disorder resistant to the usual therapeutic approaches.

The negative effects of prolonged sensory deprivation and the destructive results clinically observed in some patients and other groups such as prisoners subjected to isolation have been cited as contraindications to the therapeutic use of sensory deprivation. Our findings imply that negative effects such as these could be prevented if the interpersonal influences preceding and following sensory deprivation were suitably prestructured. Conflicting reports of changes following sensory deprivation may depend more on the interpersonal context in which the deprivation occurs than the physical characteristics of the deprived environment.

A cognitive learning interpretation of the effects of sensory deprivation might equally well apply to other techniques which produce a breakdown of orienting social hypotheses and a revision of social expectations. Such techniques include many depth psychotherapies, insulin, electroshock, and chemotherapeutic techniques using LSD or mescaline.

Our results raise questions concerning reinforcement therapies which regard rewarding or punishing events as reinforcers and ignore the interpersonal confrontations in which the rewards or punishments are given. A strong possibility exists that the social role of the therapist serves to reinforce the molar social behavior of Ss with the events described as reinforcers serving primarily as cues to the therapist's expectations.

Finally, the implication of this study has extension beyond sensory deprivation to the training of therapists and reevaluation of interviewing. If therapists' roles could be specified and performed to produce predictable shifts in client behaviors, individual psychotherapeutic techniques with more precision and wider applicability might be developed.

### REFERENCES

Abramson, E. E., & Cooper, G. D.: The interpersonal role as a reinforcer in verbal conditioning: a pilot study. *Newsletter for Research in Psychology, 12*(1):30-31, 1970.

Adams, H. B.: "Mental illness" or interpersonal behavior. *American Psychologist, 19*:191-197, 1964(a).

Adams, H. B.: Therapeutic potentialities of sensory deprivation procedures. *Institute of Mental Health Research Newsletter, 6*(4):7-9, 1964(b).

Adams, H. B.: A case utilizing sensory deprivation. In L. Krasner & L. Ullmann (Eds.), *Case Studies in Behavior Modification.* New York, Holt, 1965, pp. 164-170.

Adams, H. B., Carrera, R. N., Cooper, G. D., Gibby, R. C., & Tobey, H. R.: Personality and intellectual changes in psychiatric patients following brief partial sensory deprivation. Cleveland Convention Reports Duplication Service, 1960.

Adams, H. B., Cooper, G. D., & Carrera, R. N.: Individual differences in behavioral reactions of psychiatric patients to brief partial sensory deprivation. *Perceptual and Motor Skills, 34*:199-217, 1972.

Adams, H. B., Robertson, M. H., & Cooper, G. D.: Facilitating therapeutic personality change in psychiatric patients by sensory deprivation methods. In *Proceedings of the 17th International Congress of Psychology.* Amsterdam, North Holland Publ., 1964, pp. 108-109.

Adams, H. B., Robertson, M. H., & Cooper, G. D.: Sensory deprivation and personality change. *Journal of Nervous and Mental Disorders, 143*:256-265, 1966.

Brownfield, C. A.: *Isolation.* New York, Random House, 1965.

Carson, R. C.: *Interaction Concepts of Personality. Perspectives in Personality.* No. 1, Chicago, Aldine, 1969.

Cooper, G. D.: Changes in ego strength following brief perceptual and social deprivation. Unpublished doctoral dissertation, Duke Univer., 1962.

Cooper, G. D.: Sensory deprivation and therapy for inadequate personalities. *Frontiers of Hospital Psychiatry, 17*:3, 1970.

Cooper, G. D., Adams, H. B., & Cohen, L. D.: Changes in personality after sensory deprivation. *Journal of Nervous and Mental Disorders, 140*:103-118, 1965.

Cooper, G. D., Adams, H. B., & Gibby, R. G.: Ego strength changes following perceptual deprivation. *A.M.A. Archives of General Psychiatry, 7*:213-217, 1962.

Ferster, C. B., & DeMyer, M. K.: The development of performances in autistic children in an automated controlled environment. *Journal of Chronic Disorders, 13*:312-345, 1964.

Foa, U. G.: Convergences in the analysis of the structure of interpersonal behavior. *Psychological Review, 68*:341-353, 1961.

Gaines, L. S., & Vetter, H. J.: Sensory deprivation and psychotherapy. *Psychotherapy: Theory, Research and Practice, 5*:7-12, 1968.

Gibby, R. G., & Adams, H. B.: Perceptiveness of psychiatric patients to verbal communication. *Archives of General Psychiatry, 5*:366-370, 1961.

Gibby, R. G., Adams, H. B., & Carrera, R. N.: Therapeutic changes in psychiatric patients following partial sensory deprivation. *Archives of General Psychiatry, 3*:33-42, 1960.

Heider, F.: *The Psychology of Interpersonal Relationships.* New York, Wiley, 1958.

Krasner, L., & Ullmann, L. P.: Variables in the verbal conditioning of schizophrenic subjects. *American Psychologist, 13*:355-367, 1958.

Leary, T.: *Multilevel Measurement of Interpersonal Behavior: A Manual for the Use of the Interpersonal System.* New York, Psychological Consultation Service, 1956.

Leary, T.: *Interpersonal Diagnosis of Personality.* New York, Ronald, 1957.

Rice, P. K.: The modification of interpersonal roles. Unpublished doctoral dissertation, West Virginia Univer., 1969.

Rosenthal, R.: *Experimenter Effects on Behavioral Research.* New York, Appleton-Century-Crofts, 1966.

Suedfeld, P.: Changes in intellectual performance and in susceptibility to influence. In J. P. Zubek (Ed), *Sensory Deprivation: Fifteen Years of Research.* New York, Appleton-Century-Crofts, 1969, pp. 126-166.

Tolman, E. C.: *Purposive Behavior in Animals and Men.* New York, Appleton-Century-Crofts, 1932.

# PART TWO

## Bed Confinement: An Increased Susceptibility to External Influence

# INTRODUCTION

$T$ HE experiments in this section attempted to expand the influence of bed confinement on personality by introducting a taped message designed to alter the subject's opinion of himself, his attitudes or behavior. The researchers believed the stimulus hunger that develops in isolation would make the subjects more susceptible to their message. Some of these studies come close to the original issue of brainwashing in that they attempted to influence the subject in a deliberate and premeditated fashion. However, the tapes in these experiments were prepared from previous psychological assessment of the subjects and were considered to be beneficial. This therapeutic aspect of the messages makes generalization to brainwashing procedures inferential, for a subject is probably more open to a message that does not conflict with his ethical or ideological values.

## Experimental Variables

### Degree of Stimulus Reduction

All of the studies in this section reduced the intensity of available stimuli to a level necessary to produce regression and disorganization in their subjects. This condition is generally sufficient to produce personality change in and of itself.

### Contents of Taped Message

While some studies gave the same, hopefully therapeutic message to each subject, others created individual messages for each subject in an effort to further refine the technique. These two methods did not differentiate the experiments that found personality change from those that did not. Successes and failures were

163

reported using both approaches, suggesting other variables were more influential in determining results. It may be concluded from available research that precise individualization of the message does not appreciably affect outcome.

### Time Spent in Isolation

Robertson (chapter 11) used three, three-hour sessions whereas other experimenters used single sessions lasting between three and twenty-four hours. He reported no personality changes in his subjects. While it is possible the use of multiple isolation experiences may affect outcome, this conclusion is masked by another unique feature of his experiment. Robertson's posttesting took place one week after the last session. The potential effect of a delayed posttest is not easy to assess. It appears to suggest that therapeutic gains, if present, did not last a week. However, Suedfeld and Ikard (chapter 13) found effects from their antismoking treatment intact after two years. Also, Adams (1964) made a follow-up investigation of a single subject in his study, and concluded the isolation and tape treatment had created lasting therapeutic effect. Further research is needed to substantiate the duration of bed confinement isolation and tape induced personality change.

### Experimental Set

The findings regarding the importance of set were consistent with the conclusions of the first section. It appears a neutral or positive set is necessary for therapeutic personality change, but in and of itself is not a determining variable for that change. Robertson (chapter 11), who gave his subjects a positive set, did not find any personality change. As in the preceding section, set is not reported in the successful experiments. However, it may again be assumed the set was at least neutral given the hospital setting and the aims of the researchers.

### Theoretical Constructs

The psychoanalytic rationale prevalent in the chapters of Part

One is absent in this section. The researchers investigating the use of taped messages in isolation relied exclusively on the concept of stimulus hunger; a phenomenon well represented in the sensory isolation literature. It is worthwhile to digress briefly here to review the trend of findings in this area.

The original studies by the McGill group were concerned in part with the creation of attitude change in isolation. They found that subjects in isolation requested to hear taped messages (radio soap commercials, stock market reports, and the like) that they had previously considered aversive. Some subjects requested many repetitions of the tapes and in this sense, their attitude change toward the messages was considered evidence of their stimulus hunger. Scott, Bexton, Heron and Doane (1959) found mildly skeptical subjects expressed increased belief in psychic phenomena after having heard messages in isolation promoting that belief. Not only did they demonstrate more attitude change than the controls, but they also requested to hear the tapes many more times. Myers, Murphy and Smith (1963) attempted to change attitudes toward the Turkish Nation by presenting a boldly persuasive tape during isolation, but failed to produce predicted results. They did conclude that less intelligent subjects tended to have more attitude change than their brighter counterparts; presumably the more intelligent subjects resisted such a frontal attack on their opinions. Suedfeld (1963) and Suedfeld and Vernon (chapter 12) disguised the manipulative aspect of the pro-Turk tapes and concluded attitude change had been effected. In a summary of the literature dealing with this topic, Suedfeld concluded:

> Susceptibility to external influence, including both primary suggestibility and persuasibility is clearly increased in sensory deprivation. The data indicate that this phenomena originates with lack of informational anchors in the sensory deprivation situation; the subject is at loose ends, without guidelines for his behavior, unable to concentrate, and in a state of stimulus and information hunger .... This condition has the effect of maximizing the impact and reward value of whatever information is made available to him (1969 p. 166).

Before leaving this discussion, a potential conflict between stimulus hunger and the psychoanalytic explanations should be illuminated. The latter hypothesizes that the secondary processes of the ego depend upon a continual contact with external reality, and regression to the primary process is concurrent with a suspension of this contact. It can be inferred that the messages delivered during isolation could renew this contact with external reality and prevent the emergence of the primary process. In short, the satiation of stimulus hunger with a message or any other means may enable the individual to ward off the regression considered to be therapeutic. Thus the successful assimilation of a message may negate the regressive pull of isolation experience. This gives rise to the tentative conclusion that stimulus hunger and regression are two separate variables that act, but may not effectively interact in the therapeutic application of sensory isolation. This conclusion was substantiated by the findings of Suedfeld and Ikard (chapter 13) who reported the frequent disruption of isolation with a tape may have blunted the effect of both.

## Individual Differences

The findings in Part One that the most disturbed subjects improve the most was further substantiated. Using normal subjects, Henrichs (this volume, chapter 10) concluded "Suggestibility, a phenomena frequently noted in SR experiences, was not apparently notably increased under the present experimental conditions."

This is in accord with an investigation reported by Adams, Robertson and Cooper (chapter 9) in which normal subjects did not benefit from the isolation and tape treatment as had disturbed subjects. Further clarification was provided by Suedfeld and Vernon (chapter 12) who found simple, concrete subjects tended to internalize the contents of a message more readily than their complex, abstract counterparts, who demonstrated relatively little attitude change.

## Conclusions

It appears two major variables in isolation environments can be used therapeutically: (1) regression and ego diffusion and (2) stimulus hunger. Further research is needed to compare the effectiveness of these two approaches and to investigate the effect of varying the time at which the messages are given. Evidence from both of the preceding sections indicates bed confinement with or without a taped message is not generally effective in creating personality change in normal subjects. However, Suedfeld (chapter 13) found bed confinement to be effective in reducing cigarette smoking. While such a behavioral change could be considered evidence of personality change, no psychological testing was employed in the study, leaving the possible concurrent effects on personality open to debate. From available evidence it appears the presence of intact and differentiated defenses tends to resist regression and ego diffusion, and decrease susceptibility to external influence.

### References

Adams, H. B.: A case utilizing sensory deprivation procedures. In Krasner, L. and Ullman, L. P. (Eds.): *Case Studies in Behavior Modifications*. New York, Holt, Rinehart and Winston, 1964.

Myers, T. I., Murphy, D. B., and Smith, S.: The effect of sensory deprivation and social isolation on self-exposure to propaganda and attitude change. Paper read at the American Psychological Association. *American Psychologist, 18*:440, 1963. (Abstract)

Scott, T. H., Bexton, W. H., Heron, W., and Doane, B. K.: Cognitive effects of perceptual isolation. *Canadian Journal of Psychology, 13*:200, 1959.

Suedfeld, P.: Changes in intellectual performance and in susceptibility to influence. In Zubeck, J. P. (Ed.): *Sensory Deprivation: Fifteen Years of Research*. New York, Appleton Century Crofts, 1969.

Suedfeld, P.: Attitude manipulation in restricted environments: I. Conceptual structure and response to propaganda. *Journal of Abnormal and Social Psychology, 68*:242, 1964.

# Chapter 8

# RECEPTIVENESS OF PSYCHIATRIC PATIENTS TO VERBAL COMMUNICATION*
## An Increase Following Partial Sensory and Social Deprivation

ROBERT G. GIBBY, Ph.D. and HENRY B. ADAMS, Ph.D.

THIS paper reports an investigation of changes in the receptiveness of psychiatric subjects to verbal communication following brief partial sensory deprivation. A previous study by the present authors reported that a group of psychiatric patients exposed to a few hours of brief partial sensory and social deprivation subsequently showed less overt symptomatology, enhanced ego functioning, greater capacity to relate to others, improved reality testing, and more effective intellectual functioning, as measured by I.Q. scores.[1, 2, 5] However, there were marked individual differences in reactions during deprivation and in the nature and extent of changes afterward. The personality correlates of these individual differences have been thoroughly investigated and reported elsewhere.[1]

One of the changes most frequently observed by the present experimenters was an increased need of the subjects for social contacts in general, particularly with the professional staff. This need for increased social stimulation seems to be one manifestation of a general phenomenon of "stimulus hunger," which has been found in nearly all subjects exposed to sensory deprivation procedures. On the basis of these earlier observations the present study was set up to investigate the hypothesis that exposure to sensory deprivation induces a stimulus hunger and thereby in-

*Reprinted from the *Archives of General Psychiatry*, October 1961, Volume 5, pp. 366-370. Copyright 1961, American Medical Association.

susceptibility of subjects to a prerecorded verbal message. It was postulated that meaningful stimulus material presented under experimentally controlled conditions of sensory deprivation would be more likely to influence the thoughts, attitudes, and subsequent behavior of the subjects than the same message presented under more familiar, commonplace circumstances.

## Method

*Subjects.* The subjects were forty-two hospitalized white male veteran patients. All were either patients on the neuropsychiatric wards of a veterans' general medical and surgical hospital or patients on medical wards whose behavior had caused them to be referred for psychiatric evaluation. Every patient carried a psychiatric diagnosis, although some had initially been hospitalized and treated for various nonpsychiatric medical disorders. Patients with a diagnosis of organic brain or central nervous system pathology were excluded from the sample. The subjects ranged in age from twenty-six to fifty-nine, with a median age of 36.5 and a mean of 38.1 (S.D. 8.0). The psychiatric diagnosis of the forty-two subjects are set forth in Table 8-I.

*Procedures.* Four groups of subjects were formed. These groups

TABLE 8-I

PSYCHIATRIC DIAGNOSIS OF THE SUBJECTS

| | |
|---|---|
| Involutional psychotic reaction | 1 |
| Schizophrenic reaction, paranoid type | 3 |
| Schizophrenic reaction, chronic undifferentiated type | 6 |
| Schizophrenic reaction, unclassified | 2 |
| Psychotic reaction, unclassified | 2 |
| Psychophysiologic autonomic and visceral reaction | 5 |
| Anxiety reaction | 11 |
| Conversion reaction | 2 |
| Neurotic depressive reaction | 5 |
| Inadequate personality | 2 |
| Schizoid personality | 1 |
| Paranoid personality | 1 |
| Sociopathic personality disturbance, alcoholism | 1 |
| Total | 42 |

did not differ significantly in mean age or diagnostic composition. The Self-Rating Inventory developed by Brownfain[3] was administered on two successive days to every subject in each group, with various combinations of intervening conditions for each of the groups. The four groups and experimental conditions were as follows:

Group 1 (Tape plus Sensory Deprivation): Subjects in this group were given the Brownfain Self-Rating Inventory on the first day. On the morning of the second day they were exposed to more than four hours of partial sensory and social deprivation, during which a message prerecorded on a tape was played to each subject. Thus they experienced both the taped message and deprivation.

The deprivation conditions were similar to those utilized by the investigators in previous studies.[1,2,5] The subjects lay on a bed in a quiet, air-conditioned room. Each subject's eyes were covered, glycerin-soaked cotton plugs were inserted into his ears, and his head was wrapped in a gauze bandage. A small bone conductivity speaker was placed inside the head coverings and held in place by adhesive tape. During the entire period he was observed continuously by an experimenter, but the experimenter did not speak to the subject at any time during the period of deprivation. If during deprivation any subject complained repeatedly of the need to urinate, a urinal was silently placed in his hand, but there was no other social interaction between the subject and experimenter during deprivation. Thus, there was social deprivation just as there was sensory deprivation.

Under these conditions the subject received no verbal, auditory, or visual stimulus cues to remind him of the continuous presence of the observer. Meaningfully patterned visual and auditory stimuli were reduced to a minimum by means of the head, ear, and eye coverings. The air conditioner kept temperature and humidity at a constant level, while the sound of the machine supplied a steady monotonous blowing sound just loud enough to mask other extraneous noises. Visual, auditory, and temperature stimuli were thus kept relatively fixed at a constant low or moderate level. However, no attempt was made to diminish tactual or kinesthetic stimulation. Each subject was free to move around while lying on the bed, with his arms, legs, hands, and feet being free of any cuffs or other restraints. The experimental conditions could thus be characterized as creating partial sensory and social deprivation for a relatively short period of time, as compared with the conditions reported in many of the other published studies in sensory deprivation.

After the subject had remained in sensory deprivation for four hours, a prerecorded fourteen minute stimulus tape was played to him through the bone conductivity speaker buried in the blindfold bandages. The tenor of the message was reassuring, having been phrased so as to encourage a more favorable self-concept in the subject. The message was couched in very general terms which might be applicable to almost any hospitalized psychiatric patient. It stressed the points that (1) the subject did not view himself as a worthwhile person; (2) there was a discrepancy between the way he saw himself and the way he was actually seen by others; and (3) that he was more acceptable to others and personally more likeable than he himself realized.

Fifteen minutes after the conclusion of the tape message the subject was removed from sensory deprivation by the experimenter. The subject then had lunch, and immediately afterward he was given the Brownfain Self-Rating Inventory a second time.

Group 2 (Sensory Deprivation but No Tape): All the subjects in this group received four hours of sensory deprivation under the same conditions as those in Group 1. The only difference was that the stimulus tape was not presented; this group was exposed to deprivation but not to the tape. The subjects were administered the Brownfain Self-Rating Inventory the day before deprivation, and, following the same procedures as Group 1, the Self-Rating Inventory was repeated afterward.

Group 3 (Stimulus Tape, No Sensory Deprivation): Each subject in this group was exposed to the tape but not to deprivation. The Self-Rating Inventory was administered on the first day. On the following day the subject was taken into a private interviewing room, where he was told that a tape-recorded message had been prepared for him. He was then seated in a comfortable armchair, and told that the message would be presented to him on a tape recording. As soon as the experimenter had started the playing of the message on the tape recorder, he left the room, leaving the subject alone for the fourteen-minute period during which the stimulus tape was presented. After hearing the tape message, each subject was then given the Brownfain Self-Rating Inventory for the second time.

Group 4 (No Tape and No Deprivation): In order to assess the amount of change in self-ratings over a two-day period in which there were no other experimental events (neither stimulus tape nor sensory deprivation), the Self-Rating Inventory was administered on two successive days to a fourth group of subjects. This group could be described as a test-retest group.

## Results and Comment

In filling out the Brownfain Self-Rating Inventory the subject was instructed to make four separate sets of judgments. He was first asked to rate himself on twenty personality traits as he really thought he was. Numerical ratings on each of the twenty items ranged from 1 (very low) to 8 (the highest or most favorable rating possible). He was then told to rate himself the highest he considered realistically possible on the same twenty traits, giving himself the benefit of any doubts. He then rated himself a third time on the same twenty traits, this time being instructed to rate himself the lowest he realistically considered possible. Finally he was asked to estimate as accurately as he could how people in his own peer group would rate him on the same twenty traits. This last rating was the patient's self-picture, as he believed he would appear to others who knew him well.

The mean pretest scores on the four ratings did not differ significantly from group to group. Since the four groups were essentially equivalent in their initial ratings, it may be inferred that any differential changes in the ratings reflected differences in the conditions to which the various groups had been exposed be-between pre- and posttesting. In analyzing the data, scores on the twenty items were added together for each of the four ratings. The lowest possible score on any rating was twenty and the highest possible was 160. The analysis was focused on changes between the first and second administrations of the Self-Rating Inventory

TABLE 8-II

PRE-POST CHANGES IN RATINGS ON BROWNFAIN
SELF-RATING INVENTORY: MEANS AND STANDARD
DEVIATIONS OF CHANGE SCORES FOR FOUR GROUPS
EXPOSED TO VARIOUS EXPERIMENTAL CONDITIONS

| Group* | n | Initial Self-Rating Change Scores | | Highest Possible Self-Rating Change Scores | | Lowest Possible Self-Rating Change Scores | | Self as Perceived by Others Change Scores | |
|---|---|---|---|---|---|---|---|---|---|
| | | Mean† | S.D. | Mean‡ | S.D. | Mean† | S.D. | Mean† | S.D. |
| 1 | 10 | 13.0 | 21.9 | 11.4 | 22.6 | 8.2 | 21.5 | 11.6 | 17.7 |
| 2 | 7 | 4.6 | 10.7 | - 0.7 | 7.8 | 0.6 | 9.6 | - 1.7 | 11.3 |
| 3 | 10 | 1.0 | 11.4 | - 5.2 | 15.6 | -2.1 | 17.1 | - 0.9 | 10.1 |
| 4 | 15 | -0.7 | 8.8 | - 3.5 | 10.8 | -0.3 | 10.8 | - 4.1 | 14.2 |

*Group 1: Tape plus sensory deprivation
 Group 2: Sensory deprivation, no tape
 Group 3: Tape, no deprivation
 Group 4: No tape, no deprivation (test-retest only)
†Differences between means of Group 1 and means of Groups 2, 3 and 4 were all significant at the
0.01 level by Duncan's test of multiple contrasts between groups of means. Differences in means
between Groups 2, 3, and 4 were not significant.
‡Difference in means between Group 1 and Group 2 was significant at 0.05 level by Duncan's test.
Differences between Group 1 and Groups 3 and 4 were significant at 0.01 level. Differences between
Groups 2, 3, and 4 were not significant.

in these four total rating scores.

Table 8-II summarizes the means and standard deviations of the
change scores (differences between pre- and postratings) in each
group for each of the four ratings. The mean change was much
greater in the group which heard the stimulus tape during deprivation than in any of the other three groups. This held true for
each of the four ratings. The significance of differences between
the groups in mean changes was evaluated using Duncan's test of
multiple contrasts between groups of means.[4] This statistical test
showed that the differences between the mean changes in Group 1
(stimulus tape plus deprivation) and the corresponding means in
the other three groups were all significant at the 0.01 level for the
initial self-rating, the lowest possible self-rating, and the rating of
self as perceived by others. Differences between the means of the

other three groups were not statistically significant. For the most favorable self-rating the difference between Group 1 (tape plus deprivation) and Group 2 (sensory deprivation but no tape) in mean change was significant at the 0.05 level. The differences in means between Group 1 and Groups 3 and 4 were significant at the 0.01 level for the most favorable self-rating, but differences between the means of Groups 2, 3, and 4 were not significant.

It may be concluded that exposure to sensory deprivation led to increased acceptance of a prerecorded verbal stimulus designed to alter the subject's self-concept in a higher, more favorable direction. Particularly noteworthy is the contrast between Group 1, which received the prerecorded message under conditions of deprivation, and Group 3, to whom the identical message was presented under conditions of no sensory deprivation. The effect on Group 3 seems to have been essentially no change in the subject's self-concept, whereas there was a marked rise in Group 1.

The results thus support the hypothesis that exposure to sensory and social deprivation, even under mild conditions of relatively brief duration, serves to increase the subject's receptiveness to new stimulus material presented in the form of a verbal message. Such a communication is more readily assimilated than when it is presented under more commonplace conditions without deprivation.

The findings definitely imply that there was a factor of stimulus hunger in the subjects exposed to deprivation which produced the above effects. This factor has already been indirectly alluded to by other writers. Kubzansky[6] in reviewing the literature suggests that social isolation and sensory deprivation tend to increase the receptivity of subjects to external environmental influences. He notes that most studies in this area agree in the implication that stimulus deprivation produces stimulus hunger, which subjects in deprivation experience phenomenally as a "lack of things to see, hear, do or think about." He relates the concept of stimulus hunger to the general concept of a "curiosity-exploratory drive," which grew out of earlier animal experimentation. In any case, conditions of social isolation and sensory deprivation have been shown experimentally to "increase receptivity to otherwise dull, uninteresting material." Kubzansky suggests that the altered subjective state resulting from sensory deprivation "would seem to make one quite vulnerable to new input from a controlled source."

The present results may be regarded as having potentially significant psychotherapeutic applications. It has been repeatedly demonstrated by other investigators that one of the distinguishing characteristics of psychiatric patients as a group is that they have a relatively unfavorable, unsatisfying picture of themselves. For this reason measures of the effectiveness of psychotherapy often involve assessments of positive changes in the patient's self-concept. The present findings indicate that a message designed to enhance the self-concept is more readily accepted and assimilated under conditions of sensory deprivation. It is suggested that applications of sensory deprivation procedures such as those utilized in this investigation may be profitably used to overcome resistances, hasten the acquisition of insight, and increase the patient's self-understanding and self-acceptance. The process of psychotherapy might be speeded up and generally facilitated by the timely and appropriate use of sensory deprivation techniques.

## Summary

An experiment was conducted to investigate the hypothesis that brief partial sensory and social deprivation would enhance the receptiveness of psychiatric patients to verbal communication. Four groups of subjects were exposed to various experimental conditions. Group 1 received a taped message during deprivation; Group 2 received deprivation but not the tape; Group 3 received the tape but not the deprivation; and Group 4 received neither the tape nor the deprivation. The effects of differences in the experimental conditions were assessed by means of the Brownfain Self-Rating Scale, which was administered to every subject before and after exposure to the experimental conditions.

The subjects who heard the tape during deprivation changed their subsequent ratings significantly more in the directions suggested by the taped message than any of the other 3 groups. The hypothesis that sensory deprivation increases receptivity, acceptance, and assimilation of meaningful verbal materials was upheld. It was suggested that there is an increase in stimulus hunger during deprivation which accounts for the greater receptiveness of subjects to new stimulus material. It was also suggested that the findings may have useful applications in certain phases of psychotherapy.

## REFERENCES

1. Adams, H. B., Carrera, R. N., Cooper, G. D., Gibby, R. G., and Tobey, H. R.: Personality and intellectual changes in psychiatric patients following brief partial sensory deprivation. Cleveland, Convention Reports Duplication Service, 1960.
2. Adams, H. B., Carrera, R. N., and Gibby, R. G.: Behavioral reactions of psychiatric patients to brief sensory deprivation. Cleveland, Convention Reports Duplication Service, 1960.
3. Brownfain, J. J.: Stability of the self-concept as a dimension of personality. *J. Abnorm. Social Psychol., 47*:597-606, 1952.
4. Duncan, D. B.: Multiple range and multiple F tests. *Biometrics, 11*:1-42, 1955.
5. Gibby, R. G., Adams, H. B., and Carrera, R. N.: Therapeutic changes in psychiatric patients following partial sensory deprivation, *Arch. Gen. Psychiat., 3*:33-42, 1960.
6. Kubzansky, P. E.: The effects of reduced environmental stimulation on human behavior. Washington, D. C., Bureau of Social Science Research, 1959.

# Chapter 9

# SENSORY DEPRIVATION AND
# PERSONALITY CHANGE*

HENRY B. ADAMS, Ph.D., MALCOLM H. ROBERTSON, Ph.D.
AND G. DAVID COOPER, Ph.D.

## Introduction

DURING the past fifteen years there has been a growing interest and a rapidly expanding literature on the subject of sensory deprivation.[6,10,13,16,17] This broad general area, which goes by a variety of names (Brownfield, pp. 126-127), including sensory deprivation, perceptual deprivation, isolation, sensory restriction and confinement, deals with the phenomena which result from reduction in the absolute level and/or degree of structure in sensory input.

The earliest reports tended to stress the dramatic negative and disruptive effects on personality and mental functioning which had been observed in some subjects under some experimental conditions of reduced sensory input.[10,13,18] These early reports gave rise to a widespread belief that any long-sustained reduction of meaningfully patterned sensory input must inevitably be stressful, harmful or disruptive in its effects on organized mental functioning.

However, the authors of two recent books have challenged this belief. Both Brownfield[6] and Schultz[16] have discussed the beneficial, facilitating and therapeutic effects of sensory deprivation

*From *The Journal of Nervous and Mental Disease*. 143, 1966. Courtesy of The Williams and Wilkins Co. This paper is a revision of a preliminary report which was presented at the 17th International Congress of Psychology in Washington, D.C., on August 21, 1963. The authors acknowledge with thanks the cooperation and assistance of the staff of the Veterans Administration Hospital in Richmond, Virginia, including Dr. R.J. Scott, Hospital Driector, Dr. Andrew Davis, Chief of the NP Service, and Dr. R. G. Gibby, Chief Clinical Psychologist. The investigation described in this paper was conducted in the Richmond VA Hospital.

reported in several recent publications. Citing these published reports, Brownfield observed that "some doubt has been generated about the seemingly inevitable deteriorative consequences" of exposure to sensory deprivation and perceptual isolation. He noted that "more recent evidence, especially in connection with the possible therapeutic application of isolation to disturbed individuals, has suggested ... a facilitative or enhancing effect. ... As a matter of fact, an evaluation of the mass of literature on the topic produced thus far ... has logically led to the conclusion that whatever the requirements of the adult human organism for external and varied stimulation, reduction or monotonous patterning of stimulus input will not alone produce major disruptive psychological effects; such results are the product of a complex interaction of personality, anxiety, expectation, and situational structuring, as well as amount and patterning of external sensory input.[3] ..." (Brownfield, p. 90).

Elsewhere in his review Brownfield declared that the recent empirical studies have been in "nearly unanimous agreement as to the therapeutic value of partial sensory deprivation with psychiatric patients" (p. 131). He listed nineteen studies reporting positive, beneficial or therapeutic results, and only one study reporting negative or inconclusive results. Several additional reports of beneficial effects have appeared since Brownfield's review was published, some of which were summarized by Schultz.[16]

On the basis of these findings, it seems at present that the most profitable research strategy would be to shift away from the general question whether sensory deprivation procedures can have beneficial effects. The evidence now available indicates an affirmative reply. A more appropriate and more fruitful strategy today would involve questions of greater specificity, e.g. how, under what conditions, and for what types of individuals may these procedures be most effectively applied?

The writers have been engaged in an extensive program of research investigating the effects of various experimental sensory deprivation procedures on hospitalized psychiatric patients. Previous findings have already been reported in detail elsewhere.[1-5, 7-9, 11, 12] Briefly, it was found that most of the psychiatric patients exposed to a few hours of relatively mild experimental conditions of sensory deprivation and social isolation subsequently showed reduced psychiatric symptomatology and evidence of improved personality and mental functioning on a variety of measures. However, there was a wide range of individual differences. Some subjects showed substantial improvement, some little or none. A few showed impaired functioning and increased symptomatology after deprivation.

In the course of these investigations the writers had occasion to note the same "stimulus hunger" which many other investigators have observed in subjects during and immediately after exposure to sensory deprivation. Subjects in a state of "stimulus hunger" are rendered more accessible and receptive to new environmental stimuli. It was therefore suggested that experimentally induced stimulus hunger might be utilized in the treatment of psychiatric patients to render them more receptive to verbal communications of a socially re-educational nature. This state of enhanced receptiveness to verbal stimuli might be used to overcome resistances in the course of psychotherapy, enhance insight and self-awareness, foster conscious self-acceptance, and generally facilitate the processes of personality change.

These suggestions were incorporated into a controlled experiment in which a standardized prerecorded verbal message was presented to a group of psychiatric patients under conditions of mild sensory deprivation of relatively brief duration.[11] Measures of pre-post change on a self-concept inventory showed significantly greater alterations in the self-concepts of subjects in the experimental group, to whom the message was presented during deprivation, than in a control group to whom the same standardized message was presented under nondeprivation conditions.

In view of these results, an additional modification was proposed. Instead of a single standardized and rather generalized message, it was decided to observe the effects of individually prepared messages discussing the unique personal problems of each patient. These individual messages could be written out in advance, prerecorded, and phrased in such a way as to have maximum influence on each person when presented under experimental deprivation conditions. The present paper reports results obtained with this modification.

Two kinds of personality changes were investigated. The first were those which could be attributed exclusively to the effects of sensory deprivation and social isolation, as reflected in pre-post changes on objective personality measures. It was expected that changes on these measures among subjects exposed to deprivation alone would differ from those in a control group of subjects tested and retested without receiving deprivation. The second set of changes were those occurring in subjects to whom the individually prepared messages were presented during exposure to the same experimental deprivation conditions. It was expected that subjects presented with these messages would show personality changes different from those which could be attributed to deprivation alone, and also different from those occurring in the test-retest control group.

## Procedures

### Subject

The subjects were forty-three white male inpatients in a veterans general medical and surgical hospital. All were patients on psychiatric wards or medical ward patients whose hospital behavior had caused them to be referred for psychiatric evaluation. Although some of these subjects had initially been hospitalized for nonpsychiatric medical disorders, every patient selected as a subject carried a functional psychiatric diagnosis. Patients with a diagnosis or known history of organic brain or central nervous system pathology were excluded, as well as those receiving tranquilizing drugs, insulin or electroconvulsive therapy.

Three groups of subjects were formed. Table 9-I gives age, educational and diagnostic characteristics of each group. Although the means and standard deviations of the three groups were not identical, there were no differences between groups in means or standard deviations large enough to be statistically significant. Differences between groups in relative frequency of psychiatric diagnosis were not significant. It may be mentioned here that an earlier paper in this series reported that age, education and psychiatric diagnosis were found to be unrelated to any measures

TABLE 9-I

AGE, EDUCATION AND PSYCHIATRIC DIAGNOSIS
OF SUBJECTS IN THREE GROUPS*

| | Group I (N = 12) | Group II (N = 15) | Group III (N = 16) |
|---|---|---|---|
| Age | | | |
| Mean | 34.5 | 38.5 | 39.1 |
| SD | 3.8 | 7.5 | 7.5 |
| Yrs of school | | | |
| Mean | 11.0 | 9.6 | 9.4 |
| SD | 3.2 | 4.1 | 3.0 |
| Diagnosis | | | |
| Schizophrenic reaction | 2 | 3 | 4 |
| Manic depressive reaction | 1 | 1 | |
| Anxiety reaction | 4 | 1 | 2 |
| Obsessive compulsive reaction | 2 | | |
| Psychoneurotic depressive reaction | 1 | 1 | 2 |
| Dissociative reaction | 1 | 1 | |
| Conversion reaction | | 2 | |
| Psychoneurotic reaction, unclassified | | | 1 |
| Inadequate personality | 1 | 2 | 2 |
| Psychophysiological gastrointestinal disorder | | 1 | 1 |
| N P Unclassified | | 3 | 4 |

*Group I = stimulus tape message plus sensory deprivation; Group II = sensory deprivation only; Group III = no tape or sensory deprivation, test-retest only. There were no significant differences between groups in age, education or psychiatric diagnosis.

of reactions during sensory deprivation or changes afterward.[4]

## Conditions

All subjects were administered the Minnesota Multiphasic Personality Inventory (MMPI) and the Interpersonal Check List (ICL) twice, two days apart. In filling out the ICL each subject was asked first to check the items which he believed described himself and then to check those which in his opinion described the ideal person. The two tests were scored according to the published procedures for the Multilevel System of Interpersonal Diagnosis.[14, 15] This system is an objective combination of methods for the assessment of personality and the evaluation of changes resulting from psychotherapy and other techniques of personality modification. After the first test administration the subjects in each group were exposed to the experimental conditions described below.

*Group I (tape plus sensory deprivation):* On the first day the two personality tests were scored immediately after they were administered. An individual message based on the results of testing was then arranged for each subject. The theoretical rationale for the interpretation of the Multilevel System of Interpersonal Diagnosis was followed in preparing these individual messages. Although the specific content and general tone of each message necessarily varied as a function of the personality characteristics of individual subjects, each message included the following points: 1) the subject's typical overt behavior in new interpersonal relationships (i.e. his "presenting operations") predicted from his Level I-M scores on the MMPI; 2) his Level II conscious self-description, drawn from the ICL; 3) his covert, preconscious attitudes, as inferred from his Level III-MM pattern of scores on the *Pd* and *Mf* scales of the MMPI; 4) his Level V description of the ideal person on the ICL; and 5) the discrepancies between these levels, their significance as indicators of difficulties in interpersonal relationships, and their relevance to the personal problems which had initially led the subject to seek hospitalization or to be referred for psychiatric attention.

The messages were deliberately made repetitious and redundant in order to minimize the possibility of misunderstanding and distortion. The specific points considered most important for each individual subject were reiterated and restated several times in a variety of ways. Space forbids the inclusion of any of these lengthy, repetitious messages here, but a summary of the message presented to one of the subjects in Group I has been published elsewhere.[2] The individual messages were recorded on tape to be presented the following day during sensory deprivation.

On the second day each subject in Group I was exposed to not more than three hours of partial sensory deprivation and social isolation. The conditions of deprivation, the physical facilities and the rooms used for the experiment were the same as those which have been fully described in previous publications.[1,3,4,7,9] [11,12] Each subject lay on a bed in a quiet, air-conditioned room with his eyes covered, ears plugged with cotton and head wrapped in gauze. After two hours the prerecorded tape message was presented through a bone-conductivity speaker which had been placed in the gauze wrapped around the subject's head. Each message ran for about fifteen minutes. The subject was kept in deprivation for another forty-five minutes after the conclusion of the message in order to have time to assimilate its contents without the intrusion of extraneous or distracting stimuli. He was then removed by the experimenter.

On the third day the MMPI and the ICL were administered to each subject a second time for posttesting.

*Group II (sensory deprivation only, no tape):* All the testing procedures and experimental deprivation conditions scheduled for Group I were also followed for Group II, except that no tape messages were presented during the three hours in sensory deprivation.

*GROUP III (test-retest):* The same two tests were administered on the same three-day schedule as the other two groups in order to assess test-retest changes on these objective personality measures when there were no intervening experimental events (no sensory deprivation and no tape messages). On the day between pretesting and posttesting the subjects in Group III continued their usual routine ward activities.

### Analysis of Data

The pretest and posttest scores on the MMPI and the ICL were tabulated according to the scoring procedures for the Multilevel System.[15] In addition to the ten clinical scales and the four validity scales normally scored on the MMPI, five special scales were also scored. These included the Welsh *A* (anxiety) and *R* (repression) scales, the Baron *Es* (ego strength) scale, and the Leary Dominance-Submission and Love-Hostility scales. ICL scores on the two overall dimensions of Dominance-Submission and Love-Hostility were computed according to the descriptions of the ideal person.[15] The algebraic discrepancies between these two ICL measures were then calculated, providing a self-ideal discrepancy measure.

This gave a total of nineteen MMPI measures and six ICL measures. Pre-post changes on all twenty-five measures were computed by subtracting the pretest and posttest scores. The resulting pre-post change scores were then subjected to statistical analysis. Differences between groups in mean change scores were evaluated by the single-classification analysis of variance technique. The significance of mean changes within each group of subjects was determined by the T-test for repeated within-group measurements. The analysis of variance technique was also used to determine whether there were any significant overall differences between groups in the means of the pretest scores. No statistically significant differences in mean pretest scores were found for any of the MMPI or ICL measurements.

## Results

It was predicted that the pre-post changes on the objective personality measures in Group I following presentation of the individually prepared messages would be different from those in Group II after exposure to sensory deprivation alone, and also from Group III, where the subjects were tested and retested after a two-day interval. The results were generally consistent with these predictions.

Table 9-II shows mean raw score changes on the ICL for the three groups in self-ratings, ideal ratings, and self-ideal discrepancies. Three of the six *F* ratios were significant at the .05 level, showing that the differences between groups in mean changes following exposure to the three sets of experimental conditions were far greater than would be expected by chance alone.

The footnote symbols alongside the mean change scores in Table 9-II designate statistically significant within-group

TABLE 9-II

MEAN PRE-POST CHANGES ON INTERPERSONAL CHECK
LIST IN SELF-RATINGS, IDEAL RATINGS AND
SELF-IDEAL DISCREPANCIES* (RAW SCORES)

| | Group I | Group II | Group III | F | p |
|---|---|---|---|---|---|
| Self-ratings | | | | | |
| Dominance-Submission | -.04 | 2.57‡ | -2.09 | 5.08 | .05 |
| Love-Hostility | -2.06 | -.79 | -2.63† | 2.04 | - |
| Ideal ratings | | | | | |
| Dominance-Submission | -2.52 | .20 | 2.11 | 3.28 | .05 |
| Love-Hostility | .18 | 1.02 | .00 | .16 | - |
| Self-ideal discrepancy scores | | | | | |
| Dominance-Submission | -2.47 | -3.61‡ | .58 | 2.00 | - |
| Love-Hostility | 2.78 | -7.54‡ | .62 | 4.48 | .05 |

*The mean pretest scores of the three groups did not differ significantly on any of the six measures.
†Mean change within group significant at .10 level.
‡Mean change within group significant at .01 level.

changes. Group II showed an increase in self-ratings on the Dominance-Submission dimension which was significant at the .01 level. This indicates that when posttested the subjects in Group II described themselves on the average as significantly more dominant after exposure to sensory deprivation alone. In contrast, subjects in Group III described themselves as substantially less dominant when posttested, although the mean within-group change was not statistically significant. The subjects in Group I who heard the taped messages during sensory deprivation showed virtually no change on this dimension. The overall differences in mean change scores between the three groups were significant at the .05 level for the Dominance dimension. On the Love-Hostility dimension all three groups showed mean changes in the negative direction, the subjects in each group describing themselves on the average as less affectionate when posttested.

The differences between groups on this dimension were too small to be significant. However, the within-group change for Group III approached significance at the .10 level.

For the ideal ratings, none of the separate within-group changes was statistically significant. However, the significant *F* ratio for the Dominance-Submission dimension was large enough to show that conceptions of the ideal person were differentially altered as a result of the intervening experimental conditions. After hearing the individual messages during deprivation, subjects in Group I described the ideal person as less dominant; those in Group II after deprivation only showed little or no change, while the subjects in Group III described the ideal person as more dominant when posttested.

On the self-ideal discrepancy scores Group II showed within-group decreases on both personality dimensions that were significant at the .01 level. Differences between groups were particularly marked with respect to the Love-Hostility dimension. Here Group II showed a statistically significant mean decrease; the other two groups showed increases; and the overall *F* ratio was significant at the .05 level. Since a decreased self-ideal discrepancy score may be interpreted as reflecting an increase in conscious self-acceptance, it may be inferred that exposure to the deprivation-only condition made for much greater conscious self-acceptance than either of the other two conditions.

Table 9-III shows the mean pretest scores and mean pre-post changes in *K*-corrected T-scores on the MMPI. The analysis of variance showed no significant differences between pretest group means on any of the nineteen scales. As for mean pre-post changes, the *F* ratios for two scales were significant at the .01 level, considerably better than chance expectancy. These results indicate that the three experimental conditions produced significantly different effects on the three groups with respect to the personality variables measured by those two MMPI scales.

One of the two significant *F* ratios was on the *Ma* scale, where Group I and Group II showed significant within-group increases on posttesting, while Group III showed a drop. Inspection of the pretest mean scores on *Ma* in Table 9-III makes it evident that the differences in pre-post changes were not due to any tendency for scores to regress to the mean on posttesting. In psychological

TABLE 9-III

MEAN PRETEST SCORES AND MEAN PRE-POST CHANGES
ON MMPI (T-SCORES, K-CORRECTED)

| Scale | Pretest Means* | | | Pre-Post Changes | | | | |
|---|---|---|---|---|---|---|---|---|
| | Group I | Group II | Group III | Group I | Group II | Group III | F | p |
| Hs | 79.25 | 78.27 | 77.81 | -2.25 | -.27 | -2.19 | .17 | - |
| D | 84.83 | 81.67 | 78.81 | -1.50 | -5.47‡ | -1.94 | .09 | - |
| Hy | 79.33 | 73.53 | 72.31 | -3.17 | -2.20 | 1.56 | 1.24 | - |
| Pd | 75.42 | 66.27 | 69.31 | -4.17 | 2.47 | -2.12 | 1.73 | - |
| Mf | 65.58 | 56.00 | 57.44 | -1.67 | .00 | .69 | .59 | - |
| Pa | 65.68 | 61.93 | 61.50 | -1.83 | -2.73 | .81 | 1.00 | - |
| Pt | 76.50 | 69.60 | 71.75 | -1.08 | .20 | -1.62 | .12 | - |
| Sc | 75.83 | 64.93 | 69.31 | -1.50 | 3.33 | .75 | .77 | - |
| Ma | 61.42 | 53.00 | 56.56 | 2.42† | 4.00† | -3.25 | 7.36 | .01 |
| Si | 60.92 | 55.07 | 55.65 | -.75 | -1.07 | -.56 | .03 | - |
| ? | 39.58 | 43.20 | 34.75 | -.17 | -1.87 | 1.31 | 1.74 | - |
| L | 48.83 | 54.47 | 53.75 | -1.67 | .20 | -2.62‡ | 1.17 | - |
| F | 61.58 | 56.27 | 61.19 | 1.25 | .53 | -.06 | .27 | - |
| K | 50.25 | 56.67 | 55.81 | -1.92 | 4.00‡ | 4.06§ | 5.73 | .01 |
| A | 64.25 | 54.87 | 54.12 | .17 | -3.20 | -2.75† | 1.04 | - |
| R | 59.83 | 59.73 | 56.38 | -2.67 | -.47 | .44 | 1.11 | - |
| Es | 35.33 | 40.80 | 38.75 | 2.42 | 4.40‡ | 1.81 | 1.18 | - |
| Dom | 52.83 | 51.27 | 52.44 | -.92 | 2.93† | .50 | .62 | - |
| Lov | 49.42 | 55.80 | 51.50 | -2.42 | -1.00 | .06 | .39 | - |

*None of the overall differences between groups in pretest mean scores was statistically significant.
†Mean change within group significant at .10 level.
‡Mean change within group significant at .05 level.
§Mean change within group significant at .01 level.

terms increased *Ma* scores indicate greater mental energy and activity while lower scores suggest an opposite trend. This interpretation would suggest that Groups I and II showed evidence of increased mental energy after deprivation, while the test-retest control group showed a reduction.

Differences between groups in pre-post changes on *K* were also significant. Here again the differing changes in the three groups were clearly not due to regression toward the mean. Group I, which had the lowest pretest score, showed a drop on *K* after exposure to the experimental conditions. Both Groups II and III, whose pretest *K*-scores were well above the theoretical mean T-score of 50, showed statistically significant within-group increases on posttesting. An increase on *K* may be interpreted as reflecting an enhanced sense of personal adequacy and increased self-acceptance, along with greater defensiveness, less inclination to admit personal shortcomings and more reluctance to discuss emotional difficulties. It would appear that there were substantial differences with reference to these personality changes between the subjects who were presented individually prepared messages and those who were not.

The within-group changes for the three groups are also of interest, since the three groups showed different patterns of change on the various MMPI scales. For Group I only one change even approached statistical significance at the .10 level. Yet in comparison with the other groups, Group I showed the most consistent direction of change, at least on the ten clinical scales. On nine of these scales Group I showed lower mean scores on posttesting, the chance probability of which is only .022 by the two-tailed sign test. The other two groups did not show any comparable overall directional trend. But Group II showed the greatest number of statistically significant changes on individual scales. Four were significant at the .05 level and one at the .10 level. There was a drop on *D* and increases on the *Ma, K, Es* and Dominance-Submission scales. These results suggest that, on the average, subjects in the group receiving deprivation alone showed less depression, more mental activity, energy and alertness, enhanced ego strength, greater dominance and an increased tendency to describe themselves in favorable terms after the experience. For Group III there were three scales on which the within-group's changes approached or attained statistical significance: *L* and *A* dropped, while *K* rose. These changes indicate that, when retested without any intervening sensory deprivation, the test-retest group showed significantly less of the gross dissimulation reflected in the *L* scale, greater tendencies to deny anxiety, and an increase in defensiveness, coupled with more proneness to present themselves to others in a favorable light.

To sum up the results, there were several significant differences between the three groups on objective measures of personality change, reflecting differences in the effects produced by the three experimental conditions. After presentation of the individually prepared prerecorded messages, the subjects in Group I showed more insight, greater self-understanding, less defensiveness and the most consistent generalized improvement. The subjects in Group II also changed in directions that could be regarded as "improved," since their test responses after exposure to deprivation alone indicated more dominance, increased ego strength, more conscious self-acceptance, less depression and an enhanced sense of personal adequacy. However, Group II showed less of an increase than Group I on measures reflecting conscious insight and self-understanding. The contrasts between Group III and the other two groups indicated that exposure to sensory deprivation alone and to deprivation with the individual messages brought about measurable personality changes which cannot be attributed exclusively to the effects of testing and retesting.

## Discussion

This study was conducted to demonstrate various uses of sensory deprivation procedures with psychiatric patients. It showed 1) that exposure to a few hours of mild sensory deprivation alone produced significant changes on objective measures of personality which did not appear in a control group; and 2) that the presentation of individual messages to subjects exposed to these sensory deprivation conditions produced changes on the personality measures which differed from those obtained from subjects receiving deprivation alone.

This demonstration was part of a larger, more extensive research program which investigated therapeutic applications of sensory deprivation procedures in the treatment of hospitalized psychiatric patients. The twelve experimental subjects in Group I were scheduled to begin individual psychotherapy immediately after they completed the posttesting. The messages were prepared for presentation to the subjects with these considerations in mind. The therapists who worked with these twelve individuals agreed that presentation of these messages definitely did act as a facilitant for subsequent individual psychotherapy sessions. Sensory deprivation conditions increased the generalized receptiveness of these subjects to all forms of verbal stimulation, and, as a result, their receptiveness was at a maximum when the individually prepared messages were presented. At the outset of therapy their attention was thereby directed toward verbal communications aimed at fostering insight into their most important problems in interpersonal relationships.

These novel insights were immediately followed up when the subjects began individual therapy. The therapists who subsequently worked with them expressed the opinion that progress in therapy was faster, resistances and defensiveness were reduced, there was more insightful self-awareness, and fewer misconceptions arose as to the aims, purposes and goals of psychotherapy, in comparison with other patients from the same hospital population.

A case study on one of these twelve subjects has been published elsewhere.[1] A follow-up thirty months after the presentation of the messages showed that he had entered into intensive, prolonged outpatient psychotherapy for the first time immediately after the experience. After he commenced psychotherapy, his overall social adjustment was improved and the need for subsequent hospitalization as an inpatient reduced. There was evidence that the experience of hearing the prerecorded individual message while undergoing sensory deprivation had been a crucial factor, since he had previously been reluctant to enter into any form of intensive personal counseling or psychotherapy.

In considering the results reported in this paper it should be remembered that wide individual differences in responses to sensory deprivation phenomena have been found. As Brownfield observed, these differences may be due to any of a multiplicity of factors.[6] The many contradictory, inconsistent research findings reported in the literature might be a consequence of the wide range of individual differences in the ways subjects are affected by exposure to the same objective experimental conditions of reduced sensory input. For this reason, it is quite possible that a replication of this study might show different results with different subjects. As a matter of fact, the writers did conduct some informal small-scale investigations using "normal" subjects rather than psychiatric patients. The "normals" did not show the kinds of changes on personality measures which were found in psychiatric patients, which would imply that emotionally disturbed individuals are affected by exposure to sensory deprivation differently than normal subjects.

Inevitably a large number of potentially relevant variables will have to be considered in future research on sensory deprivation. The writers believe that the most fruitful strategy would call for careful, systematic investigations of promising variables, specifying the objective stimulus conditions, characteristics of individual subjects, techniques used, and the nature of changes observed in personality, mental functioning and overt behavior for different types of individuals. No one study can reasonably be expected to provide a definitive answer to all these questions. However, the steady accumulation and pooling of results from many independent investigations could in time lead to the development of an extensive body of systematic knowledge and a repertoire of techniques for the effective utilization of what now appears to be a promising new therapeutic approach.

In his review Schultz discussed techniques much like those used in this study involving the presentation of verbal stimulus messages to subjects undergoing exposure to sensory deprivation. In one chapter he summarized the results of studies dealing with attitude changes under conditions of both sensory and perceptual deprivation, and noted contradictory findings.[16] But in a later chapter he suggested that techniques used to change attitudes under sensory deprivation conditions "might be applicable in the therapeutic context" (p. 122). After describing these techniques he concluded the chapter by posing the question: "Might not the same techniques be applied to the therapy situation in inducing the patient to attend to 'therapeutic propaganda' and engage in dialogue with the therapist if these are the only forms of stimulation and contact afforded him?"

## Summary

Many investigators have reported positive beneficial changes in personality and mental functioning among psychiatric patients exposed to brief periods of sensory deprivation and social isolation. The present study investigated the effects produced in a group of hospitalized psychiatric patients receiving partial sensory deprivation and social isolation, contrasted with 1) a control group receiving no deprivation, and 2) an experimental group of patients to whom individually prepared stimulus tape messages were presented under conditions of sensory deprivation and social isolation.

Subjects in the experimental group (Group I) were exposed to three hours of deprivation during which they were presented individually prerecorded taped verbal messages aimed at facilitating insight, self-understanding, and self-acceptance. Pre-post personality changes were assessed by objective scores on the Interpersonal Check List and the Minnesota Multiphasic Personality Inventory. Subjects in the other two groups were pretested and posttested with the same two instruments. Group II was exposed to the same deprivation conditions as Group I, but no stimulus messages were presented. Group III, the control group, was tested and retested only.

The number of significant differences between groups in measured pre-post changes was several times chance expectancy. Subjects in Group I showed more self-acceptance, their conceptions of the ideal person changing so as to become more like their own conscious self-descriptions. There was evidence of improved inner controls, less severe psychiatric symptomatology, and a reduction in defensiveness and repression after exposure to the experimental conditions.

Subjects in Group II also showed statistically significant changes in "improved" directions, but the pattern of changes was different from Group I. While their conscious self-concepts altered positively, their conceptions of the ideal person remained unchanged. Although Group II showed evidence of greater dominance, enhanced ego strength, less depression, and an outer facade of increased personal adequacy when posttested, increases on measures reflecting conscious insight and self-understanding were less than in Group I, while tendencies to deny personal shortcomings became greater.

Group III showed few significant changes, suggesting that the significant changes in the other two groups resulted from the two experimental conditions of sensory deprivation rather than from testing and retesting alone.

The procedures used in this study and the results obtained were interpreted by the authors as illustrating practical ways in which mild conditions of sensory deprivation and social isolation might be utilized beneficially for psychiatric patients.

## REFERENCES

1. Adams, H. B.: A case utilizing sensory deprivation procedures. In Krasner, L. and Ullman, L., eds. *Case Studies in Behavior Modification*, Holt, Rinehart and Winston, New York, 1965, pp. 164-170.
2. Adams, H. B.: Therapeutic potentialities of sensory deprivation procedures. *Int. Ment. Health Res. Newsletter, 6*(4):7-9, 1964.
3. Adams, H. B., Carrera, R. N., Cooper, G. D., Gibby, R. G. and Tobey, H. R.: Personality and intellectual changes in psychiatric patients following brief sensory deprivation. *Amer. Psychol., 15*:448, 1960.
4. Adams, H. B., Carrera, R. N. and Gibby, R. G.: *Behavioral Reactions of Psychiatric Patients to Brief Sensory Deprivation.* Convention Reports Duplication Service, Cleveland, 1960.
5. Adams, H. B., Robertson, M. H. and Cooper, G. D.: Facilitating therapeutic personality change in psychiatric patients by sensory deprivation methods. In *Proceedings of the 17th International Congress of Psychology*, North Holland Publishing, Amsterdam, 1964, pp. 108-109.
6. Brownfield, C. A.: *Isolation.* Random House, New York, 1965.
7. Cooper, G. D.: Changes in ego strength following brief perceptual and social deprivation. Doctoral dissertation. Duke University, Durham, 1962.
8. Cooper, G. D., Adams, H. B. and Cohen, L. D.: Changes in personality after sensory deprivation. *J. Nerv. Ment. Disc., 140*:103-118, 1965.
9. Cooper, G. D., Adams, H. B. and Gibby, R. G.: Ego strength changes following perceptual deprivation. *Arch. Gen. Psychiat.,* (Chicago), 7:213-217, 1962.
10. Fiske, D. W.: Effects of monotonous and restricted stimulation. In Fiske, D. W. and Maddi, S. R., eds. *Functions of Varied Experience,* Dorsey Press, Homewood, Illinois, 1961, pp. 106-144.
11. Gibby, R. G. and Adams, H. B.: Receptiveness of psychiatric patients to verbal communication. *Arch. Gen. Psychiat.,* (Chicago), 5:366-370, 1961.
12. Gibby, R. G., Adams, H. B. and Carrera, R. N.: Therapeutic changes in psychiatric patients following partial sensory deprivation. *Arch. Gen. Psychiat.,* (Chicago), 3:33-42, 1960.
13. Kubzansky, P. E.: The effects of reduced environmental stimulation on

human behavior: A review. In Biderman, A. D. and Zimmer, H., eds. *The Manipulation of Human Behavior*, Wiley, New York, 1961, pp. 51-95.

14. Leary, T.: *Interpersonal Diagnosis of Personality*. Ronald, New York, 1957.
15. Leary, T.: *Multilevel Measurement of Interpersonal Behavior*. Psychological Consultation Service, Berkeley, 1956.
16. Schultz, D. P.: *Sensory Restriction*. Academic Press, New York, 1965.
17. Svab, L. and Gross, J.: *Bibliography of Sensory Deprivation and Social Isolation*. Psychiatric Research Institute, Prague, 1964.
18. Wexler, D., Mendelson, J., Leiderman, P. H. and Solomon, P.: Sensory deprivation: A technique for studying psychiatric aspects of stress. *A.M.A. Arch. Neurol. Psychiat., 79:*225-233, 1958.

# Chapter 10

# THE EFFECTS OF BRIEF
# SENSORY REDUCTION ON
# OBJECTIVE TEST SCORES*

THEODORE HENRICHS

## Introduction

$S$UBSEQUENT to some of the earliest experimental
investigations of sensory reduction (SR) experiences[6, 7], numerous experiments have been reported which attempt to delineate
important characteristics of a human being's response to what
Kubie terms "experimentally induced afferent isolation"[9]. In
many instances, particularly in the early research activity, the
parameters of the various experimental situations varied markedly, making accurate assessment of the important variables difficult. Solomon et al.[11] reviewed the literature and reported that the
common features of an individual's responses to an SR experience
seemed to be: (a) an intense desire for extrinsic sensory stimuli, (b)
increased suggestibility, (c) impairment of organized thinking,
and (d) depression and in extreme cases, hallucinations and delusions.

Suggestibility implies, in part, susceptibility to influence by
external verbal stimuli. Heron[8] had noted susceptibility in his Ss
in an SR experience with regard to arguments for the existence of
supernatural phenomena. If, as Solomon, et al.[11] posit, Ss are
more suggestible in an SR experience, this could be investigated
and an attempt made to systematically utilize this characteristic
via a factorial design involving SR and selected verbal stimuli.
The results of such an investigation could have numerous ramifi-
cations for further systematic research on changes in the psycho-

*From *The Journal of Clinical Psychology.* 19: 172-176, 1963. Courtesy of Clinical
Psychology Publishing Company, Inc.

logical functioning of Ss during SR.

This study investigated brief periods of SR where an attempt was made to influence psychological functioning through the presentation of information relevant to personality characteristics and self-attitudes. Changes and comparisons of experimental groups on their responses to two psychological inventories constituted the dependent variables.

## Method

### *The Sensory Reduction Experience*

The experimental room used for the SR experience was located in an isolated area of the hospital, partially soundproofed and completely lightproofed. The temperature was kept relatively constant by heating and conditioning units. The equipment in the room included a bed with clean linen and pillow. Next to the end of the bed was a stand which contained materials used to blindfold S. In the corner of the room farthest from S was a shielded hospital bed lamp. On the ledge next to the bed there was a two-way speaker which, along with a ceiling speaker, was used for monitoring the room. A bone conduction speaker was connected to the two-way speaker next to the bed, and this could be controlled by E via the monitoring system. This pillow speaker was wrapped into the bandage of the Ss and transmitted the personality information from a tape recorder in the adjoining observation room.

Observation of S was possible through a panel of four one-way windows. The small lamp in the experimental room provided enough light to observe distinctly the movement of S.

When S entered the experimental room he was told that E was interested in what people do when they cannot see or hear for a while. He was told to relax on the bed — that ear plugs would be inserted and a blindfold would be put in place. Glycerine-soaked cotton was placed in S's ears and a blindfold consisting of a sterile cotton gauze pad and a small cotton towel was placed over his eyes and secured with elastic bandage. The speaker was placed behind his left ear if he was to receive the personality information. E told

S to remain on the bed until the blindfold was removed. He was informed that he could talk if he wished, but nobody would respond to him. Unless S withdrew voluntarily, the session was terminated by E after five hours, but no deadline was given.

### The Personality Information

A fourteen-minute tape recording of a standard personality analysis specifically created for this experiment was played to S via the bone conduction speaker. The content of the recording was based, in part, on the personality traits employed by Brownfain, e.g. emotional maturity and flexibility, and, in part, on an interpretation of the Oedipal conflict. The recording was structured to convey a complimentary or ego-enhancing message.

### Subjects

Forty male, undergraduate volunteers were assigned to four equal groups on the basis of self-rating values. In addition, these groups were found to be closely matched on age, intelligence, and socio-economic level.

## Procedures

Two psychological inventories were selected for use in this study: the Minnesota Multiphasic Personality Inventory (MMPI) and Brownfain's [3] Self-Concept scales which require each person to rate himself on twenty personality variables four different ways: as he really believes himself to be (the private self), as he really hopes he is (the positive self), as he really fears he is (the negative self), and as other see him (the social self).

On the basis of the self-rating scales which were completed during a preliminary testing session, the forty Ss were assigned to four experimental groups. The Ss in the first group (TD), after first completing the MMPI, went through the SR experience for five hours. The tape recording was played to each of them after four and one-half hours of isolation. Immediately following this experience they were retested with both inventories. The Ss in the second group (D) went through the same procedure without hearing the tape recording. The Ss in the third group (TC) listened to the tape recording four and one-half hours after completing the MMPI and retested one-half hour later without experiencing SR. The Ss in the fourth group (C) completed the MMPI and were retested approximately five hours later without going through the SR experience or hearing the tape recording. Follow-up testing was completed on all Ss after four weeks.

Time intervals between successive repetitions of the MMPI were five hours between the first occasion and the second, and twenty-eight days between the second occasion and the third. Time intervals between the first and second occasions on the Brownfain Self-Concept scales were approximately twenty days, and twenty-eight days between the second and the third occasion.

## Results

The procedure of this study suggested a basic approach of separate analyses of the two psychological inventories, primarily because of the inherent differences in the construction and in the interpretation of the inventories, as well as the differences in the time of their administration to the Ss.

In the absence of a priori experimental evidence or theoretical formulations, the more traditional analyses of these inventories in terms of individual scales and/or specific relationships between individual scales or groups of scales were discarded in favor of a simultaneous analysis of all scales of each inventory for each repetition of that inventory. This kind of analysis is made possible by a multivariate analysis of variance computer program devised by Bock[1,2] for high speed computing equipment. The purpose of this program is to compute mean-squares or -products, scalar or vector contrasts of effects, and univariate and multivariate test statistics for any analysis of variance design and any choice of effect contrasts. In the multivariate case, discriminant functions are computed. Contrasts were selected to study both the general level of the responses of the Ss and changes over the three test administrations. The substantial scale intercorrelations which were ultimately noted for both instruments would necessitate a multivariate approach to the analysis of the data.

The basic self-rating data provided for the analysis of variance program were the total scores for the groups on the individual self-concept scales. The program provided a means of evaluating three effects: a mean effect, a linear effect, and a quadratic or curvilinear effect. This was accomplished through the use of orthogonal polynomials.

The test statistics, which, in the present case of hypotheses with one degree of freedom, are $F$ ratios, the degrees of freedom, and the tests of significance for the effects, are shown in Table 10-I. It can be seen that the linear deprivation and tape effects are both statistically significant beyond the .05 level of confidence.

TABLE 10-I

FOUR-VARIATE ANALYSIS OF VARIANCE OF
THE BROWNFAIN SELF-CONCEPT
SCALE SCORES

| Effect | df | $F_{(4/33)}$ | $p$ |
|---|---|---|---|
| Mean | | | |
| Deprivation | 1/36 | 1.12 | ns |
| Tape | 1/36 | .44 | ns |
| Interaction | 1/36 | 2.41 | ns |
| Linear | | | |
| Deprivation | 1/36 | 3.06 | <.05 |
| Tape | 1/36 | 3.35 | <.05 |
| Interaction | 1/36 | 8.6 | ns |
| Quadratic | | | |
| Deprivation | 1/36 | .60 | ns |
| Tape | 1/36 | .65 | ns |
| Interaction | 1/36 | .76 | ns |

Estimation procedures to determine the source of the mean differences, involving the use of critical ratios and standardization of discriminant function coefficients, indicated that the two groups undergoing the SR experience (Group TD and D) rated themselves significantly lower, i.e. less positive, over time on Scale 1 (the private self) than did the other two groups.

Groups TD and TC, the two groups who listened to the personality information, subsequently rated themselves significantly higher, i.e. more positive, over time on Scale 4 (the social self) than did the other two groups. This change was more pronounced for Group TD.

The basic MMPI data provided for the computer program were the non-*K*-corrected T-scores for the groups on the ten standard clinical scales and Welsh's[4] A and R scales. The scores for the groups on the validity scales were within the screening criteria suggested by Meehl[10] and separate comparisons revealed no statistically significant differences between the groups on these scales.

The analysis applied to these data provided a means of evaluating three effects: a mean effect, a contrast of scores of the preliminary testing session to the experimental session (Contrast A), and a contrast of scores of the first session to the follow-up session (Contrast B). These contrasts assess the general level of the groups, the short-term changes, and the long-term changes respectively.

The *F* ratios, the degrees of freedom and the tests of significance based on a multivariate analysis of variance in Table 10-II show that the short-term (Contrast A) tape effect and interaction are statistically significant. The same estimation procedures previously indicated were also employed in this analysis. The

TABLE 10-II

TWELVE-VARIATE ANALYSIS OF VARIANCE
OF THE MMPI SCALE SCORES

| Effect | df | $F(12/25)$ | $p$ |
|---|---|---|---|
| Mean | | | |
| Deprivation | 1/36 | 1.08 | ns |
| Tape | 1/36 | .71 | ns |
| Interaction | 1/36 | .39 | ns |
| Contrast A | | | |
| Deprivation | 1/36 | .98 | ns |
| Tape | 1/36 | 2.19 | <.05 |
| Interaction | 1/36 | 2.21 | <.05 |
| Contrast B | | | |
| Deprivation | 1/36 | 1.85 | ns |
| Tape | 1/36 | .58 | ns |
| Interaction | 1/36 | .57 | ns |

conclusions obtained indicated that the two groups who heard the personality information (Groups TD and TC) subsequently lowered their scores, i.e. showed more positive changes, on the Hypochondriasis (Hs) scale than the other two groups. This change was more pronounced in Group TC.

The interaction was more complex and seemed principally to result from the larger reduction in the Hs scale score for Group TC as compared to the other groups, as well as a noticeable increase in the Depression (D) scale score for Group D as compared to a reduction in this same scale score for the other three groups.

## Discussion

In terms of the parameters of this experiment and the instruments chosen to assess change, the hypothesis that a brief period of SR would produce either no improvement in the level of psychological functioning of the Ss or negative changes received only minimal support. There were no significant changes noted on the MMPI scales and only one of the self-rating scales revealed negative change as a function of SR.

A second hypothesis, that the personality information provided by the tape recording would produce improvement in the level of psychological functioning of the Ss, gained some support from both instruments used in this study. Scale H of the MMPI and Scale 4 of the self-rating scales both revealed significant positive changes as a function of the personality information. The former was a short-term change, the latter was long-term.

A third hypothesis was that there would be a significant enhancement of the effect of the personality information on psychological functioning if the tape recording followed a period of SR. This hypothesis did not receive unequivocal support. The significant change noted on the self-rating scales as a function of the personality information would support the hypothesis; whereas, the change noted on the MMPI would militate against it.

It would thus appear that suggestibility, as assessed in this study, is not appreciably increased in several hours under the prevailing experimental conditions. In addition, there was no apparent interference with reality orientation. These findings are quite comparable to the results obtained by Goldberger and Holt[5]. The duration of the experiment and the methodology, with the noticeable exception of the use of a masking noise and translucent goggles, are also similar.

## Summary

This study was designed to assess the effects of brief sensory reduction (SR) experiences on objective test scores — specifically on the MMPI and self rating scale scores. Forty normal male volunteers comprised the experimental sample. According to the assessment methods, the SR experiences employed in this study seemed to have little permanent or significant effect on the psychological functioning of the Ss. Suggestibility, a phenomenon frequently noted in SR experiences, was not appreciably increased under the present experimental conditions. Our results suggested that further investigation involving changes in experimental parameters, e.g. longer periods of SR and/or changes in the verbal stimuli may prove rewarding.

## REFERENCES

1. Bock, R. D.: A computer application of a completely general univariate and multivariate analysis of variance. Research Memorandum No. 2 Chapel Hill, The Psychometric Laboratory, 1960.
2. Bock, R. D.: Multivariate and univariate analysis of variance for any design — a computer program for the Royal McBee LGP-30. Research Memorandum No. 3. Chapel Hill, The Psychometric Laboratory, 1960.
3. Brownfain, J. J.: Stability of the self-concept as a dimension of personality. *J. Abnorm. Soc. Psychol,* 47:101-112, 1952.
4. Dahlstrom, W. G. and Welsh, G. S.: *An MMPI Handbook.* Minneapolis, University of Minnesota Press, 1960.
5. Goldberger, L. and Holt, R. R.: Experimental interference with reality contact (perceptual isolation): Method and group results. *J. Nerv. Ment. Dis.,* 127:99-112, 1958.
6. Hebb, D. O., Heath, E. S. and Stuart E. A.: Experimental deafness. *Canad. J. Psychol.,* 8:152-156, 1954.
7. Heron, W., Bexton, W. H., and Hebb, D. O.: Cognitive effects of a decreased variation in the sensory environment. *Amer. Psychol.,* 8:366, 1953.
8. Heron, W.: The pathology of boredom. *Sci. Amer.,* 196:52-56, 1957.

9. Kubie, L. S.: Theoretical aspects of sensory deprivation. In P. Solomon et al. (Eds.) *Sensory Deprivation*. Cambridge, Harvard University Press, 1961, Pp. 208-220.

10. Meehl, P. E.: Profile analysis of the MMPI in differential diagnosis. *J. Appl. Psychol., 30*:517-524, 1946.

11. Solomon, P., Leiderman, P. H., Mendelson, J., and Wexler, D.: Sensory deprivation: a review. *Amer. J. Psychiat., 114*:357-363, 1957.

# Chapter 11

# THERAPEUTIC EFFECTIVENESS
# OF VERBAL COMMUNICATION
# UNDER CONDITIONS OF
# PERCEPTUAL ISOLATION*

M. ROBERTSON, Ph.D.

SEVERAL studies have indicated that a modified perceptual isolation condition has a beneficial, even therapeutic
effect on psychiatric patients (Azima & Cramer-Azima, 1956;
Cooper et al., 1962; Gibby et al., 1960; Harris, 1959; Shurley,
1960). Furthermore, two studies have shown that verbal communication presented to psychiatric patients during short periods of
partial isolation enhances the therapeutic effects of isolation.
Gibby and Adams (1961) found that a fifteen-minute prerecorded
tape message which encouraged a more favorable self-concept,
and which was phrased in very general terms so as to be applicable
to almost any hospitalized psychiatric patient, was very effective
when administered under conditions of isolation. A group of ten
patients who heard the tape message during a four-hour period of
isolation changed their subsequent ratings on the Brownfain
Self-Rating Scale significantly more in the direction suggested by
the tape message, than did a group who received the message but
not the isolation, a group who received isolation but no message,
and a group who received neither isolation nor the tape message.
In a second study by Adams et al. (1964), twelve psychiatric patients were given a single treatment consisting of a three-hour
period of isolation, during which an individually prepared,

*From the *APA Convention Proceedings*. 1965: 259-260. Copyright 1965 by the American
Psychological Association. Reprinted by permission.
This research was supported in whole by the Research Foundation of the National
Association for Mental Health. The author wishes to thank the professional and staff
personnel of the Kalamazoo State Hospital for their cooperation in the project.

prerecorded tape message was administered after two and one-half hours of isolation. The MMPI and the Leary Interpersonal Checklist were administered to each patient one day before and one day after the treatment condition. The tests were scored and interpreted according to Leary's (1956) multilevel system of interpersonal diagnosis. A second group of fifteen patients was exposed only to the isolation condition, and a third group of sixteen patients received only the pre- and post-test battery. Analysis of the data indicated that only the isolation-message group and the isolation-only group showed significant improvement, though the nature of the improvement was different for the two groups.

The present investigation had three objectives. The most important one was to study the effect of three treatment sessions instead of a single treatment. The second objective was to include a group who would receive individualized therapeutic messages without any isolation condition. A third objective was to obtain interview data in addition to test data in the assessment phases of the project.

## Method

The sample consisted of fifty-one psychiatric patients from the Kalamazoo State Hospital. Patients with a diagnosis of organic brain or central nervous system pathology were excluded, as were patients who were receiving psychotherapy or shock therapy. Patients were randomly assigned to four groups. Each patient understood that the treatment was part of the hospital's total rehabilitation program, and that his *participation was voluntary.*

### Group I: Isolation-Message

There were fifteen patients in this group. Following a twenty- to thirty-minute interview, each patient was given the MMPI and the Leary Interpersonal Checklist. The tests were scored and interpreted according to Leary's multilevel system of interpersonal diagnosis. Using data from the interview, tests, and case history, 3 twenty-minute therapeutic messages were prepared for each patient and put on tape. In the first message, the results of the tests were presented in a modified form. The patient was told how he acts with others, how he describes his actions with others, how he fantasies his actions with others, and how he idealizes his actions with others. The second message reviewed the major points of the first message, and then gave the patient some understanding of how and why he had developed his particular problems of adjustment. The third message reviewed the content of the second message, and then gave specific suggestions to the patient about how he could improve his adjustment.

One week after the tests and interview, each patient returned from his first isolation-message treatment. The isolation condition consisted of the patient lying on a bed with his eyes covered with cotton-lined eye pieces, glycerin-soaked cotton plugs inserted in his ears, and his head covered with a gauze bandage. A small ear speaker through which the tape message is played was inserted in the head covering. After two hours of isolation, the tape message was presented. Approximately thirty minutes later the treatment session was terminated. The second isolation-message treatment was given two days later, the third was given four days later. One week following the third treatment, the interview and testing were repeated.

### Group II: Message

The twelve patients in this group received three treatments, each consisting of a twenty-minute therapeutic message. The patient was seated alone in a room similar to the isolation room. He listened to each message through the same type of ear speaker that was used for Group I patients. After the message was completed, the patient remained in the room for thirty minutes. In all other respects, the procedures were the same as those for the isolation-message group.

### Group III: Isolation

The twelve patients in this group received three treatments, each consisting of three hours of isolation. In all other respects, the procedures conformed to what has been described for Groups I and II.

## Group IV: Test-Retest

The twelve patients in this group were tested and interviewed twice, with the same interval between test and interview sessions as was used for the other three groups. During the interval between the two test and interview sessions, the patients followed their customary hospital routine.

## Results

The patient's pre- and postinterview behavior were rated on each of the twenty items of the Symptom Rating Scale (Jenkins et al., 1959). Pre- and posttest data were evaluated in terms of **self-perception** (discrepancy between the patient's self-description and description by others), **self-acceptance** (discrepancy between the patient's self-description and description of ideal self), and **self-actualization** (discrepancy between the patient's description of ideal self and description by others).

In the statistical analysis, Dunnett's test was used to compare the test-retest group with each of the three treatment groups. Where more than one treatment group differed from the test-retest group, the Newman-Keuls test was used to compare two treatment groups. The .05 level was used as the criterion of significance. The results are summarized below.

The three treatment groups showed significantly fewer negative (regressive) changes on the interview ratings than did the test-retest group, but the three treatment groups did not differ from one another. The message-only group and the isolation-only group showed significantly more positive (improvement) changes on the interview ratings than did the test-retest group, but the isolation-message group did not differ from the test-retest group.

The three treatment groups did not differ significantly from the test-retest group in the amount of improvement in accuracy of self-perception or in self-actualization. In terms of self-acceptance, the isolation-only group showed significantly more improvement than did the test-retest group, and the improvement of the message-only group over the test-retest group was very close to significance. On the other hand, the isolation-message group showed very little improvement over the test-retest group in self-acceptance.

None of the groups showed a significant change in how they described their actions with others or in how they fantasied their actions with others, however, the message-only group did show a significant change in how others describe them and in their ideal self. In both cases the change was in the direction of more dominant, assertive behavior.

## Discussion

The principal finding of this research was that the combination of isolation and therapeutic communication does not result in more improvement than isolation by itself or therapeutic communication by itself. In terms of negative changes in the interview, the isolation-message group showed no improvement over the other two treatment groups. In terms of positive changes in the interview, the isolation-message group did not do as well as the other two treatment groups. For the test data, the isolation-message group did no better than the other treatment groups in accuracy of self-perception or in self-actualization. In terms of self-acceptance, the isolation-message group did not do as well as the other two treatment groups.

Thus, the combination of isolation and therapeutic communication did not benefit patients as much as it did in the Gibby study and in the Adams study. The present study cannot, however, be directly compared to the other two. While there are some similarities in the design of the three studies, there are also important differences. For example, in the Gibby study the isolation period was four hours instead of three; different assessment measures were employed; and a standardized, nonindividualized message was used. In the Adams study, patients were given one treatment session instead of three; patients were tested one day after the treatment instead of one week later; and the design did not include a group who received only a tape message.

## REFERENCES

Adams, H., Robertson, M., & Cooper, G.: Facilitating therapeutic personality changes in psychiatric patients by sensory deprivation methods. In *Proceedings of the XVIIth International Congress of Psychology.* Amsterdam, North Holland, 1964.

Azima, H., & Cramer-Azima, F. J.: Effects of partial perceptual isolation in mentally disturbed individuals. *Diseases of the Nervous System, 17*:117-122, 1956.

Cooper, G., Adams, H., & Gibby, R.: Ego strength changes following perceptual deprivation. *Archives of General Psychiatry, 7*:213-217, 1962.

Gibby, R., Adams, H., & Carrera, R.: Therapeutic changes in psychiatric patients following partial sensory deprivation. *Archives of General Psychiatry, 3*:33-42, 1960.

Gibby, R. & Adams, H.: Receptiveness of psychiatric patients to verbal communication. *Archives of General Psychiatry, 5*:366-370, 1961.

Harris, A.: Sensory deprivation and schizophrenia. *Journal of Mental Science, 105*:235-237, 1959.

Jenkins, R., Stauffer, J., & Hester, R.: Symptom rating scale of psychiatric patients. *Archives of General Psychiatry, 1*:197-204, 1959.

Leary, T.: *Multilevel Measurement of Interpersonal Behavior.* Cambridge, Unitas Publications, 1956.

Shurley, J.: Profound experimental sensory isolation. *American Journal of Psychiatry, 117*:539-545, 1960.

Chapter 12_____

# ATTITUDE MANIPULATION IN RESTRICTED ENVIRONMENTS: CONCEPTUAL STRUCTURE AND THE INTERNALIZATION OF PROPAGANDA RECEIVED AS A REWARD FOR COMPLIANCE*

PETER SUEDFELD, Ph.D. and JACK VERNON

Conceptually complex (abstract) and simple (concrete) Ss underwent twenty-four hours of sensory deprivation (SD) or non-confined control (NC) treatment. Towards the end of this period, each S had to evaluate the meaning of each of seven passages which presented two-sided information about Turkey. If S responded so as to show that the passage was pro-Turk, he was rewarded by the presentation of the next passage; otherwise, the questions were repeated. This was a test of compliance; internalization was measured by changes on an attitude scale presented several weeks before, and again immediately after, the experimental session. Abstract SD Ss showed a greater degree of compliance than abstract controls and concrete SD Ss; there was no difference between the two concrete groups. Concrete Ss evidenced more attitude change (internalization) than abstracts; in SD, abstract Ss were less and concretes more persuasible than in NC (where the two groups were about equal). The results were interpreted in terms of conceptual structure theory.

SEVERAL studies have investigated the effects of

*From the *Journal of Personality and Social Psychology*. Volume 3, No. 5: pp. 586-589. Copyright 1966 by the American Psychological Association. Reprinted by permission. This research, carried out at Princeton University, was financed by Grant G-27162 from the National Science Foundation.

sensory deprivation (SD) upon susceptibility to persuasive messages (see Suedfeld, 1963). In the most recent of these (Suedfeld, 1964a), it was suggested that the heightened persuasibility of SD subjects may be the result of the suboptimal availability of information which characterizes the deprivation situation and which leads to the increased importance of the information presented in the message itself. As a corollary of this explanation, individual differences in persuasibility were hypothesized. Using the theoretical approach of Schroder, Driver, and Streufert (in press), it was predicted that abstract persons (individuals who are able to make complex integrations of information) would be less responsive to propaganda than would concrete subjects (whose conceptual structure is less complex and flexible). The results showed that SD subjects did change their attitudes more than nonconfined controls (NC) after hearing a taped propaganda passage, and further that concrete subjects evidenced more change than abstracts.

The current study is concerned with the extension of this problem. Vernon (1963) has described a method for producing attitude change in sensorially deprived subjects. Among other things, this method involves reinforcing the subject who shows the desired attitude change by "a little light . . . a novel food item . . . social contacts [pp. 30-31]." While this technique would probably be quite effective in producing change, another type of reinforcement may be more subtle and more powerful.

In an excellent series of papers, Jones and his associates (Jones, 1964a, 1964b; Jones & McGill, 1963; Jones, Wilkinson & Braden, 1961) have demonstrated that SD subjects are motivated to obtain informational stimuli. If we consider the propaganda material as information, we could then reinforce subjects who evidence compliance by giving them a new propaganda message. Thus, we would have a spiral process in which each piece of propaganda would present another opportunity for compliance, with the next piece of propaganda as the reward.

The question arises whether behavioral compliance would lead to actual attitude change — internalization, as described by Kelman (1961). Obviously, it would be quite easy to respond to propaganda in the "desired" way for the sake of the reinforcer;

this would not necessarily involve actual attitude change.

A related question is that of personality differences. Again referring to the theory of Schroder et al. (in press) we would say that abstract individuals — whose need for information is relatively high and who find SD more unpleasant than do concretes (Suedfeld, 1964b) — would consequently show a higher degree of compliance in order to obtain information; being capable of more complex conceptual functioning, however, they would not feel the need to change their actual attitudes towards the subject matter. We thus predicted that among abstract subjects the SD condition will result in greater compliance but less internalization than the NC treatment; in the concrete group, SD subjects should evidence more compliance *and* more internalization than NCs.

## Method

### Subjects and Procedure:

A group of 248 male undergraduates of Rutgers University volunteered to undergo twenty-four hours of SD. From this group, we chose subjects whose opinions about Turkey and the Turks were neutral (see Suedfeld, 1964a). Fourteen abstract and fourteen concrete subjects, all of whom met the neutrality criterion, were then selected by use of the Sentence Completion Test (Schroder & Streufert, 1962). Half of each group was randomly assigned to the SD (darkness, silence, and restricted mobility) and half to the NC (nonconfined control) treatment (for complete description of these two treatments, see Suedfeld, 1964a).

### Propaganda Material:

The material was the same as had been used in the previous study (Suedfeld, 1964a), which had been derived from passages originally devised by Murphy and Hampton (1962). In the current experiment, however, the combined pro- and anti-Turk passage was broken down into seven brief statements. Each of these consisted of a pro-Turkish item followed by a negative item related to the same aspect of Turkish life (e.g., "Turkish justice is swift and impartial, as seen when ... On the other hand, the police force and the courts are sometimes overhasty and harsh; for example ..."). After each two-sided statement, three evaluative items of the Turk attitude scale were presented on the tape, and the subject responded by pressing a button from one to three times. The passages were presented during a one-hour period beginning twenty-three hours after the start of the experimental session.

### Instructions to Subjects:

Before beginning the experimental session, each subject was instructed as follows:

> We are interested in what happens to cognitive efficiency under unusual conditions. You have probably taken tests where you were supposed to answer questions about a passage which you had just read; we will ask you to do something similar. Sometime during the session, you will hear some passages; at the end of each one, you will be asked some questions about it. If you get the majority of the answers *right*, there will be a short pause; then you will hear a new passage, will be asked questions about what it said, and so on. If you get the majority of the answers *wrong*, there'll be a longer pause; then the questions, but not the passage itself, will be repeated. This will go on until you do get the answers right, at which time we'll go on to the next passage. Remember, we're not interested in your own opinion about the topic — just tell us what the passage said.

These instructions were repeated and explained until all subjects understood the scheme; subjects were also taught how to indicate their answers.

After these instructions had been given, all subjects were told that the "comprehension test" would be administered approximately twenty-three hours after the beginning of the experiment. SD subjects were then confined and were left undisturbed until, twenty-three hours later, they were alerted by a buzzer and the propaganda tape began. Control subjects were conditionally dismissed (see Suedfeld, 1964a) and heard the passages begin as soon as they were put into the SD chamber for that purpose twenty-three hours afterwards. At no time during the experimental session did the experimenter know whether a given subject was abstract or concrete.

Pro-Turkish responses were arbitrarily treated as "correct." Figure 12-I shows the process graphically. (These time sequences were used for all subjects.) Technically, there was no limit on the number of "errors" (negative evaluation) possible; in actuality, the number ranged from zero to ten, with higher numbers indicating less compliance.

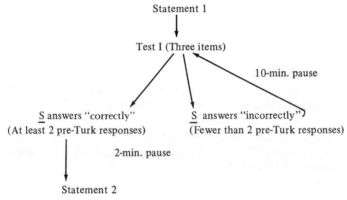

Figure 12-1. Presentation of propaganda material.

At the end of the session, all subjects were presented with the Turk attitude scale used in the earlier study; they were told that we wanted to know their own personal opinions about the Turks, since it was possible that their performance on the passage tests might be related to their attitudes. As before, the maximum degree of internalization of the propaganda was indicated by a change of

TABLE 12-I

MEAN NUMBER OF "INCORRECT" RESPONSES

| Conceptual structure | SD | NC |
|---|---|---|
| Concrete | 3.71 | 3.57 |
| Abstract | 1.00 | 4.29 |

plus twelve points (change in the opposite direction would be minus twelve points at most).

## Results

As a measure of the degree of compliance, we counted the number of "incorrect" (i.e., anti-Turk) responses given as evaluations of the two-sided propaganda messages (see Table 12-I). Because the distribution of scores was not normal, nonparametric methods were used to evaluate the data. When we applied Wilson's (1956) analysis of variance, significance was on the borderline for both the treatments effect ($\chi^2 = 3.59$, $p = .059$) and the interaction effect ($\chi^2 = 3.60$, $p = .057$). SD subjects in general were more compliant than NCs; furthermore, abstract SD subjects were significantly more compliant than concrete subjects in the same condition (corrected for ties, $U = 5.5$, $p < .01$, one-tailed). NC-SD differences were not significant for concrete subjects, but were significant in the abstract group (corrected for ties, $U = 9.5$, $p = .036$, one-tailed).

Table 12-II shows mean attitude change from the initial to the postexperimental test. Analysis of variance of these data indicates that concrete subjects changed significantly more than abstracts ($F = 4.659$, $p < .05$) and that there was a significant interaction effect ($F = 5.897$, $p < .05$); while SD resulted in more change than NC for concrete subjects, the opposite was the case for the abstract group.

## Discussion

In this experiment, noncompliance was measured by the

TABLE 12-II

MEAN ATTITUDE CHANGE

| Conceptual structure | SD | NC |
|---|---|---|
| Concrete | 5.86 | 2.14 |
| Abstract | 1.00 | 2.43 |

number of "incorrect" (anti-Turk) responses the subject made in evaluating the passages. As expected, abstract subjects who had undergone SD showed a higher degree of compliance than did abstract controls; within the SD treatment, abstract individuals complied to a higher degree than concretes. Both of these findings are in accord with theoretical predictions: being highly information oriented, abstract subjects are stressed by low-information environments and thus would be expected to strive harder for an information reward than either concretes in the same environment or than abstract individuals who are in a relatively information-rich situation. It is possible, of course, that the difference between the two SD groups resulted from differential ability to recognize the correct response — but this reasoning fails to explain the difference between the confined and the nonconfined abstract groups.

The fact that concrete subjects complied no more in the SD than in the NC treatment was not in accordance with predictions. Two possible explanations present themselves. One is that concrete individuals are so low in information motivation that environments as severely suboptimal as SD do not raise information need to an appreciable degree; this hypothesis is contradicted by a finding that in a relatively mildly suboptimal game situation concrete subjects do increase their information-search activity (Suedfeld & Streufert, 1964). The second interpretation is based upon previous findings that relatively extreme environmental pressures are needed to produce compliance in concrete subjects (Allen, 1962; Janicki, 1960). It may be that the pressure provided by the SD situation is insufficient to overcome their strong resistance to change, which may be a dissonance-avoiding technique. In this view, compliance may be seen as a relatively complex response in which the subject takes an "as-if" attitude and acts contrary to his own beliefs (thus arousing dissonance) in order to obtain a reward. Subsequent internalization, by the same token, is a simple (or at least simplifying), dissonance-reducing behavior.

The attitude change (internalization) data are generally as hypothesized. As in the earlier study (Suedfeld, 1964a), there was no difference between the abstract and the concrete subjects in the NC condition. After SD, however, the abstract and the concrete groups diverged. Greater attitude change on the part of concrete SD subjects had been predicted as a result of behavioral simplification. Abstract SD subjects evidenced relatively little attitude change; this datum may be explained by positing that the SD situation caused less behavioral simplifcation in abstract than in concrete subjects.

## REFERENCES

Allen, L. H.: The effects of instructional variation and stress on the perception of aniseikonic distortion. Unpublished senior thesis, Princeton University, 1962.

Janicki, W. P.: The effects of variation in conceptual structure on dyadic interaction. Unpublished doctoral dissertation, Princeton University, 1960.

Jones, A.: Drive and incentive variables associated with the statistical properties of sequences of stimuli. *Journal of Experimental Psychology, 67*:423-431, 1964a.

Jones, A.: How to feed the stimulus hunger: Problems in the quantification of an incentive. Paper read at American Psychological Association, Los Angeles, 1964b.

Jones, A., and McGill, D.: Auditory information satiation in humans. Paper read at Eastern Psychological Association, New York City, 1963.

Jones, A., Wilkinson, H. J., and Braden, I.: Information deprivation as a motivational variable. *Journal of Experimental Psychology 62*:126-137, 1961.

Kelman, H. C.: Processes of opinion change. *Public Opinion Quarterly, 25*:57-78, 1961.

Murphy, D. B., and Hampton, G. L. A.: A technique for studying attitude change. In *Collected papers related to the study of the effects of sensory deprivation and social isolation.* (Task Pioneer VI — Endorse) Alexandria, Va.: Human Resources Research Office, 1962.

Schroder, H. M., Driver, M. J., and Streufert, S. *Personality structure, information processing, and social organization.* New York, Holt, Rinehart and Winston, in press.

Schroder, H. M., and Streufert, S.: The measurement of four systems varying in level of abstractness (sentence completion method). *Off. Naval Res. Tech. Rep.*, 1962, No. 11.

Suedfeld, P. Conceptual and environmental complexity as factors in attitude change. *Off. Naval Res. Tech. Rep.*, 1963, No. 14.

Suedfeld, P.: Attitude manipulation in restricted environments: I. Conceptual structure and response to propaganda *Journal of Abnormal and Social*

*Psychology, 68*: 242-247, 1964a.

Suedfeld, P.: Conceptual structure and subjective stress in sensory deprivation. *Perceptual and Motor Skills, 19*:896-898, 1964b.

Suedfeld, P., and Streufert, S.: Information search as a function of conceptual and environmental complexity. Unpublished manuscript, University of Illinois, 1964.

Vernon, J.: *Inside the black room.* New York: Potter, 1963.

Wilson, K. V.: A distribution-free test of analysis of variance hypotheses. *Psychological Bulletin, 53*: 96-101, 1956.

Chapter 13 _____

# USE OF SENSORY DEPRIVATION IN FACILITATING THE REDUCTION OF CIGARETTE SMOKING*

PETER SUEDFELD, Ph.D. AND FREDERICK F. IKARD

Twelve months after a twenty-four-hour period in a socially isolated, monotonous environment, subjects had reduced their rate of cigarette smoking by an average of 48 percent, compared with 16 percent for control subjects. A smaller sample reported similar results at the end of twenty-four months. A set of anti-smoking messages had no permanent effect. Sensory deprivation can apparently be used as a powerful facilitator of long-term behavioral change in human beings.

IN spite of the strong evidence that cigarette smoking is a health hazard, and in spite of the tremendous amount of publicity that has been given to that fact, many smokers who want to quit find it extremely difficult to do so. It has been reported that between 1966 and 1970, 22 million adult smokers in the United States alone have tried unsuccessfully to stop smoking (Horn, 1973). Consequently, many individuals and groups have developed, tested, and sometimes offered to the public methods by

*From the *Journal of Consulting and Clinical Psychology*. Volume 42, No. 6: pp. 888-895. Copyright 1974 by the American Psychological Association. Reprinted by permission. This study is Number 6 in a series with the generic title, "Attitude manipulation in restricted environments." Special thanks are due to G.J. Johnson ("Computational procedures for the unweighted-means analysis of multifactor experiments having repeated measures." Manuscript in preparation), who devised and performed the major data analysis. The assistance of the following people was also instrumental in completing the project: S.S. Tomkins, D. Luciano, Delores Mazurkewica, Cessna Kaye, Darylynn Rank, and Phyllis Denegar. Financial support was received from the National Institutes of Health Biomedical Sciences Support Program, The American Health Foundation, and the Research Committees of Rutgers — The State University and the University of British Columbia.

which smoking cessation could be facilitated: At least half a dozen scientific books and hundreds of articles in the past few years have addressed themselves to this problem.

Among the techniques that have been used in this context are the use of alternative or antagonistic drugs (Bridel, 1970, Davison & Rosen, 1972); hypnosis (Johnson & Donoghue, 1971, Spiegel, 1970a); group therapy (Bozzetti, 1972, Guilford, 1972, Tamerin, 1972); and a wide variety of behavior modification techniques (Berecz, 1972a, 1972b, Best & Steffy, 1971, Hunt, 1973, Lichtenstein, Harris, Birchler, Wahl, & Schmahl, 1973, Livingston, Shapiro, Schwartz, & Tursky, 1971, Mausner, 1971, Miller & Gimpl, 1971). Reviews of this voluminous literature indicate serious shortcomings both in the potency of the techniques and in the adequacy of the research (Bernstein, 1969, Hunt & Matarazzo, 1973, Lichtenstein, 1971, Lichtenstein & Keutzer, 1971, Schwartz, 1969).

The study reported here derives from evidence that a period of sensory deprivation leads to generally increased persuasibility and responsiveness to external cues (Suedfeld, 1969). As a part of a series of experiments investigating this phenomenon, a previous study presented to subjects a two-minute message mentioning some of the health hazards associated with smoking. This message was combined with twenty-four hours of sensory deprivation in a 2 X 2 design, the message being presented at the end of the period to deprived subjects (Suedfeld, Landon, Pargament, & Epstein, 1972). Surprisingly, three months after the experiment the subjects in the deprivation group reported a mean 38 percent reduction in the number of cigarettes smoked per day, compared with a 23 percent reduction in the group that heard the message without having been previously deprived and with an increase in the smoking rate of the untreated control group. This finding justified further testing of the effectiveness of sensory deprivation as a tool in long-term behavioral change.

In a second study, using five psychologically addicted smokers (Suedfeld & Ikard, 1973), a new approach to the persuasive material was adopted. The number of messages was first increased to eighteen; after the third subject was run, this was reduced to twelve in order to avoid the excessively frequent interruption of the deprivation situation. The messages dealt with health hazards of smoking, problems such as weight gain or nervousness, which people are afraid that they will experience should they stop smoking (Barefoot & Girodo, 1972); a simple relaxation exercise; and a message taken from Spiegel (1970b) stressing the responsibility of the subject to avoid poisoning his body by smoking. In spite of the psychological addiction of these subjects to cigarettes, three of the five had quit completely three months after the session (two of these having requested and received brief "booster" deprivation sessions two months after the first).

The current study was designed as a larger scale and more definitive test of the hypothesis that sensory deprivation can facilitate the cessation and/or the reduction of cigarette smoking among subjects with heavy psychological commitments to smoking. The factorial Message X Deprivation design used in the first study was combined with the greater number of messages used in the second previous experiment.

## Method

### Subjects

As a result of the report of our previous research, articles appeared in approximately fifteen newspapers concerning our techniques. These stories indicated that we were seeking subjects for a further study using various types of procedures, including sensory deprivation. All of the material emphasized that the latter was essentially a relaxing, not unpleasant, experience. Several hundred volunteers responded. Each of these was sent a biographical data sheet, a questionnaire concerning smoking habits, and the Tomkins-Ikard Smoking Scale (Ikard & Tomkins, 1973).

The final selection of subjects was based on two considerations. First, we wished to obtain maximally generalizable results. We therefore selected a sample that was approximately equally split between males and females, with an age range of twenty-five to fifty-five, a wide variety of occupations, educational levels, communities, etc. Thus, the final sample included mostly adult workers and housewives, with a few college students. They came from rural, suburban, and urban settings from all over the State of New Jersey.

Second, the group was to be evenly split among psychologically addicted and preaddictive smokers according to the Tomkins-Ikard scale. Psychologically addicted smokers are those who are distressed by the awareness of not smoking, and who experience a craving for cigarettes whenever they are not in the act of smoking; preaddictive smokers are close to addiction and rely heavily upon smoking as an aid in coping with emotionally arousing experiences. While there has been some question as to the independence of "addictive" smoking as a category (McKennell, 1973), subjects here fit the operational definition not only of Tomkins-Ikard scores but also in that they smoked "to reduce negative feelings and smoke[d] automatically [McKennell, 1973, p. 508]."

These two categories make up the most difficult types of smokers to treat successfully (Ikard & Tomkins, 1973). The final group of subjects was made up of thirty-five addicted and forty-two preaddictive smokers. The daily smoking rate of these individuals ranged from approximately one to three packs, with a mean of about thirty-two cigarettes per day; they had been smoking from three to thirty-five years, with a mean of about fifteen years.

## Messages

Seven of the messages used by Suedfeld and Ikard (1973) were retained, with three additions. These consisted of a technique similar to that traditionally used in systematic desensitization: The subject was asked to remember the last time that he had been in an emotional situation that had led him to crave a cigarette and to try to relive that situation in his imagination with the substitution of a simple relaxation exercise at the point where in the real event he had begun smoking. There were three of these messages, one each for the affects of anger, anxiety, and joy. The messages in this set of persuasive inputs lasted from one to three minutes each. In addition, there were five "reward" messages of approximately ten seconds each congratulating the subject when he had completed a period of six, ten, fifteen, twenty, and twenty-three hours of sensory deprivation.

### Design and Procedure

The subjects were randomly assigned to one of four conditions: sensory deprivation-messages (twenty-four hours of sensory deprivation with messages presented approximately one every one and one-half hour), sensory deprivation-no messages (confinement under the same conditions as the previous group but without any messages), messages-no sensory deprivation (subjects were instructed to remain "confined — with reduced sensory variation" — that is, at home, close to a telephone, for twenty-four hours, with the persuasive messages transmitted by telephone on the same schedule as used for sensory deprivation-messages), and no messages-no sensory deprivation (subjects were informed — as was true — that our facilities did not allow us to include them in the deprivation treatment at this time, and were encouraged to seek other forms of treatment). Three sensory deprivation subjects quit shortly after the beginning of the session, and two no-sensory deprivation subjects failed to respond to one or more of the follow-up questionnaires. Thus, the final data analysis is based on seventy-two subjects, with twenty subjects in the sensory deprivation-messages condition, eighteen in the no message-no sensory deprivation, and seventeen each in sensory deprivation-no messages and messages-no sensory deprivation conditions.

The sensory deprivation treatment was administered in a shielded, completely dark, sound-reducing chamber (Industrial Acoustics Model 404-A) located next to the Rutgers University Psychological Clinic. The subjects were lying on a hospital bed, wearing pajamas, nightgowns, leotards, or other simple garments. All pockets were emptied, and watches, jewelry, etc., were removed. No physical restraints, cuffs, goggles, or earphones were used. A chemical toilet was located near the bed; water and vanilla-flavored liquid diet food were available ad lib and could be obtained by turning one's head on the pillow and sucking on a plastic tube. Subjects were thoroughly oriented to the chamber, the equipment, and the route to the door if they should desire to quit, and they were told that there would always be a monitor next door to make sure everything was all right. They were also informed that most people found the experience somewhat boring at worst, and some enjoyed it; but some found it unpleasant and wanted to terminate it ahead of schedule. This was perfectly all right, and no reflection on the subject, but he should be sure that he wanted to quit before he walked out, since once he walked out he could not be allowed to reenter the room. Also, subjects were told to try to remain lying fairly (but not necessarily completely) still and quiet on the bed, except when using the toilet; the monitor would listen in on them from time to time, and the session would be terminated immediately if he heard them walking around, moving excessively, singing, talking aloud, etc. All sensory deprivation subjects were interviewed and debriefed after leaving the chamber. None reported any severe discomfort or distress as a result of sensory deprivation.

After the session, follow-up telephone calls were made every day for a week, with mail follow-ups after two weeks, four weeks, and then every month for a year. A final mail follow-up was conducted at the end of two years. Further phone and mail communications were initiated if the subject did not respond at first. All orientation material heavily emphasized that the technique was experimental and that its proper evaluation through *accurate* self-reports of smoking rate was crucial in avoiding either the error of perpetuating a useless treatment or abandoning a promising one. While it is of course possible that some subjects were not completely truthful, there seems to be no reason to think that this was likely. The research nature of the project, the lack of definite preconceptions on the part of the project staff, and the need for unbiased data were all referred to repeatedly. In a few cases where subjects knew each other, or where a subject was known to acquaintances of the project staff, the verbal reports were confirmed as truthful. Furthermore, subjects usually gave spontaneous explanations for major changes in smoking rate (e.g. "I went to Smokenders, and quit" or "I started smoking again when I was laid off on the job"). Many also sent long introspective statements as to why they thought the treatment did or did not work for them.

## Results

Changes in the number of cigarettes smoked per day from the baseline (presession) level are shown in Figure 13-1. There were no significant intergroup differences in smoking rate prior to treatment. Throughout the first year, sensory deprivation had a highly significant effect ($F = 14.82$, $df = 1/63$, $p < .001$). The time variable was also significant ($F = 7.81$, $df = 12/756$, $p < .001$), as were the Time X Message ($F = 2.03$, $df = 12/756$, $p < .05$) and the Time X Message X Deprivation interactions ($F = 2.78$, $df = 12/756$, $p < .01$). Messages versus no messages, type of smoker (i.e. addicted vs. preaddictive), sex, and age of subjects were not significant.

There was an almost 100 percent complete cessation rate for the first week after sensory deprivation, after which individuals began smoking again but at low rates. These initial decreases

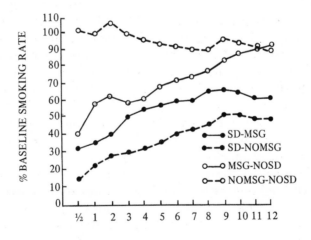

POST-SESSION MONTH

Figure 13-1. Mean changes in smoking rate. (Abbreviations: SD = sensory deprivation, MSG = messages, NoMSG = no messages, NoSD = no sensory deprivation.

were reduced over time. Examination of Figure 13-1 indicates that all three treated groups showed substantial decreases in smoking rate within the first two weeks after treatment, ranging from a 60 percent decrease in the messages-no sensory deprivation group to a decrease of approximately 88 percent in the sensory deprivation-no message group. The rate of the no-message-no-sensory deprivation group was essentially unchanged during the same period. Twelve months after the session, the changes in smoking rates (-15 percent and -17 percent) were virtually identical for the two no sensory deprivation groups, and quite similar for the two sensory deprivation groups (-45 percent and -52 percent). Thus, at the end of one year, sensory deprivation subjects on the average were smoking approximately 48 percent less than they had before the session, the equivalent figure for no-sensory deprivation subjects being approximately 16 percent.

The two-year follow-up occurred after the major data analysis had been completed. Since, unfortunately, only about half of the original subjects responded (many had moved in the meantime), it was decided to analyze this return separately. At the end of the second postsession year, mean decreases in smoking rate were: sensory deprivation-message ($n$ = 10), 57.8 percent; sensory deprivation-no message ($n$ = 8), 52.5 percent; message-no sensory deprivation ($n$ = 9), 23.6 percent; no message-no sensory deprivation ($n$ = 10, 13.6 percent. Analysis of variance showed a significant effect only for the sensory deprivation factor ($F$ = 4.55, $df$ = 1/32, $p < .05$).

The proportion of totally abstinent subjects during the first postcontact week was close to 100 percent in the sensory deprivation groups and close to zero in the no-sensory deprivation groups; the rates continued to show significant intergroup differences throughout the first three postsession months (see Table 13-I). At the end of the twelve-month follow-up period, ten of the thirty-seven (27%) sensory deprivation subjects were maintaining total abstinence, as compared to four of the thirty-five (11.4%) no-sensory deprivation subjects. Of the reduced sample at the end of two years, seven sensory deprivation subjects (39%) and three no-sensory deprivation subjects (16%) were complete abstainers. This difference is not significant by chi-square test; because of the attrition of almost half of the original subjects, it is also difficult to interpret. Nine of the eventually nonabstaining sensory deprivation subjects remarked on follow-up forms that repeated and/or longer deprivation sessions would have enabled them to maintain cessation.

TABLE 13-I

NUMBER OF TOTAL ABSTAINERS

| Group | $n$ | Postsession month | | | | |
|---|---|---|---|---|---|---|
| | | ½ | 3 | 6 | 9 | 12 |
| SD-MSG | 20 | 11(55) | 7(35) | 7(35) | 6(31) | 6(31) |
| SD-no MSG | 17 | 8(47) | 7(41) | 5(29) | 4(24) | 4(24) |
| MSG-no SD | 17 | 3(18) | 4(24) | 2(12) | 1(6) | 1(6) |
| No MSG-no SD | 18 | 0(0) | 1(6) | 2(11) | 3(17) | 3(17) |
| $x^2$ ($df = 3$) | | 20.13** | 6.75* | 4.85 | 3.91 | 3.91 |

*Note.* Percentages are in parentheses. Abbreviations: SD = sensory deprivation; MSG = messages.
*$p < .05$.
**$p < .001$.

Gross direction of change showed significant intergroup differences at the end of the first year, with more sensory deprivation than no sensory deprivation subjects indicating reduction as opposed to no change or increase ($x^2 = 14.32$, $df = 6$, $p < .05$). To check whether subjects perceived differences in having received "treatment," we compared the sensory deprivation and no-sensory deprivation groups in the frequency of seeking other forms of help after contact with us. The only significant difference was a much higher frequency of such behavior in the no-messages-no sensory deprivation group than in the other three ($x^2 = 5.47$, $df = 1$, $p < .02$). The no-messages-no-sensory deprivation group was, of course, the one that had been encouraged by us to try other forms of therapy. The finding implies that the changes in smoking rate between the sensory deprivation groups and the messages-no-sensory deprivation group were due to the sensory deprivation treatment rather than to a difference in the subjects' perception of involvement or of having been treated. Incidentally, there had been no presession differences in help seeking among the groups. Among those subjects who did not undergo sensory deprivation but sought other forms of treatment, we found the mean reduction in number of cigarettes smoked per day to be 14.1 percent, about the same change as was reported by the two no-sensory deprivation groups in our study.

## Discussion

The mean reduction in cigarette consumption by approximately one half and the continued abstinence of over a quarter of the subjects one year after a single session with abstinence by over a third of a reduced sample two years later are very encouraging findings compared to the effects of most commonly used treatments. Although a number of methods appear to obtain high rates of reduction or cessation during or shortly after active treatment, in most of these cases' recovery of smoking behavior appears to be relatively rapid.

While, of course, it would have been desirable to obtain a higher rate of total abstinence, our approach seems to be a promising one on the basis of these data. Those subjects who did not manage to stay off cigarettes completely, but who maintained a significantly lowered smoking rate (one-third to two-thirds less than baseline), have reduced the adverse health effects of smoking. Some of them have reported a decrease or elimination of such symptoms as chronic coughing, and a generally improved sense of well-being. Thus, partial success also appears to be worth the effort. The one-year abstention rate in our study is not strikingly different from those found with behavior modification (Hunt & Matarazzo, 1973); but it should be pointed out that our subjects were selected to have poor rather than good prognoses, and that there was no significant dropout rate during treatment.

As in most programs, self-selection in terms of initial motivation to stop smoking was a factor here; but since most participants in smoking-cessation studies presumably share this motive to some degree, its effect is not crucial in evaluating the technique. One exception to this common motivational factor is found in the original study of our series (Suedfeld et al., 1972), where the subjects were volunteers merely for an experiment "involving lying in a dark, quiet room for twenty-four hours" for a payment of $20. As mentioned previously, a three-month reduction rate of 38 percent was obtained with this procedure. The equivalent postsensory deprivation figure in the current experiment was approximately the same, indicating that motivation to quit was not an overriding factor in the more recent results. In all, it appears that the treatment used here compares favorably with any other technique that has been adequately tested to date.

Furthermore, the sensory deprivation technique is much briefer, simpler, and more economical than most. A single session, a method that can be almost completely automated and requires only a monitor technician, and a facility that can be converted to treat any number of patients simultaneously from one central control room, represent significant savings. For example, the time of patients and of highly trained therapists can be reapportioned more flexibly than in a technique requiring group interaction and supervision over an extended period.

Several explanations can be developed for our findings. It is known that even usually heavy smokers can tolerate the unavailability of cigarettes during sensory deprivation. While no systematic data collection seems to have been performed on this phenomenon, anecdotal reports have indicated that it is quite common (Tomkins, 1968, Vernon, 1963, J. P. Zubek, personal communication, December 16, 1970). There is a plethora of evidence that in a normal environment abstaining from smoking for twenty-four hours is both stressful and ineffective in inducing long-term change; but it may be that the experience of having gone for twenty-four hours in sensory deprivation, without smoking and without having felt an excessive amount of stress, has a greater impact on posttreatment behavior.

Presumably, the painless cessation of smoking in sensory deprivation is due at least in part to the absence of familiar smoking cues. Afterward, the knowledge of successful completion may help to bolster one's resistance when smoking cues are encountered in the normal environment. Continued resistance may also avoid the arousal of cognitive dissonance from relapsing after having successfully completed, and usually discussed with friends and relatives, a rather strange and perhaps somewhat awesome experience.

Going through sensory deprivation appears to be a very personal thing for many subjects. While almost everyone loves to talk about it afterward, there is an emphasis on one's own reactions rather than on the features of the environment. Thus, a change in smoking patterns achieved with the help of this procedure may be perceived as more of a personal achievement, and more under the individual's own control, than changes induced by aversive reinforcement or group pressure. This may be the reason why transfer to normal life seems to be unusually successful, in spite of the brevity of the treatment and the discontinuity between the therapeutic and the everyday *milieux*. This hypothesis will be tested in future research.

Neither in the Suedfeld et al. (1972) data nor in those obtained in the present study was there a lasting increment in the desired behavioral change as a result of adding explicit persuasive messages to the sensory deprivation treatment. This is an unexpected finding, since the theoretical base of our work was the increase in persuasibility that occurs after deprivation. Such an increase has been documented quite reliably (Suedfeld, 1969) and ascribed to a two-component process (Suedfeld, 1972). According to this explanation, increased need for information (Jones, 1969) leads the subject to attend to otherwise uninteresting or even aversive messages. Sensory deprivation simultaneously functions as a general attitude "unfreezer" (Lewin, 1958), disrupting complex cognition so that the recipient finds it difficult to maintain the stability of his belief system (Koslin, Pargament, & Suedfeld, 1971; Koslin, Suedfeld, & Pargament, 1973).

The disconfirmation of this prediction in the Suedfeld et al. (1972) study could logically be explained as a function of the brevity and blandness of the message. In the current study, however, the material was designed to be useful, informative, and persuasive. According to many spontaneous comments, furthermore, it was in fact judged by our subjects to have these characteristics. While the hypothesis may be wrong, the negative result may have been due to the fact that the messages actually worked in two contradictory directions: First, the material was useful and persuasive, which would have tended to facilitate smoking cessation or reduction; but on the other hand, the message presentations provided an excessively frequent (although brief) disruption of the deprivation situation, thus reducing their own impact. This possibility will be tested by the presentation of all messages close together during the session, with the remainder of the twenty-four hours being uninterrupted.

Plans for further experiments also include making the messages obtainable on a self-demand basis. Presumably, this procedure would ensure that the messages are heard when stimulus hunger is at its highest, and at the same time would increase the subject's feeling that he is in control. The use of longer periods of deprivation, and the opportunity to return for brief "booster" periods, may also be helpful. Although repeated sensory deprivation sessions show adaptation effects on a variety of experimental dependent variables (Zuckerman, 1969), a second, shorter deprivation experience did help subjects in a previous study (Suedfeld & Ikard, 1973) to stop smoking again after having relapsed. Correlations between success as a result of sensory deprivation and various personality measures (e.g. of sensation seeking) should also be useful in identifying people who are most likely to benefit from this method.

In spite of the popularized image of sensory deprivation as a threatening and stressful environment, there is a fairly large body of evidence that it can be a useful method, and a useful adjunct to other methods, in clinical contexts (Suedfeld, in press). The current study indicates that in situations such as the amelioration of psychologically addicted smoking, it may be a powerful, simple, and economical modifier of behavior (Suedfeld, 1973). Presumably, the effects could be magnified by methodological improvements and by combining sensory deprivation with other, more traditional, forms of therapy. At any rate, further testing and possible application in a variety of therapeutic situations, and the extension of this model to other forms of addiction, appear to be warranted.

## REFERENCES

Barefoot, J. C., & Girodo, M.: The misattribution of smoking cessation symptoms. *Canadian Journal of Behavioral Science,* 4:358-363, 1972.

Berecz, J. M.: Modification of smoking behavior through self-administered punishment of imagined behavior: A new approach to aversion therapy. *Journal of Consulting and Clinical Psychology,* 38:244-250, 1972a.

Berecz, J. M.: Reduction of cigarette smoking through self-administered aversion conditioning: A new treatment model with implications for mental health. *Social Science and Medicine,* 6:57-66, 1972b.

Bernstein, D. A.: Modification of smoking behavior: An evaluative review. *Psychological Bulletin,* 71:418-440, 1969.

Best, J. A., & Steffy, R. A.: Smoking modification procedures tailored to subject characteristics. *Behavior Therapy,* 2:177-191, 1971.

Bozzetti, L. P.: Group psychotherapy with addicted smokers. *Psychotherapy and Psychosomatics,* 20:172-175, 1972.

Davison, G. C., & Rosen, R. C.: Lobeline and reduction of cigarette smoking. *Psychological Reports,* 31:443-456, 1972.

Guilford, J. S.: Group treatment versus individual initiative in the cessation of smoking. *Journal of Applied Psychology,* 56:162-167, 1972.

Horn, D.: What's happening to smoking behavior? Cited in J. S. Tamerin, Recent increase in adolescent cigarette smoking. *Archives of General Psychiatry,* 28:116-119, 1973.

Hunt, W. A. (Ed.): Special issue: New approaches to behavioral research on smoking. *Journal of Abnormal Psychology,* 81(2), 1973.

Hunt, W. A., & Matarazzo, J. D.: Three years later: Recent developments in the experimental modification of smoking behavior. *Journal of Abnormal Psychology,* 81:107-114, 1973.

Ikard, F. F., & Tomkins, S. S.: The experience of affect as a determinant of smoking behavior: A series of validity studies. *Journal of Abnormal Psychology,* 81:172-181, 1973.

Johnston, E., & Donoghue, A. R.: Hypnosis and smoking: A review of the literature. *American Journal of Clinical Hypnosis,* 13:265-272, 1971.

Jones, A.: Stimulus-seeking behavior. In J. P. Zubek (Ed.), *Sensory Deprivation: Fifteen Years of Research.* New York, Appleton-Century-Crofts, 1969.

Koslin, B. L., Pargament, R., & Suedfeld, P.: An uncertainty model of opinion change. In P. Suedfeld (Ed.), *Attitude Change: The Competing Views.* Chicago, Aldine-Atherton, 1971.

Koslin, B. L., Suedfeld, P., & Pargament, R.: Belief instability as a mediating variable in opinion change. *British Journal of Social and Clinical Psychology,* 12:18-33, 1973.

Lewin, K.: Group decision and social change. In E. E. Maccoby, T. M. Newcomb, & E. L. Hartley (Eds.), *Readings in Social Psychology.* (3rd Ed.) New York, Holt, 1958.

Lichtenstein, E.: Modification of smoking behavior: Good designs — Ineffective treatments. *Journal of Consulting and Clinical Psychology,* 36:163-166, 1971.

Lichtenstein, E., Harris, D. E., Birchler, G. R., Wahl, J. M., & Schmahl, D. P.:

Comparison of rapid smoking, warm, smoky air, and attention placebo in the modification of smoking behavior. *Journal of Consulting and Clinical Psychology, 40*:92-98, 1973.

Lichtenstein, E., & Keutzer, C. S.: Modification of smoking behavior: A later look. In R. D. Rubin, H. Fensterheim, A. A. Lazarus, & C. M. Franks (Eds.), *Advances in Behavior Therapy*. New York, Academic Press, 1971.

Livingston, B. L., Shapiro, D., Schwartz, G. E., & Tursky, D.: Smoking elimination by gradual reduction. *Behavior Therapy, 2*:477-487, 1971.

Mausner, B.: Some comments on the failure of behavior therapy as a technique for modifying cigarette smoking. *Journal of Consulting and Clinical Psychology, 36*:167-170, 1971.

McKennell, A. C.: Is addictive smoking an independent trait? *International Journal of the Addictions, 8*:505-509, 1973.

Miller, A., & Gimpl, M.: Operant conditioning in self-control of smoking and studying. *Journal of Genetic Psychology, 119*:181-186, 1971.

Schwartz, J. L.: A critical review and evaluation of smoking control methods. *Public Health Reports, 84*:483-506, 1969.

Spiegel, H.: A single-treatment method to stop smoking using ancillary self-hypnosis. *International Journal of Clinical and Experimental Hypnosis, 18*:235-250, 1970a.

Spiegel, H.: Termination of smoking by a single treatment. *Archives of Environmental Health, 20*:736-742, 1970b.

Suedfeld, P.: Changes in intellectual performance and susceptibility to influence. In J. P. Zubek (Ed.), *Sensory Deprivation: Fifteen Years of Research*. New York, Appleton-Century-Crofts, 1969.

Suedfeld, P.: Attitude manipulation in restricted environments: V. Theory and research. Symposium presented at the XXth International Congress of Psychology, Tokyo, Japan, August 1972.

Suedfeld, P.: Sensory deprivation used in the reduction of cigarette smoking: Attitude change experiments in an applied context. *Journal of Applied Social Psychology, 3*:30-38, 1973.

Suedfeld, P.: The clinical relevance of reduced sensory stimulation. *Canadian Psychological Review*, in press.

Suedfeld, P., & Ikard, F. F.: Attitude manipulation in restricted environments: IV. Psychologically addicted smokers treated in sensory deprivation. *British Journal of Addiction, 68*:170-176, 1973.

Suedfeld, P., Landon, P. B., Pargament, R., & Epstein, Y. M.: An experimental attack on smoking: Attitude manipulation in restricted environments, III. *International Journal of the Addictions, 7*:721-733, 1972.

Tamerin, J. S.: The psychodynamics of quitting smoking in a group. *American Journal of Psychiatry, 129*:589-595, 1972.

Tomkins, S. S.: A modified model of smoking behavior. In E. Borgatta & R. Evans (Eds.), *Smoking, health, and behavior*. Chicago, Aldine, 1968.

Vernon, J. A.: *Inside the Black Room*. New York, Potter, 1963.

Zuckerman, M.: Variables affecting sensory deprivation results. In J. P. Zubek

(Ed.), *Sensory Deprivation: Fifteen Years of Research.* New York, Appleton-Century-Crofts, 1969.

# PART THREE

## Water Suspension Environments and Ego Diffusion

# INTRODUCTION

THE experiments in this section used water suspension isolation environments in which the subject was suspended
in a tank of water heated just below body temperature. Air was
provided through a mask, and a combination of weights and
floatation achieved the desired neutral buoyancy. This is a less
common form of isolation than the bed confinement method,
thus these studies were primarily exploratory. While they did not
directly seek to demonstrate that water suspension isolation can
be therapeutic, they did report evidence of ego diffusion in subjects and thus inferred potential psychotherapeutic value.

## Experimental Variables

### Degree of Stimulus Reduction

The water suspension environments in these studies decreased
the intensity of available stimuli to levels that are not possible in
bed confinement isolation. The environment used by Barnard,
Wolff and Graveline (chapter 16) included apparatus which provided stimulation not present in the other water suspension experiments. This stimulation may account for the fact that
Barnard et al. found less ego diffusion in subjects than did the
other researchers in the area.

### Time Spent in Isolation

Time does not appear to be particularly influential in determining outcome, a finding consistent with those of bed confinement experiments. A wide range of effects were reported across the
two and one-half to ten hour durations. However, it is not clear

whether the effects reported would be achievable in less than two and one-half hours.

### Experimental Set

Consistent with bed confinement research, set appears to have bearing on experimental outcome in water suspension experiments. Shurley (chapter 15) was careful to provide his subjects with an elaborate set stressing their ability to limit participation and choice of experimental procedures. He also introduced them to the environment in a series of time-limited runs. In effect, he created a positive set without " . . . any suggestion to the subject . . . of what might or might not occur." The result of this effort was described by a subject as " . . . massive comfort with built-in confidence and security, yet with an air of fascinating mystery about the outcome." This attempt to create comfort and confidence in subjects is in contrast to Barnard et al. who were primarily interested in the negative effects shown by their Air Force Volunteers, i.e. the potential hazards of prolonged space flights. This context suggests a neutral, perhaps even negative expectation as to effects and outcome that may well have been passed on to their subjects.

As might be expected, the reports of Barnard's subjects during the experience differ from those of Shurley. The Air Force subjects used techniques of self-stimulation to maintain time orientation, sustain concentration and avoid imagery, whereas the subjects of Shurley and Lilly appeared to enjoy the experience and consider it an adventure. It appears Barnard's set implicitly encouraged his subjects to resist the effects of the experience.

While set may be primarily responsible for these differences in behavior, other variables may also have played a part. The stimulation available in Barnard's environment along with the personality differences between Air Force and civilian subjects are both factors that may have been equally influential.

### Theoretical Constructs

References to both stimulus hunger and psychoanalytic theory appear in these experiments. Lilly (chapter 14) noted stimulus hunger preceded fantasy, imagery and other features of the primary process. He suggested the hunger for stimuli must be resisted if an individual is to regress to the primary process. Substantiating this conclusion, Barnard's subjects did employ various methods of self-stimulation and were relatively successful in resisting the ego-diffusing influence of the environment.

An interesting aspect of both Lilly's and Shurley's experiments are references to subjective experiences concurrent with ego diffusion that appear to be more than simple regression to the primary process. In a startling passage, Shurley reproduced the tape recording of the associate stream of a man in water suspension isolation which clearly illustrates unconscious material flowing into consciousness. It is apparent that regression to primary-process thinking does take place, and there is reference to another, deeper level of experience.

> Apparently (the subject) dropped off in a short (less than two minute) nap; he woke with a start and had the eerie feeling he had just been 'out of this world' and with a very vivid long dream, which he struggled to recall.

The subject was not able to recall the dream into which he fell in the midst of a song he was singing! The text of the tape from this experience onward takes on a different texture with more affect, a two-party dialogue, auditory hallucinations and the like. The two minutes are intriguing for they suggest another level of experience available in the environment that needs classification and further exploration. A similar phenomenon may have been uncovered by Barnard, who found seven of his subjects reported sleeping, while the EEG recordings showed evidence of sleep in only five.

Exploring further into the effects of water suspension sensory isolation, Lilly (1970) combined the environment with LSD. He compared the processes of the mind to a programmed and programmable computer in which what is believed to be true is true or becomes true. It is possible Lilly's reports described unconscious experience observable without LSD, but at this time further research is necessary to substantiate these hypotheses. A few brief excerpts are presented for consideration.

> Later lessons to be learned involve a boundary between one's own computer and the unknown. Experiences at this boundary

may cause anxiety in some professionals. This is the boundary where we run out of explanatory models during these experiments. Certain phenomena take place which are "as if" one or several of the following: mental telepathy, spiritualism, extraterrestial science fiction, paranoid systems or psychosis.

It turns out in our experiments that one can run an experiment by preprogramming with a given unfamiliar and strange set of beliefs (for example, those of some science fiction) and during the experiment, experience most of the phenomena described in the science fiction literature (Lilly, p. 102).

Is all this taking place totally inside one human brain isolated, confined, in solitude, or are unknown influences from currently unknown sources entering into the programs? (Lilly, p. 102).

If one looks very carefully at the quantum mechanical considerations of our brains and their operations, we cannot say we know all of the influences which can be brought to bear on the brain's operations, in all of the states which we can induce by hypnosis, by physical isolation and/or various chemical agents (Lilly, p. 103).

## Individual Differences

The studies in this section used normal subjects. Although evidence in previous sections indicated normal subjects show few effects when exposed to a few hours of bed confinement, brief periods of water suspension isolation have been generally effective in creating ego diffusion in this subject group.

As has been discussed, the content and affect of subjective reports during isolation differed between the groups used by Shurley and Barnard, with the latter subjects generally resisting the regressive pull. This difference may be partly a function of the individual differences between civilian and Air Force volunteers. This conclusion is masked by other factors mentioned that appeared in the Barnard study: the additional stimulation and the neutral or negative set.

## Conclusions

Most significant in the data presented in this section is the phenomenon concurrent with ego diffusion reported by normal subjects. This gives rise to the possibility of personality change in those with intact defensive systems, and by inference suggests water suspension isolation may be more effective than bed confinement in treating disturbed individuals. Moreover, the environment appears to be a potential tool for investigating levels of unconscious experience that may lie below the primary process.

Lilly and Shurley demonstrated the usefulness of proper and adequate treatment of subjects. Their conscientious experimental set apparently allowed for a deeper penetration into unconscious material. Their subjects were able to relax the defensive vigilance of the ego amidst the security generated by the experimenters. Thus this preparation may be a critical factor in maximizing the effectiveness of isolation treatment.

## REFERENCES

Lilly, J. C.: Solitude, isolation and confinement and the scientific method. In Madow, L., and Snow, L. H. (Eds.): *The Psychodynamic Implications of Physiological Studies on Sensory Deprivation.* Springfield, Thomas, 1970.

# Chapter 14

# MENTAL EFFECTS OF REDUCTION
# OF ORDINARY LEVELS OF
# PHYSICAL STIMULI ON
# INTACT, HEALTHY PERSONS*

John C. Lilly, M. D.

## Introduction

**W** E have been seeking answers to the question of what happens to a brain and its contained mind in the relative absence of physical stimulation. In neurophysiology, this is one form of the question: Freed of normal efferent and afferent activities, does the activity of the brain soon become that of coma or sleep, or is there some inherent mechanism which keeps it going, a pacemaker of the "awake" type of activity? In psychoanalysis, there is a similar, but not identical problem. If the healthy ego is freed of reality stimuli, does it maintain the secondary process, or does primary process take over? For example, is the healthy ego independent of reality or dependent in some fashion, in some degree, on exchanges with the surroundings to maintain its structure?

In seeking answers, we have found pertinent autobiographical literature and reports of experiments by others, and have done experiments ourselves. The experiments are psychological ones on human subjects. Many psychological experiments in isolation have been done on animals, but are not recounted in detail here; parenthetically, the effect on very young animals can be an almost completely irreversible lack of development of whole systems, such as those necessary for the use of vision in accomplishing tasks put to the animal. No truly neurophysiological isolation experiments on either animals or man have yet been done.

---

*From *Psychiatric Research Reports.* 5:1-9,. 1956. Courtesy of American Psychiatric Association.

## Autobiographical Accounts

The published autobiographical material has several draw-backs: In no case is there a sizeable reduction of all possibilities of stimulation and action; in most cases, other factors add complications to the phenomena observed. We have collected eighteen autobiographical cases from the polar and sea-faring literature (see References) which are more frank and revealing than most. We have interviewed two persons who have not published any of their material. In this account, we proceed from rather complicated situations to the more simple ones, i.e. from a maximum number of factors to the most simple experimental situation.

From this literature we have found that isolation per se acts on most persons as a powerful stress. The effects observed are similar to those of any extreme stress, and other stressful factors add their effects to those of isolation to cause mental symptoms to appear more rapidly and more intensely. As is well known, stresses other than isolation can cause the same symptoms to appear in individuals in an isolated group.

Taking our last point first, we have the account by Walter Gibson given in his book, "The Boat." This is the case in which four persons out of an initial 135 survived in a lifeboat in the Indian Ocean in World War II. Gibson gives a vivid account of his experiences, and the symptoms resulting from loss of hope, dehydration, thirst, intense sunburn, and physical combat. Most of the group hallucinated rescue planes and drank salt water thinking it fresh; many despaired and committed suicide; others were murdered; and some were eaten by others. The whole structure of egos was shaken and recast in desperate efforts at survival. (It is interesting to note that many of those who committed suicide tried to sink the boat by removing the drain plugs before jumping overboard, i.e. sink the boat [and other persons] as well as the self; this dual destruction may be used by some of the non-surviving solitary sailors; see below.)

I cite this case because it gives a clue as to what to expect in those who do survive isolation in other conditions: Gibson survived — how? He says: (1) by previous out-of-doors training in the tropical sun for some years; (2) by having previously learned to be able to become completely passive (physically and mentally); (3) by having and maintaining the conviction that he would come through the experience; and, we add, (4) by having a woman, Doris Lim, beside him, who shared his passivity and convictions.

In all cases of survivors of isolation, at sea or in the polar night, it was the first exposure which caused the greatest fears and hence the greatest danger of giving way to symptoms; previous experience is a powerful aid in going ahead, despite the symptoms. Physical passivity is necessary during starvation, but, in some people, may be contraindicated in social isolation in the absence of starvation. In all survivors, we run across the inner conviction that he or she will survive, or else there are definite reassurances from others that each will be rescued. In those cases of a man and a woman together, or even the probability of such a union within a few days, there is apparently not only a real assurance of survival, but a love of the situation can appear. (Such love can develop in a solitaire.) Of course, such couples are the complete psychological antithesis of our major thesis of complete isolation; many symptoms can be avoided by healthy persons with such an arrangement.

Solitary sailors are in a more complex situation than the group of polar isolates. The sailing of a small boat across oceans requires a good deal of physical exertion, and the situation may be contaminated by a lack of sleep which can also cause symptoms. The solitary sailors, of which Joshua Slocum and Alain Bombard are outstanding examples, relate that the first days out of port are the dangerous ones; awe, humility, and fear in the face of the sea are most acute at this time. Bombard states that if the terror of the first week can be overcome, one can survive. Apparently, many do not survive this first period. Many single-handed boats have not arrived at their transoceanic destination. We have clues as to the causes from what sometimes happens with two persons on such crossings. There are several pairs of ocean-crossing sailors in which one of the couple became so terror-stricken, paranoid, and bent on murder and/or suicide, that he had to be tied to his bunk.

Once this first period is past, other symptoms develop, either from isolation itself or from isolation plus other stresses. In the

South Atlantic, Joshua Slocum had a severe gastro-intestinal upset just before a gale hit his boat; he had reefed his sails, but should have taken them down. Under the circumstances, he was unable to move from the cabin. At this point he saw a man take over the tiller. At first he thought it was a pirate, but the man reassured him and said that he was the pilot of the Pinta and that he would take his boat safely through the storm. Slocum asked him to take down sail, but the man said, no, they must catch the Pinta ahead. The next morning Slocum recovered, and found his boat had covered ninety-three miles on true course, sailing itself. (His boat was quite capable of such a performance; he arranged it that way for long trips without his hand at the helm.) In a dream that night the pilot appeared and said he would come whenever Slocum needed him. During the next three years the helmsman appeared to Slocum several times, during gales.

This type of hallucination — delusion seems to be characteristic of the strong egos who survive: a "savior" type of hallucination rather than a "destroyer" type. Their inner conviction of survival is projected thoroughly.

Other symptoms that appear are: superstitiousness (Slocum thought a dangerous reef named M Reef was lucky because M is the thirteenth letter of the alphabet and thirteen was his lucky number. He passed the reef without hitting it. Bombard thought the number of matches necessary to light a damp cigarette represented the number of days until the end of the voyage. He was wrong several times.); intense love of any living things (Slocum was revolted at the thought of killing food-animals, especially a goat given to him at one port. Ellam and Mudie became quite upset after catching and eating a fish that had followed the boat all day, and swore off further fish-eating); conversations with inanimate objects (Bombard had bilateral conversations with a doll mascot); and a feeling that when one lands, one had best be careful to listen before speaking to avoid being considered insane. (Bernicot refused an invitation to dinner on another yacht after crossing the Atlantic alone, until he could recapture the proper things to talk about.) The inner life becomes so vivid and intense that it takes time to readjust to the life among other persons and to reestablish one's inner criteria of sanity. (When placed with fellow prisoners, after 18 months in solitary confinement, Christopher Burney was afraid to speak for fear that he would show himself to be insane. After several days of listening he recaptured the usual criteria of sanity, and then could allow himself to speak.)

Life alone in the polar night, snowed-in, with the confining surroundings of a small hut is a more simple situation. However, there are other complicating factors: extreme cold, possibilities of carbon monoxide poisoning, collapse of the roof, etc. Richard Byrd, in his book "Alone," recounts in great detail his changes in mental functioning, and talks of a long period of CO poisoning resulting in a state close to catatonia. I refer you to his book for details. He experienced, as did Slocum and many others, an oceanic feeling, the being "of the universe," at one with it.

Christiane Ritter ("A Woman in the Polar Night") was exposed to isolation for periods up to sixteen days at a time. She saw a monster, hallucinated her past as if in bright sunshine, became "at one" with the moon, and developed a monomania to go out over the snow. She was saved by an experienced Norwegian who put her to bed and fed her lavishly. She developed a love for the situation and found great difficulty in leaving Spitzbergen. For a thorough and sensitive account of symptoms, I recommend her book to you.

From these examples and several more (see References), we conclude the following:

(1) Published autobiographies are of necessity incomplete. Social taboos, discretion to one's self, suppression and repression of painful or uncomfortable material, secondary elaboration, and rationalization severely limit the scope of the material available. (Interviews with two men, each of whom lived alone in the polar night, confirm this impression.)

(2) Despite these limitations, we find that persons in isolation experience many, if not all, of the symptoms of the mentally ill.

(3) In those who survive, the symptoms can be reversible. How easily reversible, we do not know. Most survivors report, after several weeks exposure to isolation, a new inner security and a new integration of themselves on a deep and basic level.

(4) The underlying mechanisms are obscure. It is obvious that

inner factors in the mind tend to be projected outward, that some of the mind's activity which is usually reality-bound now becomes free to turn to phantasy and ultimately to hallucination and delusion. It is as if the laws of thought are projected into the realm of the laws of inanimate matter and of the universe. The primary process tends to absorb more and more of the time and energy usually taken by the secondary process. Such experiences either lead to improved mental functioning or to destruction. Why one person takes the healthy path and another person the sick one is not yet clear.

Experiments to clarify the necessary conditions for some of these effects have been done. One of the advantages of the experimental material is that simpler conditions can be set up and tested, and some of the additional stresses of natural life situations can be eliminated.

## Experimental Isolation

The longest exposure to isolation on the largest number of subjects has been carried out in Dr. Donald Hebb's Department of Psychology at McGill University by a group of graduate students. We started a similar project independently with different techniques at the National Institute of Mental Health. In the Canadian experiments, the aim is to reduce the *patterning* of stimuli to the lowest level; in ours, the objective is to reduce the *absolute intensity* of all physical stimuli to the lowest possible level.

In the McGill experiments, a subject is placed on a bed in an air-conditioned box with arms and hands restrained with cardboard sleeves, and eyes covered completely with translucent ski goggles. The subjects are college students motivated by payment of $20 per day for as long as they will stay in the box. An observer is present, watching through a window, and tests the subject in various ways verbally through a communication set.

In our experiments, the subject is suspended with the body and all but the top of the head immersed in a tank containing slowly flowing water at 34.5° C. (94.5° F.), wears a blacked-out mask (enclosing the whole head) for breathing, and wears nothing else.

The water temperature is such that the subject feels neither hot nor cold. The experience is such that one tactually feels the supports and the mask, but not much else, a large fraction of the usual pressures on the body caused by gravity are lacking. The sound level is low; one hears only one's own breathing and some faint water sounds from the piping; the water-air interface does not transmit air-borne sounds very efficiently. It is one of the most even and monotonous environments I have experienced. After the initial training period, no observer is present. Immediately after exposure, the subject writes personal notes on his experience.

At McGill, the subjects varied considerably in the details of their experiences. However, a few general phenomena appeared. After several hours, each subject found that it was difficult to carry on organized, directed thinking for any sustained period. Suggestibility was very much increased. An extreme desire for stimuli and action developed. There were periods of thrashing around in the box in attempts to satisfy this need. The borderline between sleep and awakedness became diffuse and confused. At some time between twenty-four and seventy-two hours most subjects couldn't stand it any longer and left. Hallucinations and delusions of various sorts developed, mostly in those who could stay longer than two days.

The development of hallucinations in the visual sphere followed the stages seen with mescaline intoxication. When full-blown, the visual phenomena were complete projections maintaining the three dimensions of space in relation to the rest of the body and could be scanned by eye and head movements. The contents were surprising to the ego, and consisted of material like that of dreams, connected stories sharing past memories and recent real events. The subjects' reactions to these phenomena were generally amusement and a sense of relief from the pressing boredom. They could describe them vocally without abolishing the sequences. A small number of subjects experienced doubling of their body images. A few developed transient paranoid delusions, and one had a seizure-like episode after five days in the box with no positive EEG findings for epilepsy.

Our experiments have been more limited both in numbers of subjects and duration of exposures. There have been two subjects, and the longest exposure has been three hours. We have much preliminary data, and have gained enough experience to begin to guess at some of the mechanisms involved in the symptoms produced.

In these experiments, the subject always has a full night's rest before entering the tank. Instructions are to inhibit all movements as far as possible. An initial set of training exposures overcomes the fears of the situation itself.

In the tank, the following stages have been experienced:

(1) For about the first three-quarters of an hour, the day's residues are predominant. One is aware of the surroundings, recent problems, etc.

(2) Gradually, one begins to relax and more or less enjoy the experience. The feeling of being isolated in space and having nothing to do is restful and relaxing at this stage.

(3) But slowly, during the next hour, a tension develops which can be called a "stimulus-action" hunger; hidden methods of self-stimulation develop: twitching muscles, slow swimming movements (which cause sensations as the water flows by the skin), stroking one finger with another, etc. If one can inhibit such maneuvers long enough, intense satisfaction is derived from later self-stimulations.

(4) If inhibition can win out, the tension may ultimately develop to the point of forcing the subject to leave the tank.

(5) Meanwhile, the attention is drawn powerfully to any residual stimulus: the mask, the suspension, each come in for their share of concentration. Such residual stimuli become the whole content of consciousness to an almost unbearable degree.

(6) If this stage is passed without leaving the tank, one notices that one's thoughts have shifted from a directed type of thinking about problems to reveries and fantasies of a highly personal and emotionally charged nature. These are too personal to relate publicly, and probably vary greatly from subject to subject. The individual reaction to such fantasy material also probably varies considerably, from complete suppression to relaxing and enjoying them.

(7) If the tension and the fantasies are withstood, one may experience the furthest stage which we have yet explored: projection of

visual imagery. I have seen this once, after a two and one-half hour period. The black curtain in front of the eyes (such as one "sees" in a dark room with eyes closed) gradually opens out into a three-dimensional, dark, empty space in front of the body. The phenomenon captures one's interest immediately, and one waits to find out what comes next. Gradually forms of the type sometimes seen in hypnogogic states appear. In this case, they were **small, strangely shaped objects with self-luminous borders. A** tunnel whose inside "space" seemed to be emitting a blue light then appeared straight ahead. About this time, this experiment was terminated by a leakage of water into the mask through a faulty connector on the inspiratory tube.

It turns out that exposures to such conditions train one to be more tolerant of many internal activities. Fear lessens with experience, and personal integration can be speeded up. But, of course, there are pitfalls here to be avoided. The opposite effects may also be accelerated in certain cases. Fantasies about the experience (such as the illusion of "return to the womb," which is quite common) are dispelled; one realizes that at birth we start breathing air and hence cannot "return to the womb." One's breathing in the tank is extremely important: as a comforting, constant safeguard and a source of rhythmic stimulation.

In both the McGill experiments and in ours, certain aftereffects are noted: The McGill subjects had difficulty in orienting their perceptual mechanisms; various illusions persisted for several hours. In our experiments, we notice that after emersion the day apparently is started over. For example, the subject feels as if he has just arisen from bed afresh; this effect persists, and the subject finds he is out of step with the clock for the rest of that day. He also has to readjust to social intercourse in subtle ways. The night of the day of the exposure he finds that his bed exerts great pressure against his body. No bed is as comfortable as floating in water.

Experiments such as these demonstrate results similar to that given above for solitary polar living and sailing alone. If one is alone long enough, and at levels of physical and human stimulation low enough, the mind turns inward and projects outward its own contents and processes; the brain not only stays active despite the lowered levels of input and output, but accumulates surplus energy to extreme degrees. In terms of libido theory, the total *amount* of libido increases with time of deprivation; body-libido reaches new high levels. If body-libido is not discharged somatically, discharge starts through fantasy; but apparently this is neither an adequate mode nor can it achieve an adequate rate of discharge in the presence of the rapidly rising level. At some point a new threshold appears for more definite phenomena of regression: hallucinations, delusions, oceanic bliss, etc. At this stage, given any opportunities for action or stimulation by external reality, the healthy ego seizes them and re-establishes more secondary process. Lacking such opportunities for a long enough interval of time, re-organization takes place; how reversibly and how permanently we do not yet know.

Apparently even healthy minds act this way in isolation. What this means to psychiatric research is obvious: We have yet to obtain a full, documented picture of the range available to the healthy human adult mind; some of the etiological factors in mental illness may be clarified and sharpened by such research. Of course, this is a limited region of investigation. We have not gone into details about loss of sleep, starvation, and other factors which have great power in changing healthy minds to sick ones. I think that you can see the parallels between these results and phenomena found in normal children and in psychotics. And, if we could give you a more detailed account, possible explanations of the role of isolation factors in involuntary indoctrination and its opposite, psychotherapy, would be more evident.

## REFERENCES

1. Small, Maurice H.: April, 1900. On some psychical relations of society and solitude. *Pedagogical Seminary,* 7(2).

### Solitary Sailors

2. Slocum, Captain Joshua: *Sailing Alone Around the World.* Rupert Hart-Davis, London, 1948.
3. Ellan, Patrick and Mudie, Colin: *Sopranino.* W. W. Norton and Co., Inc., New York, 1953.
4. Bombard, Dr. Alain: *The Voyage of the Hérétique.* Simon and Schuster,

New York, 1953.
5. Merrien, Jean: *Lonely Voyagers*. G. P. Putnam's Sons, New York, 1954.
6. Merrien, Jean: *Les Navigateurs Solitaires*. Editiones Denoël, 1954.
7. Bernicot, Louis: *The Voyage of Anahita — Single-Handed Round the World*. Rupert Hart-Davis, Soho Square, London, 1953.

## Drastic Degrees of Stress

8. Gibson, Walter: *The Boat*. Houghton Mifflin Company (The Riverside Press), Boston, Mass, 1953.

## Living in the Polar Night

9. Scott, J. M.: *Portrait of an Ice Cap with Human Figures*. Chatto and Windus, London, 1953.
10. Courtauld, A.: Living alone under polar conditions. *The Polar Record*. No. 4. University Press, Cambridge, 1932.
11. Byrd, Richard E.: *Alone*. G. P. Putnam's Sons, New York, 1938.
12. Ritter, Christiane: *A Woman in the Polar Night*. E. P. Dutton and Co., Inc., New York, 1954.

## Forced Isolation and Confinement

13. Burney, Christopher: *Solitary Confinement*. Coward-McCann, Inc., New York, 1952.
14. Stypulkowski, Z.: *Invitation to Moscow*. Thames and Hudson, London, 1951.

## The Deaf and the Blind

15. Collingswood, Herbert W.: *Adventures in Silence*. The Rural New Yorker, New York, 1923.
16. Ormond, Arthur W., C. B. E., F. R. C. S.: Visual hallucinations in sane people. *British Med. J.*, 2, 1925.
17. Bartlet, J. E. A.: A case of organized visual hallucinations in an old man with cataract and their relation to the phenomena of the phantom limb. *Brain*, 74(31):363-373, 1951.

## Experimental Isolation

18. Heron, W., Bexton, W. H., and Hebb, D. O.: Cognitive effects of a

decreased variation to the sensory environment. *The Amer. Psychol.,*
*8*(8):366, 1953.

# Chapter 15

# PROFOUND EXPERIMENTAL
# SENSORY ISOLATION*

### Jay T. Shurley, M.D.

THE nature and range of psychophysiological phenomena evoked in intact humans experimentally exposed in solitude to an environment which profoundly diminishes absolute amounts of sensory inputs has been suggested by Lilly[1]. Lilly and Shurley[2] attempted to define relevant physical, physiological, psychological and social conditions for such experiments. Beginning with Bexton, Heron and Scott in Hebb's laboratory,[3,4,5,6] many workers [7,8,9] have described effects of minimal or partial experimental interference with sensory inputs, or the normal, varied patterning of these with or without solitude. Bennett[10] and Camberari[11] have used immersion techniques; their findings are more comparable with those reported here. In an attempt to eliminate further some shortcomings of the early experiments, the author redesigned the apparatus and altered critical aspects of the technique. These modifications are briefly reported here, together with an account of some experimental findings.

### Method and Procedure

At the physical level we aimed at the provision of a constant environment allowing the maximum achievable reduction of ambient physical stimuli, plus the maintenance of a constant level of those inputs impossible to eliminate, such as temperature. A special two-room laboratory was constructed at the Oklahoma City Veterans Administration Hospital. The laboratory enabled us to achieve a marked diminution of light, sound, vibration,

---

*From the *American Journal of Psychiatry*. 1960, Volume 117, pp. 539-545. Copyright 1960, the American Psychiatric Association.

odor, and taste inputs. A large tank of slowly flowing water maintained at approximately 93.5 degrees F. (34.5°C.) provided simulated weightlessness, a uniform tactile field, elimination of body wastes, and other advantages for our purpose. Inspired air was kept at a constant low pressure, at 70°F., a relative humidity of 45 percent, and free of odor and other pollution. Automatic controls and continuous tape recorders completed a virtual self-operating system requiring infrequent attention.

At the physiological level, we aimed at the absolute elimination of all sources of pain and discomfort from body position, pressure ischemia and hollow viscus distention. The subject was positioned so as to remain comfortable, though motionless, for relatively long periods. He was under instruction to inhibit body movements to the maximum degree consistent with comfort. Design of the mask and breathing system allowed effortless breathing without reduction of oxygen tension and without carbon dioxide pile-up. Neutral buoyancy of the body was carefully achieved by appropriate, low stimulation placements of weights or buoyant, soft plastic material around the mask or body.

At the psycho-social level, we sought subjects with distinct personal attributes. The experimental situation per se required a somewhat self-selected volunteer with presumed ability for sensitive and accurate self-observation, and better than average memory, recall, and descriptive powers. In the experiment the subject needed to assume the role of a relatively passive, self-maintaining sensor, recorder, recaller and reproducer with free time, motivated to communicate his experience fully, freely, and with minimal omission and distortion to the interested, relaxed, minimally active and minimally coercive experimenter. With these qualities as relatively constant factors, we collected data related to: A.) subject variables, sex, occupational identity (lawyers, journalists, physicians, psychoanalysts, technicians, nurses, artists and performers), chronological age (twenty-four to seventy-four), and personality type; B.) four conditions, in terms of separation in time and space, of experimenter from the subject in the tank; and C.) two alternatives in reporting — immediately following the run, and during the run itself. (Subjects were permitted free choice between alternative conditions of experimenter distantiation, and of reporting.)

Certain considerations seemed relevant at this level, and were observed rigidly. The experimenter and his assistants prepared for the observer role by first using themselves as subjects; the subject was familiarized thoroughly with the experimental conditions by a step-wise series of time-limited runs prior to definitive endurance runs. The identity, and longest times of all subjects were known only to the experimenter.

Strenuous efforts were made to eliminate any suggestion to the subject by project personnel of what might or might not occur. Spontaneous reporting by the subject was encouraged and all queries by the experimenter were general and open-ended in the interviews between the subject and the experimenter. Naturally, the anonymity of each subject and the confidential nature of all personal data were made explicit to the subject and were scrupulously observed. Permission to limit or eliminate participation at any time without prejudice was specifically granted each subject in advance.

Together, these measures resulted in a state described afterwards by one subject as, "an extremely monotonous state of massive comfort, with built-in confidence and security, yet with an air of fascinating mystery about the outcome."

## Findings

Detailed consideration of the manifold aspects of the extensive data is obviously not possible here, and many of the observations lend themselves poorly or not at all to quantitative reporting. A portion of the data is here presented in two ways: first, a condensed, narrative account, much of it in the subject's own words; second, a summary of selected data from many experimental runs by many subjects.

### Findings in One Subject

The following is a chronological report from a tape recording of the experience of a 29-year-old married male, college-trained journalist, who desired to write a feature story from first-hand experience, and who felt that the experience might resemble that of the first astronaut.

The familiarization run occurred three days prior to his experimental run and only slightly dampened his enthusiasm, despite the fact that just prior to the run, he unexpectedly panicked when he placed the mask over his head (a thing he previously had done a number of times without undue anxiety). He had to remove and replace the head mask several times before he felt comfortable enough to enter the tank. The experimenter who was standing by was mildly surprised and reminded the subject that he could stop participation if he wished. The subject declined, however, and once the run started, he continued to its pre-set limit of three hours, with the observer on the outside, monitoring position. The familiarization run revealed that the mask leaked badly, and that the tank water at 92°F. was too cold, resulting in chilling. The subject experienced headache and severe stomach cramps, had a vivid fantasy of shopping for a private plane, and was startled to learn that only he had heard dogs barking at one point. He reported afterwards that "that was more peace and quiet than I've ever had by myself," and that he felt unusually calm and relaxed for the remainder of the day. He viewed the total experience as "enjoyable."

## Experimental Run

The subject appeared at the laboratory at eight A.M. on a Saturday, with a day free of obligations or plans until seven P.M. His vital signs were normal, and a half hour saw him launched on his run, with a comfortable mask which leaked considerable less than the one he had used before, yet proved to require self-bailing every half to three quarters of an hour. He denied anxiety about the mask and expressed great puzzlement as to what had caused his previous panic. With the observation that "the knowledge you are right across that wall impairs the feeling of being alone," he dismissed the experimenter from the immediate scene to a point where he would be available by telephone from ten minutes away. The subject revealed that he was determined to use his time this day to prepare in his mind an important report and a budget, both due within a week. He elected to report his experience as it occurred, with tape recorder running. "Everything," he said, "pointed to a 'good' run," and he anticipated a pleasant time.

His first half-hour was spent motionlessly, except for a monologue of his everyday thoughts and concerns. These were: anxiety over a strange and entirely unusual somnambulisitc act of his wife's two nights before; guilt over disappointing his boy's expectations of him on that day; curiosity about an unexpected letter from a girl friend unheard from for years; philosophizing about life, and over "What it all means"; pleasure and pride in his job ("I've got a front row seat at the greatest show in the world!"); irritation over and disapproval of the attitudes and behavior of the younger generation of journalists. Following each shift of thought, he would digress briefly into some childhood memory associatively connected. In listening to this tape later, the experimenter was forcibly struck by a curious quality about each remark: namely, that each was expressed in ambiguous language that, on a different level, invariably could be construed as a comment on a popular fear about the sensory isolation experience. For the above series, this went as follows: embarrassment at doing something slightly ridiculous or crazy; anxiety over loss of contact with firm ground; regret over failure to establish a good communication link with another in advance; concern over being brain-washed; frustration in the effort to derive some deeper meaning out of the apparently meaningless and ambiguous situation, (i.e. the structureless experimental sensory isolation situation), and a turning to the recollection of rich personal sensory experiences enjoyed in the past.

In the second hour his comments concerned his self-thwarted, increasing urgency for "exercise" and physical activity; amazement at his lack of appetite for a cigarette; his state of utter loneliness and solitude, save for "my very real companions, my thoughts and memories"; compassion for the little space-monkey, Sam, who received only half an apple and a glass of water for his dinner after his historic trip fifty-five miles into space; thoughts of food and sudden intense hunger pangs.

He whistled, and then sang the refrain from a popular tune which went, "I'll never get rid of that ___, ___, ___!" Apparently he dropped off into a short (less than two minutes) nap; he woke with a start and the eerie feeling he had just been "out of this world," and with a very vivid, "long" dream, which he struggled to recall. He succeeded in recalling only a part — "a sawdust cream cone."

In the third hour he questioned and then asserted he heard the very faint sound of water trickling (the tape records the sound); asserted he heard dogs barking (not present on the tape); and commented on a "crackling sound" (unable to verify from the tape). At intervals he sang, increasingly louder, the refrain from a slightly obscene ditty which began, "Roll me over ___."

Increasingly strong impulses to action came: "I had an urge to make like a porpoise, but those darned hoses (air supply) won't let me!" Briefly, he seemed to be in quite an ebullient, elated mood. Suddenly, he plunged into grief and tears with the expressed thought, "How many people really think about what it's all about? How many people ever, ever think — just once — about love?"

Within seconds, the depressed mood vanished and he was again joking, whistling, and laughing. A make-believe dialogue ensued, as he asked, anxiously, "Joe, what do you do when your engine quits at 200 feet?", and replied, in a peal of laughter, "You land the sonofabitch!"

Immediately following, his tone shifted and he uttered an angry command: "You voice! Keep quiet up there! Quiet!" He, himself, obeyed, and was silent, but only briefly. He hummed. He sang. He sighed deeply. He yawned. He seemed unutterably bored.

His thoughts turned to his plan to compose his report and his budget, and the belated recognition he had not even begun to accomplish this. In a half-hearted explanation to himself, he said, "I just allowed my thoughts to drift." Futility and resignation hung from his tone of voice. He then remarked briskly, "I seem kind of wide awake. I ought to get out!" For a period following this, there was more singing, more humming. Then, "I don't know, but it seems like I heard voices. Somewhere. Male voices. Men's voices. Too bad! (laughter). It should have been a bunch of dollies!" He laughed again. More singing came.

In a tone of extreme annoyance, he blurted out, "I might just as well be Sam, for all I can be or do or think or hear or be or smell or taste!"

Over the next ten minutes he argued himself into the position that he was "just wasting time. After all, I feel fine. This is ridiculous." (Here he referred to his being a grown man bobbing around in the dark in a tank of water in a hole under the hospital). "Besides," he added, "This run isn't producing any data for the doctor, anyway!"

Again, he commented and questioned whether he really was hearing "some noises." Abruptly, he pulled off the mask and left the tank.

Over the four and one-half hours of his run, his longest mute period had been less than six minutes.

In the observer room, he dried, dressed, took his pulse (80), his temperature (98.2°) and respiration (16). He guessed that it was now 12:35, and elated to discover, on uncovering the clock, that it was 1:00 P.M. He picked up the interview card, and dictated into the recorder his response to the first instruction: Give a spontaneous account of the run.

> This one was a calmer thing, from the beginning to the very end. I don't know if you got any material out of it you can really use. I enjoyed this one to a degree. I have no specific recollections, except that I seemed to doze quite a bit at first. I don't believe I dictated as much as last time. I don't feel as subdued as after my first run. I feel like I'd like to go out and hunt bear! I feel more exhilarated, refreshed, and rested than I did after that first one. I'm sorry, I don't have a lot to say. [Apologetically], I noticed I thought a lot about women this time.

In response to the question, why terminate now?, he replied,

> I had the feeling there were some things I ought to be doing . . . I don't know now, though, what they were . . . I felt like I was "coming to," and I was getting bored, and it just didn't seem like I should stay. That's why I quit now.

Coincidentally, the experimenter returned to the scene at this point, intending to check the operation of the automatic equipment in the outer chamber, and discovered the subject busily interviewing himself. The experimenter remained, listening passively, while the subject continued his report and occasionally injected, or replied to a question. He noted that the subject seemed unusually buoyant, gay, and energetic. He was amazed to hear the subject calmly report that on several occasions he had seen a brilliant white light, that "looked like the sun through a peephole," and once had seen an inverted "V" in brilliant blue and white flame moving through dark space toward him. This occurred about half way through the run. Shortly after this he experienced an "extremely strong" and persistent feeling that "someone" identified as friendly, had entered the chamber and was "in the room with me." After these and several similar accounts of experiences in isolation, he apologized, "I have so little to offer this time."

As he neared the end of the interview, he waxed increasingly angry. These feelings reached a climax with the vehement assertion, "I honestly believe, if you put a person in there, just kept him and fed him by vein, he'd just flat die!"

One further observation by the subject deserves mention. He commented on what was to him a curious, paradoxical fact. Although he could visualize his complete budget sheet with photographic clarity in his mind's eye (a feat he is incapable of in everyday life) he simply could not "hold on to it and work with it." "Everything I thought of came to mind much more vividly than it would outside, but I simply could not concentrate." In addition, he noted that certain mental images experienced on a previous trial run could be recalled as freshly as if they had just happened.

The postrun interview lasted an hour and a half, during which time he lit one cigarette, but took only one or two puffs (he is almost a chain-smoker in everyday life). He also ignored a proffered cup of coffee, which turned cold on the table before him — a thing he ordinarily would never have allowed.

His buoyant mood and unaccustomed energy persisted throughout the day, and he reported that "nothing else unusual — nothing at all" had occurred when he was queried a week later. However, a colleague of the experimenter's happened to hear him reading a newscast on the evening following the day of the run, and noted that the subject, usually a facile and accomplished speaker, hesitated momentarily and stumbled in pronouncing the words "water" and "Medical Center," but gave no indication of awareness that he did so.

The news feature which he planned remained uncompleted four months later.

## Findings in General

Results under the two alternatives of reporting, i.e. retrospective or both simultaneous and retrospective reporting, permit the observation that simultaneous reporting generally was much richer in detail and appeared to inhibit less the revelation of marked deviations from usual feeling states, imagery, and thought content. Retrospective accounts, however, were most revealing. Put another way, the healthy ego seemed to possess an incredible degree of ability to utilize repression and other defensive mechanisms that drastically limited the full reporting of experience. With only an occasional exception, persons having had considerable subjective experience of analytic-type psychotherapy consistently reported fuller and less distorted retrospective accounts of what is called "ego-alien" or "primary process" experience. Subjects with experience as analysts reported even more of this experience and with even less distortion.

No generalizations are possible as yet regarding the effects of temporal and spatial distantiation between subject and experimenter. It was obvious that anxieties of both were significant in determining what was requested and allowed, but other factors also are involved.

For many reasons, the reporting of findings in the area of mental imagery is exceptionally difficult, yet one of the most dramatic findings of these experiments concerns this very area. Mental imagery phenomena, broadly conceived, invariably were present in every run of every subject in our series, although conditions of reporting dictated that in some instances they were inferential, rather than direct. The variety of these experiences defies classification and description. For example, consider how one would classify this: "I strongly felt that I was stirring with my left leg, and it was a spoon in an iced tea glass, just going round and round. I 'came to' with a start to realize that my leg *was* going

round and round." By contrast, the following seems easy to classify: "I suddenly saw in the darkness before me a field of golden
toadstools, with the sunlight brightly reflected from the stem of
one." The latter experience might be described as purely visual,
three dimensional, and in color. The subject was able to paint a
picture of what she saw. A fuller discription of data on mental
imagery soon will be available elsewhere[12].

Under the extreme conditions of our experiment, clear limits of
what might be expected (for example, what might be heard) were
nonexistent. Two physician-subjects independently reported
having been startled to hear, without benefit of stethoscope, their
own heart sounds at ear-filling intensity. One of them reported
having heard repeatedly the snapping sound of his own aortic
cusps closing at the end of each systole. A third physician-subject
reported in awe that for the first and only time of his life he heard
the gliding sound made by moving his large joints. Such reports,
if verified, raise the interesting question of whether they are to be
regarded as instances of enhanced sensory acuity, lowering of
sensory thresholds, or enhanced ability to fix attention.

There was a general tendency, following a run, for pulse, respiratory rate and blood pressure to drop moderately, and for body
temperature to rise slightly, although exceptions were noted.
Nine of the twelve subjects made runs exceeding 180 minutes, but
none exceeded 400 minutes. Within this range, postexposure
feeling states varied both between subjects, and for the same subject between runs. We saw marked calmness and extreme irrita-
bility, buoyancy and lethargy, vigilance and somnolence. Most
frequently we observed a peculiar, mixed state characterized by
calm, clear mental vigilance, coupled with lethargy, muscular
relaxation and a decided disinclination for exercise, but without
any sense or sign of fatigue.

## Discussion

The single run reported here is not atypical. There are wide
individual variations in specific mental content, but much fewer
variations in form and sequence of events.

When one takes out light and sound, one perforce puts in darkness and silence; when one takes out change and structure, one puts in monotony and nonstructure. When one takes away gravity, a state of weightlessness obtains. Thus, every "negative" state has "positive" consequences. In terms of these consequences, the former (or negative) state may be far more potent, regardless of how much physical energy input, or stimulus is denied. As a matter of fact, for a conscious human, the *absolute* elimination of *any* sensory input, save for special modalities within very narrow limits (e.g. visible light), is impossible, and can be approached only asymptomatically.

## Conclusions

A feasible and effective method has been described for studying a wide range of psychophysiological phenomena under circumstances permitting exceptionally effective isolation and demonstration of discrete elements in the complicated, interconnected patterns and sequences underlying even the simplest human act or experience.

A number of hypotheses relating to very fundamental issues can be erected from these observations and can be subjected to experimental testing. In due course, such experiments may contribute to a more adequate understanding of human behavior.

### REFERENCES

1. Lilly, John C., Mental effects of reduction of ordinary levels of physical stimuli on intact, healthy persons. Psychiatric Research Reports, #5, *APA*, June 1956.
2. Lilly, J. C., and Shurley, J. T.: Experiments in solitude in maximum achievable physical isolation with water suspension of intact, healthy persons. Read, in part, at the Symposium on Sensory Deprivation, Harvard Medical School, Boston, June 1958. To be published.
3. Heron, W., Bexton, W. H., and Hebb, D. O.: *Am. Psychologist, 8*:366, 1953.
4. Bexton, W. H., Heron, W., and Scott, T. H.: *Can. J. Psychol., 8*:70, 1954.
5. Heron, W., Doane, B. K., and Scott, T. H.: *Can. J. Psychol., 10*:52, 1957.
6. Heron, W.: *Scientific American, 196*:52, 1957.
7. Vosburg, Robert L.: *Sensory Deprivation and Isolation.* Psychiatric Communications, Pittsburgh, Oct. 1958.
8. Solomon, P., Liederman, H., Mendelson, J., and Wexler, D.: *Am. J.*

*Psychiat., 114*:357, Oct. 1957.

9.  Wheaton, Jerrold L.: Fact and fancy in sensory deprivation studies, Review 5-59. *Aero-medical Reviews*. School of Aviation Medicine, USAF, Brooks AFB, Texas, Aug. 1959.
10. Bennett, A. M. H.: Sensory deprivation in aviation. Read at Symposium on Sensory Deprivation, Harvard Medical College, Boston, June 1958.
11. Camberari, J. D.: The effects of sensory isolation on suggestible and non-suggestible psychology graduate students. Unpublished Doctoral Dissertation. University of Utah, 1958.
12. Shurley, Jay T.: Mental imagery in profound sensory deprivation and isolation. To be published in the Volume Reporting AAAS Symposium on Hallucinations, Washington, D.C., Dec 1958. (L. J. West, Ed.).

\* \* \*

## Discussion

John C. Lilly, M.D. (St. Thomas, Virgin Islands). The importance of this work seems to lie, not in its testing and extension of research on isolation and confinement in water which I began in 1954, but in the fact that a group is doing profound isolation and confinement in a water immersion situation. It has been my impression, and my published opinion, that this kind of isolation, in which all possible sensory inputs and information exchanges with the physical and social surroundings are reduced towards zero, will be a fertile source of knowledge of the human mind in a short-term and in a long-term sense.

When this work was initially presented in 1956 in the *Psychiatric Research Reports No. 5* (Lilly), it was inadvertently linked with a negative aura conditioned by the brain-washing milieu in which similar studies were being carried out in the laboratory of Dr. Donald Hebb. It also suffered from being born in an atmosphere of research on mental illness. I do not feel that either of these bedfellows can benefit except by products from the research. The research itself should be on a much broader biological and psychological basis. To put it very simply, our curiosity about the functioning of human minds can be satisfied and intrigued by these techniques as by no others. The amount of information which can be, and is, generated by each subject in these experiments in a few hours can be mountainous and overwhelming, even as it can be by a freely associating person lying on a couch.

The advantage of the watertank over the couch is that the conditions are more extremely isolating and there is a greater degree of true aloneness achievable in the tank. For healthy subjects this has the distinct advantage of lessening the feeling of someone looking over one's shoulder watching one's thinking processes. One can, as it were, really be free of supervision, the necessity of exchanges and the necessity of organization of one's thinking for the purposes and activities of others.

The truly individual aloneness achievable by this method allows one to find out the following basic facts:

1. The human mind is not a solipsistic cesspool of circuitous internal feedbacks. "Pure thought thinking of itself" is not the net result of such work.

2. The human mind in this situation can be seen to be a true source of continuous new information, some recorded in the past but inevitably generating new relationships interwoven with information recently derived from social realities and from the anticipated future.

3. Demonstrations of the portions of the human psyche which are not under the immediate control of one's own self are shown in a dramatic and immediate fashion to those who are ready to see them.

4. In my own experience, and apparently in that of some others, who have been through these experiences (and similar ones in prisons, small sailing vessels and polar huts), one gains an increased awareness of, and a willingness to move with, power, speed and integrity along the lines of one's life situation along which one really and truly wishes to move. The long-term effects of repeated satisfactory exposures to these extreme conditions in several cases have been quite rewarding.

In contrast to most other isolation experiments, there seems to be an underlying thread of a reward balance in the reward and punishment account book in the immersion-type experiments. Once a satisfying solution to the technical matters is provided for the subject, I found, as have Shurley and Bennett, that the subjects want to repeat their exposures and seek out opportunities to do so. One may ask if addiction might develop. My answer is No, eventually one becomes weaned from such artificial aids for exploring one's mind. In my experience practically everyone who has been through this has been very much impressed with the experience. No one has yet called it trivial.

# Chapter 16

# SENSORY DEPRIVATION UNDER NULL-GRAVITY CONDITIONS*

GEORGE W. BARNARD M.D., HAROLD D. WOLFF, M.D.
AND DUANE E. GRAVELINE, M.D.

IN the near future a manned space vehicle will be launched. Rapid technological advances promise progressively longer flights including explorations of other planets. Individuals selected for these ventures will be exposed to such stresses as high accelerative forces, weightlessness, prolonged loud noises, vibration, radiation hazards, constant danger, confinement, monotony, isolation and sensory alteration with a lowering of sensory input. It is with these latter four stresses that the present study is concerned.

A review of the biographical and anecdotal accounts of men who have been alone and isolated at sea on rafts or in the Antarctic, reveals that many of them reacted with profound psychological alterations. At times these changes were perceptual with the person experiencing visual or auditory hallucinations. On other occasions there was intellectual impairment with an inability to concentrate and a decreased verbalization for fear that this decrement in intellectual power might be revealed. At still other times changes occurred in mood with deep feelings of loneliness and depression.

In recent years an interest has developed in trying to simulate these conditions of isolation and sensory deprivation. One of the earliest reports came from the McGill studies.[1] Subjects lay on a bed in a small room while a constant white noise was present and visual input was depatterned by use of translucent goggles. Cotton gloves and cardboard cuffs reduced tactile stimulation. Subjects experienced vivid hallucinations and showed intellec-

*From the *American Journal of Psychiatry.* 1962, Volume 118, pp. 921-925. Copyright 1962, The American Psychiatric Association.

tual impairment. A later study by Vernon[2] was conducted in a dark, soundproof room. The subjects wore earplugs and cardboard gauntlets, but had more freedom of movement than those in the McGill study. These subjects denied perceptual change and intellectual impairment was not found by testing. Lilly[3] at NIMH suspended his subject in a tank of water with temperature held constant at 34.5° C. The subject wore only a headmask which blacked out vision. Vivid hallucinations occurred in two and one-half to three hours. Subsequent experiments by Shurley[4] at Oklahoma, also using the water immersion method, have revealed that many subjects developed hallucinations and hallucination-like experiences. The isolation studies performed by Ruff, Levy and Thaler[5] at the Aero Medical Laboratory used mostly Air Force personnel. Subjects were placed in a soundproof room with vision input either depatterned by translucent goggles or blacked out with masks. These studies did not show the dramatic perceptual changes and hallucinations that were reported by the other experimenters.

## Methods

This present study was designed to study the psychophysiological reactions of Air Force pilots to sensory deprivation using a water immersion method in order to minimize sensory input. The subjects, wearing only a modified pressure helmet and urinary collection device, were submerged in a tank which measured 8 feet long, 2½ feet wide and 4 feet deep. Temperature of the water was maintained between 90° to 93° F. by a flow of warm water into the tank. A regulator on the helmet permitted balanced air pressures for the submerged subjects. Light was excluded and except for the monotonous hum of the air blower and the flow of air into the helmet, no sounds were present. Subjects lay on a webbed lounge chair in a semireclining supine position. Because of the buoyancy of the body in water, the musculo-skeletal system approached a weightless state. A pulley tie down was necessary to counterbalance the buoyancy of the helmet. A small tube in the helmet allowed the subjects to drink water from a bottle. Twenty-four gauge needle electrodes were used as EEG sensors, small surface electrodes in the mid-axillary line for ECG and respiratory sensors. Subjects were instructed to move as little as possible and to describe freely all their thoughts and feelings. A microphone in the helmet permitted all verbalizations to be recorded and cognitive function as measured by the Watson-Glaser Deduction Test and Robinson Rhymes Test was assessed before and after the experiments. All subjects were interviewed after the experiment by a psychiatrist for reactions to the experimental situation.

## Results

The ten-hour period of sensory deprivation was initiated with fourteen volunteers, four of whom aborted the mission within two hours because of leaks into the helmet or inability to void. Of the remaining ten subjects, six aborted between six and ten hours because of nausea or pain in the neck, eyes, back or head.

### *Behavioral Reactions*

Table 16-I summarizes the behavioral reactions experienced by

TABLE 16-I

REACTIONS TO SENSORY DEPRIVATION
10 SUBJECTS — 6-10 HOURS

| | |
|---|---|
| 1. Time disorientation | 10 |
| 2. Decrement in concentration | 7 |
| 3. Thoughts self-directed | 10 |
| 4. Daydreams and search for stimuli | 6 |
| 5. Unrealistic thinking | 3 |
| 6. Imagery | 6 |
| 7. Affective States | |
| (a) Loneliness | 5 |
| (b) Feelings of confinement | 6 |
| (c) Boredom | 10 |
| (d) Apprehension | 8 |
| (e) Irritation | 8 |
| 8. Need for movement and tasks | 10 |
| 9. Sleep: | |
| (a) Subjective | 7 |
| (b) Objective by EEG | 5 |

the subjects. These are grouped into nine categories:

1. *Time disorientation.* There was preoccupation by all subjects with time. The subjects controlled the anxiety growing out of the loss of time orientation by three techniques: counting numbers, counting heart beats, and guessing when the experiment would end. They would, however, subtract an epoch from their first approximation in order to avoid the anxiety generated by being confined past the hoped-for time of release. This technique was successful in that upon completion of the experiment most subjects thought less time had elapsed than actually had. Another interesting phenomenon was that toward the end of the experiment, time was experienced as passing more rapidly than it was occurring.

2. *Decrement in concentration.* Seven of the ten subjects reported a decrease in their ability to concentrate. This impairment was of such proportion in one subject that he could not remember the Lord's Prayer or a familiar hymn. Another reported that for several hours after the experiment his mind seemed "blank"

TABLE 16-II

COGNITIVE FUNCTION AFTER SENSORY DEPRIVATION

| ect | Age | Watson-Glaser Number Wrong Control | Test | Robinson Rhymes Number Wrong Control | Test |
|---|---|---|---|---|---|
| | 30 | A2 | *B7 | A1 | *B1 |
| | 30 | *B4 | A3 | A3 | B5 |
| | 38 | A2 | *B5 | A0 | *B1 |
| | 32 | *B3 | A2 | *B0 | A1 |
| | 31 | A0 | *B2 | A0 | *B1 |
| | 28 | A0 | *B2 | A2 | *B1 |
| | 35 | *B7 | A5 | *B2 | A0 |
| | 44 | *B10 | A3 | *B3 | A2 |
| | 30 | A1 | *B4 | A1 | *B1 |
| | 38 | *B11 | A6 | A1 | *B1 |

| Watson-Glaser | | Robinson Rhymes | |
|---|---|---|---|
| Improved: | 5 | Improved: | 4 |
| Worse: | 5 | Worse: | 3 |
| | | Same: | 3 |

necessitating that he visually focus on an object in order to concentrate effectively. In general, the altered concentration was in the form of thought processes being accelerated, moving rapidly from one subject to another. Although subjectively experienced by most subjects, this altered thinking was not revealed by the two cognitive function tests administered after the experiment (Table 16-II.) Possibly this cognitive alteration was only a subjective experience or perhaps the tests administered did not adequately measure this change, or that with reintroduction of meaningful stimuli, the normal intellectual function was quickly regained.

3. *Thoughts self-directed.* Although the subjects were specifically encouraged to talk freely during the experimental period, there was a tendency for some to talk very little, one individual saying but thirty words during his entire six hours in the tank. These individuals rationalized their hesitancy in various ways. In several, further inquiry revealed heavily charged emotional situations, such as a fight to reject unwanted thoughts, imagery, or feelings of claustrophobia. For most subjects there was a turning inward on the self with a great preoccupation with the body and its state of comfort. Table 16-III reflects this somatic preoccupation which in seven subjects amounted to 80 percent or more of all their verbalizations. During the early stages of the experiment,

TABLE 16-III

VERBALIZATIONS IN SENSORY DEPRIVATION

| Subject | Time in Tank | Total Number Verbalizations | % Verbalizations Somatic Comfort-Discomfort |
|---------|--------------|------------------------------|----------------------------------------------|
| A | 10 hrs. | 31 | 84 |
| B | 10 hrs. | 10 | 80 |
| C | 8 hrs. 40 mins. | 51 | 84 |
| D | 6 hrs. 20 mins. | 28 | 89 |
| E | 7 hrs. 15 mins. | 38 | 58 |
| F | 10 hrs. | 209 | 50 |
| G | 6 hrs. | 49 | 82 |
| H | 10 hrs. | 105 | 85 |
| I | 7 hrs. 15 mins. | 19 | 68 |
| J | 6 hrs. 15 mins. | 8 (30 words) | 37 |

some of the thoughts concerned things outside the tank, but gradually the focus of attention was constricted to the boundaries of the tank. Body discomfort was more easily reported than feelings of anxiety. In the postexperimental interview, this was admitted by some. Several admitted that focusing on body discomfort had prevented the occurrence of thoughts or images which upset them.

4. *Daydreams and search for stimuli.* While most subjects had fleeting thoughts of past events and people, there was but little emotional involvement with this introspection. An active search was made for sensory stimuli, such as touching fingers together, seeking for light sources or noting the sensation of bubbles moving over the skin. Many subjects were surprised that they derived so much pleasure from these ordinarily trivial stimuli.

5. *Unrealistic thinking.* Only three individuals related unrealistic and disturbing thoughts, all of which involved the body. These distortions were impressions that the body was tumbling in the water, that the head was swelling and that the needle electrodes were traversing the head.

6. *Imagery.* Although a majority of subjects reported some form of visual or auditory imagery, most experiences were without affect. Even the vivid illusion of a rattlesnake being thrown into the tank was viewed as unrealistic by the subject, and he did not become frightened. Nevertheless, this emotional detachment was not always possible for everyone and for several the images were experienced with feeling. One individual feared the images and thought that if they were "let in" he could not control them. He was able to prevent their occurrence or to dispel them by moving or looking to the side of the helmet.

7. *Affective states.* Moods varied among the subjects and also within the same subject from time to time. Loneliness was reported by five, sense of confinement by six, boredom by ten, apprehension by eight, and irritation by eight. In addition, several described a transient state resembling suspended animation, in which the subject did not desire to move or talk.

8. *Need for movement and tasks.* All subjects expressed a definite need for a task. Although specifically instructed not to move, no one was able to do this for more than a few minutes. Several

moved almost continuously throughout the test period. Involuntary flexion of the extremities was noted in most subjects after movement had been inhibited for several minutes. In some subjects there were body image and spatial changes, so that without movement, it was difficult to know where the body limits ended. This further prompted the need for movement to reassure the self where one's extremities were in space.

9. *Sleep.* When subjects slept, they did so for short periods and only rarely reached a deep state of sleep. Reawakening followed stimulation given by involuntary movements or urgency to void. Whenever the subjects awoke from sleep they were most likely to experience increased anxiety and momentary panic. They attributed these reactions to their loss of time and spatial orientation. Quickly, however, they were able to partially reorient themselves avoiding prolonged anxiety.

### Physiological and Biochemical Results

EKG, EEG, and respiration were recorded every fifteen minutes. There was much intrasubject and intersubject variation for pulse and respiration responses. One subject developed a leak in the helmet after four hours so that we were unable to obtain pulse and respiratory measurements because of electrical interferences. For the remaining nine subjects, only the initial six-hour period is used for comparison. Other than an initial mean pulse rate of seventy-nine beats per minute as compared to the experimental mean pulse rate of sixty-eight beats per minute, there was no consistent pattern. Both the initial mean respiration rate and the experimental mean respiration rate were fourteen per minute. EEG was analyzed only for the presence or absence of sleep patterns. Although seven subjects reported sleeping, there was EEG evidence of sleep in only five subjects.

Because of technical difficulties we were able to obtain satisfactory undiluted urine samples from only four subjects. These samples were bioassayed for adrenaline and nor-adrenaline in the laboratory of Dr. McChesney Goodall, Memorial Research Center and Hospital, Knoxville, Tennessee. Because the number of samples was so small, quantitative results will not be reported. One of the subjects showed a rise in both adrenaline and nor-adrenaline output, one a decrease in adrenaline and increase in nor-adrenaline and two showed a marked decrease in both adrenaline and nor-adrenaline. In one of the latter subjects, the nor-adrenaline dramatically fell from 73.44 gm. per twenty-four hours to 0.41 *u* gm. per twenty-four hours in the ten hours. Neither the increases nor decreases in adrenaline or nor-adrenaline were correlated with changes in pulse rate.

## Conclusions

In evaluating the results of this series of experiments it should be noted that we did not obtain our desired level of minimal external sensory stimulation. We do believe, however, that we did obtain a significant degree of sensory deprivation and attenuation.

Although there are trends in reactions to sensory deprivation, it remains evident that the situation will be viewed differently by various subjects. Each subject will react to the situation in accordance with his past experience and personality structure.

While intellectual and emotional changes were present in our Air Force group, the degree of alterations was not as great as in some of the previously reported experimental groups. It may be that the defense mechanisms of our group did not permit as much loss of reality contact as other experimental subjects, most of whom were college students or other non-Air Force groups. An alternate explanation might be that we were introducing so much external stimulation in the nature of physical discomfort that subjects focused on this and prevented the lapse into primary process thinking with true hallucinations. By using new facilities and techniques, our future research will determine if further lowering of sensory input causes a greater loss of contact with reality. There was a suggestion that those who remained in the deprivation environment for the ten hours were able to relate the somatic discomforts with detachment and had confidence in themselves, in the monitors and in the equipment.

## REFERENCES

1. Heron, W., Bexton, W. H., and Hebb, D. O.: *Am. J. Psychol.*, 8:366, 1953.
2. Vernon, J., and Hoffman, J.: *Science, 123*: 1074, 1956.
3. Lilly, J. C.: *Psychiat. Res. Rep.*, Am. Psychiat. Ass., 5:13, 1956.
4. Shurley, J. T.: *Am. J. Psychiat., 117*: Dec. 1960.
5. Ruff, G. E., Levy, E. Z., and Thaler, V. H.: *Aerospace Med., 30*:599, 1959.

## Discussion

Jay T. Shurley, M. D. (Oklahoma City, Oklahoma). — It is a pleasure to welcome Drs. Barnard, Wolff, and Graveline of the Wright-Patterson Aerospace Medical Laboratory to the small, but growing circle of intrepid souls who are performing, by means of the water immersion technique, these experimental interventions into the complex feedback loops normally existing between an individual and his environment. In terse aerospace language, they term this "under null-gravity conditions." Since my presentation of a fragment of my own findings here last year,* I have attempted to describe the complex nature of the experiments in operational terms, referring to the experimental variable in a short-hand way as "the HHDE," which stands for "hydro hypodynamic environment," and categorizing the experimental frame of reference as that of bionomics, or experimental human ecology.

I, like the authors of this paper, have reluctantly resigned myself to the use of the misnomer, "sensory deprivation," in referring to the product of the experimentation, since popular usage has so widely seized upon the term. The labels applied matter much less than the fact that another group of experimenters has demonstrated that curious, complex, and potentially disturbing effects upon mentation and physiology ensue in some profusion upon even relatively brief exposures of otherwise highly effective, healthy individuals to this situation.

The implication seems abundantly clear that here is a highly challenging set of facts, from both the practical and theoretical standpoints. They must be explored, tested, and thoroughly understood if man is to develop capability of personally penetrating

---

*Shurley, Jay T.: *Am. J. Psychiat., 117*:539, Dec. 1960.

ever deeper into alien environments without encountering preventable minor to major discouragements. For, I believe, disasters can occur if the implications of these experiments are ignored and necessary corrective measures not worked out to counteract insidiously developing decrements in performance.

At the same time, I feel that generally too much has been made of the hazards, and not enough attention paid to the reward side of the ledger in assessing the effects of these and similar experiments. The behavioral findings reported here are quite similar to those of my group, allowing, of course, for significant differences in details of technique, and in subjects used. The problem remains, how to account systematically for the phenomena observed! We note, too, the attempts to record concomitant physiological data — a difficult technical problem. What is reported here in this regard is interesting, but insufficiently meaningful for me.

Among the many questions left unanswered by this sparse description of preliminary findings are these: Did the experimenters use themselves as subjects? If so, was this fact known to the subjects? What motivational factors were known to be operating with the subjects, and with the experimenters? What was the nature of the explicit and implicit instructions to the subjects? How do the authors account for the discrepancy between the number of subjects reporting sleep, and the number in whom EEG evidence is found? As judged by EEG, what depth of sleep was attained? Finally, were there any peculiarities in the volumes of urine excreted by the four subjects in which this could be accurately measured?

For me, this was a fascinating, even tantalizing report. I congratulate the authors and look forward eagerly to hearing more from this group.

# PART FOUR

Water Suspension Isolation and
the Induction of Ego Diffusion

# INTRODUCTION

THE water suspension isolation discussed in this section did not require the breathing apparatus used in the preceding water suspension environments. The subject lay horizontally in a heated solution of epsom salts which provided adequate floatation without effort and kept the mouth and nose above water. This freedom from apparatus represented a twofold improvement: The comfort and security of the subject was increased, and the equipment failure noted in previous experiments was eliminated. A taped message was played at the beginning of the experience in an attempt to encourage ego diffusion.

## Experimental Variables

### Degree of Stimulus Reduction

The absence of breathing and floatation equipment in this water suspension environment brought levels of available stimuli to slightly lower levels than were achieved in previous studies.

### Contents of Taped Message

The text of the tape appears in the appendix. It combined a brief invitation to relax and free associate with *Adagio for Strings* by Samuel Barber. Music may have been effective in encouraging ego diffusion as it does not appeal directly to discursive thought, but rather articulates complexes of feeling and imagery. Music has no easily assigned connotations, and as such can overcome some limitations of word-bound thinking. The selection played for the subject may have created a shifting, amorphous, affect-laden stream of association crossing and recrossing the threshold of consciousness. In this way, *Adagio for Strings* may have func-

281

tioned as an effective bridge into the unconscious mind without the limitations of verbal programming.

## Experimental Set

An attempt was made to make each subject comfortable and confident by introducing him to the environment in an initial time-limited run of one-half hour. Previous to this experience each subject was shown the isolation tank and its heating, filtration and ventilation systems. A written introduction to the experience was given to each subject to provide a standard positive set without revealing the purpose of the study. This introduction appears in the appendix.

## Time Spent in Isolation

A one-half hour session was given before the two experimental runs of one and one-half hours each. Subjects who did not hear the taped message did not evidence personality change, suggesting multiple isolation only-sessions of this length are not adequate to create change in normal subjects. However, the subjects who received the tape encouraging ego diffusion did demonstrate personality change, indicating the efficacy of this time duration under certain conditions.

## Theoretical Constructs

In accord with much of the literature reviewed, this study relied on the therapeutic and growth-producing aspects of regression and ego diffusion to account for personality changes. The more popular psychoanalytic concepts were exchanged for Jung's model of the psyche. This position regards the integration of unconscious material into conscious awareness as beneficial and necessary for psychological development. Moreover, Jung's notion of the unconscious indicated the existence of levels below the personal unconscious, which can account for previous evidence not easily classified as primary-process material.

## Individual Differences

Water suspension isolation combined with a taped message encouraging ego diffusion was found to create personality changes in normal subjects with intact and healthy defensive systems. This may be largely due to the strong regressive pull characteristic of an almost complete absence of environmental stimulation. Normal individuals have been shown by previous research to be generally uninfluenced by bed confinement isolation. This fact suggests the regressive pull of those environments is not sufficient to bring forth unconscious material in the presence of adequate defenses.

## Conclusions

The literature reviewed in this book lends insight into the workings of the mind both in and out of sensory isolation, for we may be observing a phenomenon that also occurs in a natural and more random form.

The evidence reported in this and preceding sections indicates individuals benefit from brief periods of greatly reduced contact with environmental stimulation. Ego diffusion appears to be a central aspect of isolation experience that allows for a reorganization or rebalancing of conscious and unconscious components of the psyche. While normal individuals with differentiated defenses require greater reductions in external stimuli for the diffusion of ego processes than do disturbed individuals, in both cases therapeutic growth appears concurrent with diffusion.

Personality change taking place outside the isolation laboratory is marked by a similar phenomenon. The template for human creativity and growth seems to be lodged within the unconscious. New and higher affective and cognitive stages are reached as the ego integrates previously unrealized resources within the self. The work of developmentalists such as Sullivan, Piaget and Gowan sustains this axiom in their description of discrete stages of development that are the heritage of all men. To the developmentalist, growth proceeds in jumps and spurts characterized and marked by the emergence of new powers from within.

From the viewpoint of developmental psychologists as well as Jungians and advocates of positive disintegration such as Laing and Dabrowski, the integration of unconscious affect-imagery is the major mechanism for human personality advance. Sensory isolation can thus be considered an experimental method of developmental escalation; it diffuses some of the processes that comprise the ego, permitting an influx of unconscious material made readily accessible to direct observation and subsequent integration. Latent and unused aspects of the personality are made conscious in sensory isolation much as they arise spontaneously into consciousness as an individual matures.

Much of the experimentation presented in this book was conducted a number of years ago, and the work in experimental isolation reached a peak in the sixties. It is the editor's hope that this collection of data will stimulate further needed research in the area, for the contribution of experimental isolation to the study of man has not been fully explored.

# Chapter 17

# PERSONALITY CHANGES RESULTING FROM WATER SUSPENSION SENSORY ISOLATION*

MARK KAMMERMAN, Ph.D.

## Introduction

MOST of the published research on the therapeutic application of sensory isolation reports positive effects on personality. While the literature is fairly consistent in agreement that the limitation of external stimuli for a brief period can produce beneficial change in human beings, it is divergent in its explanation of these changes. At this time evidence has been assembled that attributes the changes produced to the temporary regression and disorganization that occurs in isolation. Other evidence suggests the stimulus hunger of an individual in isolation makes him susceptible to preplanned therapeutic stimuli introduced before or during the reduction of stimuli. Fortunately, the research has not turned to a contest between these two theoretical stances, for it is likely a both/and situation rather than an either/or. If indeed we have in grasp two of the variables that operate in isolation environments to produce personality change, effort to refine our techniques along these variables may result in the emergence of a more effective therapeutic tool.

This study was designed under the assumption that the regressive aspect of isolation experience was one of the major variables that had created personality change in previous experiments. Greatly reduced contact with external reality releases cortical regions usually influened by sensory excitation to scan internal cognitive and affective events. Below ordinary levels of conscious awareness lie vast inner unknown regions that affect personality.

*This is a condensation of a Ph.D. dissertation done at United States International University in 1975.

285

Contact with this region is evidenced by the fleeting thoughts, imagery and hallucinations reported by subjects in many isolation experiments.

While researchers studying the positive effects of sensory isolation have employed Freudian theory to imply that regression beyond certain fixation positions may initiate a progression, it appears Jungian formulations more adequately account for the positive changes in personality resulting from this regression. The Freudian notion of the unconscious suggests it consists mainly of infantile tendencies repressed through the maturation of the ego. Jung, on the other hand, held a more expansive view of the unconscious.

> The unconscious has still another side to it: it includes not only repressed contents, but all psychic material that lies below the threshold of consciousness. Moreover we know from abundant experience as well as for theoretical reasons, that the unconscious also contains all the material that has not yet reached the threshold of consciousness. These are the seeds of future conscious contents (Jung, 1953, p. 124).

This expanded model of the unconscious supported Jung's belief that collaboration with the unconscious was the central and primary task of therapy. He saw the purpose of analysis as giving the individual in treatment the ability to adapt through an intermix of conscious and unconscious tendencies. Jung felt that contact with and knowledge of the unconscious would lead to the highest developmental level, that of the transcendent function; the collaboration of conscious and unconscious data. This collaboration could not take place through mere self observation: "... mere self observation and intellectual self analysis are entirely inadequate as a means of establishing contact with the unconscious ... If there is no capacity to produce fantasies freely, we have to resort to an artificial aid." (Jung, 1960, p. 81) Nor did he consider the interpretation of such material necessary: "The danger of wanting to understand the meaning is overvaluation of the content, which is subjected to intellectual analysis and interpretation, so that the essentially symbolic character is lost." (Jung, 1960, p. 54) This model asserts the integration of unconscious material into consciousness in its raw and symbolic form is the major pathway to developmental growth and mental health. As such, it concurs with the findings of many sensory isolation experiments in which subjects were psychologically improved without interpretation, clarification or elaboration of their isolation experience. In this light, water suspension sensory isolation is a most effective isolation environment in that it provides for the maximum reduction of stimuli, and thus provides for maximum contact with the unconscious. Experimental findings have shown that in isolation, a subject's attention is powerfully drawn to residual stimuli. The external cues that exist in the other forms of sensory isolation were seen in this study as providing for the maintenance of secondary process thinking, especially in the case of normal subjects with intact defensive systems.

Also taken into consideration in the selection of water suspension isolation was the relatively high degree of comfort afforded the subjects. There are no restricting devices designed to keep movement to a minimum, no blindfolds, earplugs or noseplugs. This comfort and freedom from restraint was considered important in the subject's adaptation to the environment, his ability to relax, enjoy himself, and be free of somatic stimulation inevitably imposed by physical apparatus.

Some subjects in water suspension isolation spend much of the time engaged in tactile self-stimulation — creating sound by splashing water, attempting secondary-process thinking and problem solving (Kammerman, Bondell & Doty, 1973). To counter these efforts to create stimuli, this study employed an audio message encouraging free association, that was to provide an orientation to the experience that would attenuate activity incompatible with regression. The use of audio messages in sensory isolation has been supported in the literature in terms of increased suggestibility in the isolation environment. Tapes have been used that: (1) give the same message to all subjects, suggesting positive self-image and self-acceptance (Gibby and Adams, 1961); and (2) give individualized messages prepared from test batteries, suggesting improved insight and self-understanding (Adams, Robertson & Cooper, 1966). The present study used the same message for all subjects in one experimental group. Rather than suggesting specific personality change, the message encouraged primary process thinking. It was hypothesized that this message combined with isolation would create more opportunity for personality change than the isolation experience alone.

## METHOD OF RESEARCH

### Design

The study was a three-group x three-observation design as illustrated below.

| | | | | |
|---|---|---|---|---|
| Group I | $O_1$ | $X_1$ | $O_2$ | $O_3$ |
| Group II | $O_1$ | $X_2$ | $O_2$ | $O_3$ |
| Group III | $O_1$ | | $O_2$ | $O_3$ |
| (control) | | | | |

$X_1$ refers to the treatment which consisted of a series of three water suspension sensory isolation experiences. The first experience lasted one-half hour, and the next two experiences lasted one and one-half hours each. There was a two-week interval between the first and last experience.

$X_2$ refers to the same procedure as $X_1$ with the inclusion of an audio message designed to encourage free association.

$O_1$ refers to the pretest of all groups with the MMPI.

$O_2$ refers to posttesting immediately following the last isolation experience with the MMPI, or two weeks after the pretest for controls.

$O_3$ refers to a follow-up testing with the MMPI which took place four weeks following the last isolation experience.

Volunteers were randomly assigned to each group using a random draw until each group had ten subjects.

### Subjects

Thirty volunteer subjects were obtained through social network contacts. Many were people who had contacted the experimenter, having heard of a previous experiment in isolation a year prior. Of the thirty subjects, seventeen were male and thirteen were female; fourteen were married, fourteen were single, and two divorced. The mean age of the subjects was 27.6 (S-D 6.7) and their mean education was 15.6 years (S-D 3.6).

## Apparatus

The isolation tank was constructed of fiberglass laminated over 5/8-inch marine plywood and covered with two inches of stippled foam. Dimensions at the largest point were four feet by eight feet, and at the water level, where the subjects floated, three feet ten inches by seven feet ten inches. Flotation was provided by 375 gallons of an epsom salts solution. A large light-proof ventilator at one end provided a continuous supply of fresh air. Sound was delivered to the interior of the tank by two eight-inch coaxial speakers connected to a two-hundred watt amplifier and tape deck. The speakers were mounted to the outside of the tank. The hatch was constructed with a three-inch flange on all sides overriding a foam rubber seal to prevent light from entering the tank.

The tank was heated and filtered four hours a day to keep the temperature at 96 degrees and the solution clean.

## Procedure

### Group I (Isolation)

INITIAL CONTACT: As the subjects contacted the experimenter, they were told of the time commitment and given a date to begin the first session. Subjects' questions about the procedure were answered briefly, but those concerning the purpose or hypotheses were deterred until a debriefing session, which took place following the final MMPI administration.

SESSION ONE: The MMPI and a Personal Data Sheet requesting name, age, education, occupation, etc. were administered. Upon completion of these, the subject was asked to draw a number from a jar which determined the treatment group to which each was assigned.

The subject was then given written and physical introductions to the tank. The subject was told that after a half-hour his name would be called through the ventilator to signal the end of the session. Each subject was then left to undress and place himself in the tank. One half-hour later, the experimenter returned and terminated the session.

SESSION TWO: After having been told his name would be called in one and one-half hours, the subject was left to undress.

SESSION THREE: The subject was treated as during Session Two. After leaving the tank, the subject rinsed his hair with fresh water and was immediately administered the MMPI. An appointment was made for the subject to return four weeks in the future.

SESSION FOUR: The MMPI was administered, after which the purpose of the study was explained along with an interpretation of the MMPI results.

### Group II (Isolation with tape)

Sessions were the same as for Group I, with the addition that in Sessions Two and Three the subject was played a brief taped message shortly after entering the tank.

### Group III (Control)

INITIAL CONTACT: Same as Group I.

SESSION ONE: Same as Group I with one exception: the subject was told he would take two more MMPI's over a six-week period before beginning his tank experience. An appointment was made to take the next MMPI within two weeks.

SESSION TWO: The MMPI was administered and an appointment made for four weeks in the future for the final MMPI.

SESSION THREE: The MMPI was administered, after which appointments were made for the subjects to enter the tank.

### Results

A mixed model analysis of variance was performed with the following independent variables: (1) treatment condition (three levels — no treatment, isolation, and isolation with tape); (2) time of assessment, a repeated measure (three levels — pretest, posttest and follow-up test); and the following dependent variables: *L, F, K, Hs, D, Hy, Pd, Mf, Pa, Pt, Sc, Ma,* and *Si* (*K*-corrected T-scores on the MMPI administered in the three assessments noted above). No signficant difference in sex, age, meditation experience, drug use, medication use, marital status, health, and education was found among the treatment groups. However, in the comparison of the treatment groups on the premeasures of the MMPI scales, significant differences were found on the L ($F = 3.525$, $df = 2.27$, p .044) and Sc scales ($F = 4.979$, $df = 2.27$, p $<$ .014). The means and standard deviations for these comparisons are presented in Table 17-I. Independent one-tailed T-tests revealed no significant differences between the isolation and isolation with tape groups L prescores or Sc prescores. However, a significant difference (T = 4.687, $df = .29$, p $<$ .001) was found between mean *L* prescores of the control group and the combined mean L scores of the two experimental groups. Also, a significant difference (T = 3.95, $df =$ 1.29, p $<$ .01) was found between the mean *Sc* pretest score of the control group and the combined mean *Sc* of the two experimental treatment groups. The control subjects had initially lower *Sc* scores and *L* scores than the two treatment groups. Therefore, it was necessary to use the *Sc* and *L* pretest scores as covariants in the planned comparison in order to control the effects of these initial differences.

### Primary Analyses

#### *Controls*

Comparisons were made between pretest and posttest and

TABLE 17-I

MEANS AND STANDARD DEVIATIONS OF PRETESTS:
ISOLATION VERSUS ISOLATION AND TAPE
VERSUS CONTROL

| | Isolation | | Isolation + Tape | | Control | |
| Scale | Mean | S-D | Mean | S-D | Mean | S-D |
|---|---|---|---|---|---|---|
| L | 47.8 | 4.6 | 48.8 | 5.2 | 41.4 | 3.5 |
| Sc | 62.1 | 7.7 | 61.9 | 5.3 | 50.1 | 6.2 |

between posttest and follow-up scores. In the primary analysis of variance (without covariants) no significant differences were found for the control subjects between the pretest and posttest, or the post and follow-up measures on the MMPI scales.

### Isolation

Comparisons were made between pretest and posttest and between posttest and follow-up scores. A significant pre-post difference was found ($F$ = 4.074, $df$ = 1.54, p < .049) on the $K$ scale. The mean pretest score was 55.7 ($S$-$D$ 5.3), and the posttreatment mean for this group was 57.9 ($S$-$D$ 4.3). No other significant differences in the MMPI scores were found in the pre-post comparisons for this group. A significant post-follow-up difference was found ($F$ = 4.192, $df$ = 1.54, p < .045) on the $Ma$ scale for the isolation group. The mean posttreatment score was 60.8 ($S$-$D$ 5.6) and the mean follow-up score was 66.1 ($S$-$D$ 9.0). No other significant effects were found for the post and follow-up comparison.

### Isolation and Tape

Comparisons were made between pretest and posttest and

TABLE 17-II

SUMMARY OF ANALYSIS OF VARIANCE COMPARING
PRETEST VERSUS POSTTEST IN THE ISOLATION
AND TAPE GROUP

| Variable | df* | Mean Square | F | p Less than |
|----------|-----|-------------|-----|-------------|
| L | 1, 54 | 28.017 | 4.166 | .046 |
| F | 1, 54 | 40.071 | 3.486 | .067 |
| Pd | 1, 54 | 198.016 | 7.861 | .007 |
| Sc | 1, 54 | 56.067 | 2.853 | .097 |
| Ma | 1, 54 | 138.016 | 4.120 | .047 |

*All df = 1, 54 because all tests were within group (repeated measure) planned comparisons.

between posttest and follow-up scores. Within the isolation-with-tape treatment several significant effects were found for the pre-post treatment comparison. These results are presented in Table 17-II. Significant differences were found between the pre- and posttreatment assessments on the *L, Pd,* and *Ma* scales. The means and standard deviations for these comparisons are presented in Table 17-III. In addition, the pre-post comparisons of the *F* and *Sc* scores approached significance.

TABLE 17-III

MEANS AND STANDARD DEVIATIONS
FOR VARIABLES DISPLAYING PRE-POST
CHANGE WITHIN THE ISOLATION
AND TAPE GROUP

| | Pretest | | Posttest | |
|---|---|---|---|---|
| *Scale* | *Mean* | *S-D* | *Mean* | *S-D* |
| L [a] | 48.8 | 5.2 | 46.2 | 3.7 |
| F [b] | 59.1 | 5.3 | 57.3 | 9.1 |
| Pd [a] | 62.9 | 8.0 | 58.3 | 6.2 |
| Sc [b] | 61.9 | 5.8 | 57.6 | 8.3 |
| Ma [a] | 62.1 | 6.6 | 57.2 | 5.0 |

[a] Significant
[b] Approaching significance

## Within Assessment Time Comparisons Among Treatment Groups

As mentioned above, a significant difference was found between the control and the two treatment groups on the pretreatment assessment of *L* and *Sc* scores, with the isolation-with-tape group having significantly higher *L* and *Sc* scores than the control group. However no significant post or follow-up differences were found between treatment groups.

## Analysis of Covariance

No changes in significance were found in any of the primary comparisons when the *Sc* or *L* prescores were used as covariants, separately or together, in the same analyses. Thus all findings above were independent of any effects of differences in control *Sc* or *L* scores, separately or together.

## Summary

In summary, the following results were found. Control subjects had initially lower scale scores than the experimental groups, with the *Sc* and *L* scores significantly lower. No differences were found between control subjects and experimental groups after the treatments or in the follow-up measurement. Analysis of data revealed the treatments reduced the *L* and *Sc* scores of the experimental groups. Other significant treatment group differences in post and follow-up scores may have been masked by a biased control group sample.

In addition, the isolation treatment significantly raised *K* scores with *Ma* scores increasing significantly from the posttreatment assessment to the follow-up assessment.

Most of the changes occurred in the isolation and tape treatment group. *L, Pd* and *Ma* scores were significantly lowered following the treatment and then remained the same through the follow up measurement.

## Discussion

Typical clinical interpretation of MMPI profiles is derived either from an analysis of the individual scales, or from the configuration of scales, or both. This discussion will employ both of these standard methods of interpretation.

### *Group I — Isolation:*

The isolation treatment resulted in a significant increase in pre-post $K$ scores. The standard clinical interpretation of an increase in $K$ is either an increase in ego strength or defensiveness (Dahlstrom et al., 1972). A possible explanation for this result is that the subjects in isolation were called upon to muster their defenses to cope with the invitation to rapid regression. As has been discussed, the isolation environment can bring into consciousness novel and potentially threatening material; and that some subjects with intact and differentiated defenses can resist this influx of unconscious content (Henrichs, 1963). It can be inferred that resistance to the possible intrusion of unknown content brings the subject to a fuller employment of defensive procedures which are reflected in the increase in the $K$ scale.

The isolation treatment also resulted in a significant increase in post-follow-up $Ma$ scores. It is important to note this change occurred not as an immediate result of the isolation experience, but rather as an aftereffect. This increase in $Ma$ after the isolation treatment may be the product of the subject's reflection upon the experience interplayed with the rise in his defensiveness or ego strength which was maintained at the postisolation level. The subject has emerged from a novel and potentially threatening experience feeling more capable and less negative (as indicated by the stable increase in $K$). Even in the absence of actual personality change, the individual may feel differently about himself in terms of being less vulnerable to threatening and novel experiences, and more resistant to negative thoughts about himself. This state is reflected in an increase in enthusiasm and optimism of the sort that is based on a somewhat less sensitive and defensive posture, which are those characteristics related to an increase in the Ma scale (Dahlstrom et al., 1972).

The absence of other changes in the isolation group's clinical scales may be explained by these subjects' ability to resist the emergence of unconscious material. As this integration of unconscious content into consciousness is the theoretical basis for personality change in this study, it follows that these subjects would not evidence personality change.

### Group II — Isolation with Tape:

The changes in the clinical scales of this group of subjects may be the result of the emergence of unconscious content into consciousness. As had been hypothesized, the taped message suggesting free association may have attenuated activities in isolation that were inconducive to regression, facilitating the emergence of novel material. This group did not evidence an increase in defensiveness as had Group I, and in fact did show a decrease in several clinical scales of the MMPI, indicating positive personality changes. These changes were present immediately following the isolation experience, and were sustained throughout the four-week follow-up period. The isolation-with-tape treatment resulted in a significant decrease in pre-post $L$ scores, which was maintained through the four-week follow-up period. A decrease in the $L$ scale is generally associated with an increase in insight (Marks et al., 1974). This change can be attributed to an increase in these subjects' awareness of themselves; with less need for denial and repression. The emergence of previously unknown and alien aspects of themselves into consciousness may be represented by an increase in insight and the decrease of $L$ scores.

This treatment also resulted in a significant decrease in pre-post- $Pd$ scores which was maintained through the four-week follow-up period. Two studies conducted with this scale deserve mention, as they bear on the discussion of the findings of the present study. The lowest values found for test-retest reliabilities were found in subjects who had undergone psychiatric treatment; otherwise the scale was found to be very stable (Rosen, 1953). One other factor besides therapy that has been found to change $Pd$ scales is an important maturational change, generally occurring over a year's time (Hathaway and Monachesi, 1963). Thus the changes induced by the isolation-and-tape treatment can be likened to both therapy and maturation in terms of an increase in the scope of the ego and a subsequent deepening of its controls and responsibility. Such changes are reflected in a decrease in impulsiveness, a characteristic to which the $Pd$ scale is considered sensitive (Gilbertstadt and Duker, 1965). Jung considered the relationship between the conscious and unconscious to have a direct bearing on impulsivity. He wrote that one-sidedness (too much energy invested in conscious content) will be characterized by sudden releases of tension from the unconscious.

> ... if the tension increases as a result of too great one-sidedness, the counter-tendency breaks through into consciousness, usually just at that moment when it is most important to maintain the conscious direction ... The further we are able to remove ourselves from the unconscious through directed functioning, the more readily a powerful counterposition can build up in the unconscious, and when this breaks out it may have disagreeable consequences (Jung, 1960, p. 71).

The isolation environment may have provided for a flow of unconscious material into consciousness, thus decreasing the one-sidedness and a subsequent impulsivity.

The isolation-with-tape treatment also resulted in a significant decrease in pre-post *Ma* scores which was maintained through the four-week follow-up period. Research has related low *Ma* scores with stability of emotional adjustment (Woodworth et al., 1957). Adjectives used to describe these low types were: assuming, cool and sincere. This is in contrast to the high end of the scale, which indicates characteristics of agitation, over-optimism, defensiveness and bitterness. As a result of the treatment, subjects endorsed fewer items that described themselves as defensive and agitated; they became, it appears, better adjusted emotionally. This may be a result of the collaboration of conscious and unconscious content, as Hall and Nordby (1973, p. 52) aptly summarized from Jung:

> By making conscious that which is unconscious, man can live in greater harmony with his own nature. He will experience fewer irritations and frustrations because he recognizes their origins in his own unconscious.

The isolation-with-tape treatment resulted in a decrease in pre-post *F* scores which was maintained through the four-week follow-up period. High *F* scores correlate with several acting out patterns (Rice, 1968). On the other hand, individuals with moderately high *F* scales are typically described as restless, unstable and dissatisfied. Low *F* scales have been associated with characteristics of general compatibility with and accommodation to one's present environment (Gough, McKee, and Yandell, 1955). A lowering of the *F* scale may be attributable to an increase in personal integration, and a resultant compatibility with self and environment. An individual who has come into contact with unconscious material is less likely to project it on the world, and less likely to blame the world for his own condition.

The isolation with tape treatment also resulted in a decrease in pre-post *Sc* scores which was maintained through the four-week follow-up. The *Sc* scale contains items that include bizarre mentation, social alienation, peculiarities of perception and difficulties in concentration and impulse control. Harris and Lingoes (1955) sorted these items into three major categories; one of these they described as a lack of ego mastery in areas of cognitive functioning, conative functioning, and defects of inhibition and control. During the isolation experience, the influx of unconscious content may have provided for an improvement of ego functioning. As in analytic theory, more awareness of internal contingencies leads to greater capacity for thinking-through and impulse control. Gough et al. (1955) found high scorers on the *Sc* scale showed evidence of the subjects' being at odds with themselves, and having major internal conflicts. A decrease in this scale could thus be explained by a penetration of the conscious-unconscious barrier. If the typically polar relationship between conscious and unconscious content were modified for a few hours, the result may well be a decrease in the sense of being split within one's self.

The effect of the isolation and tape treatment can also be considered in terms of its effect on the profile configuration of the MMPI. Changes in the two clinical scales, *Pd* (4) and *Ma* (9) are interesting in light of the difficulty psychotherapy has in attempting to modify this configuration. The 4-9 is, in fact, the only code type that maintains the same profile before and after psychotherapy (Marks et al., 1974). Individuals with this profile are considered to have a deficiency in ego and superego controls, and to characteristically project their difficulties on the world. They appear incapable of controlling impulse, and act without sufficient deliberation (Marks et al., 1974). Typically, 4-9's are described as selfish, narcissistic, and incapable of establishing emotional contact and friendship. This cluster of symptomatology can be expected in individuals who are insulated from the influence of their unconscious. If the individual is deaf to his unconscious self, he is deaf to the others in his life, "... to the degree that he does not admit the validity of the other person, he denies the 'other' within himself the right to exist — and vice versa. The capacity for inner dialogue is a touchstone for outer objectivity, (Jung, 1960, p. 89)." Being in touch with the unconscious is considered a prerequisite to a regulation of one's actions. The whole of personality must be taken into account or one-sidedness predominates, making the individual egocentric and prone to high energy breakthroughs from the repressed unconscious values within himself, "Thus, in coming to terms with the unconscious, not only is the standpoint of the ego justified, but the unconscious is granted the same authority. The ego takes the lead, but the unconscious must be allowed to have its say too (Jung, 1960, p. 88)."

Without the inner dialogue, there can be no balance. The lack of success in treating the 4-9 may be the inability of psychotherapy to begin this inner dialogue. This may arise out of the 4-9's characteristic pathogenic attitude toward authority figures, their difficulty in forming relationships of any sort, and their lack of insight along with low motivation for change. While these cardinal features would obstruct traditional therapy, the isolation treatment employs them effectively. There is no authority figure present in the treatment; no need to form a relationship to effect a change. Narcissism is granted primacy; the individual in isolation is totally reliant upon internal, self-produced stimuli. In short, it would appear that the isolation treatment is a most effective means of reuniting an alienated and neglected unconscious with its isolated and self-indulgent ego.

## Summary

It was found that water suspension isolation alone did not produce positive personality change, but rather created a rise in ego strength or defensivenss, and later, an increase in feelings of overoptimism associated with a defensive position. It is postulated that the isolation was not sufficient to produce an influx of unconscious material into consciousness.

Water suspension isolation with a tape designed to encourage free association was found to produce positive personality changes in normal subjects, and the change was maintained at four weeks. This positive change was reflected in a decrease in the *L, Pd, Ma, Sc* and *F* scales of the MMPI, and may have been due to the emergence of unconscious and novel material into consciousness.

The isolation and tape treatment had a significant effect on the 4-9 profile, which implies it may be of benefit in treating personality types generally considered out of reach of conventional psychotherapy. The evidence generated by the present study in regard to the treatment of 4-9 personality types is inferential, and further research is needed to substantiate this conclusion.

## REFERENCES

Adams, H. B., Robertson, M. H., and Cooper, G. D.: Sensory deprivation and personality change. *The Journal of Nervous and Mental Disease, 143*:256, 1966.

Dahlstrom, W. G., Welsh, G. S., and Dahlstrom, L. E.: *An MMPI Handbook, Volume I, Clinical Interpretations*, 2nd ed. Minneapolis, University of Minnesota, 1960.

Gibby, R. G. and Adams, H. B.: Receptiveness of psychiatric patients to verbal communication: An increase following partial sensory and social isolation. *Archives of General Psychiatry, 5*:366, 1961.

Gilberstadt, H. and Duker, J.: *A Handbook for Clinical and Actuarial MMPI Interpretation.* Philadelphia, Saunders, 1965.

Gough, H. B., McKee, M. G., and Yandell, R. J.: Adjective check list analyses of a number of selected psychometric and assessment variables. Officer Education Research Laboratory, Technical Memorandum, *10*, 1955.

Hall, C. S. and Nordby, V. J.: *A Primer of Jungian Psychology.* New York, New American Library, 1973.

Harris, R. E. and Lingoes, J. C.: Subscales for the MMPI: an aide to profile interpretation. Department of Psychiatry, University of California, (Mimeographed) 1955.

Hathaway, S. R. and Monachesi, E. D.: *Adolescent Personality and Behavior: MMPI Patterns of Normal, Delinquent, Dropout and Other Outcomes.* Minneapolis, University of Minnesota, 1963.

Henrichs, T.: The effects of brief sensory deprivation on objective test scores. *Journal of Clinical Psychology, 19*:172, 1963.

Jung, C. G.: *The Structure and Dynamics of the Psyche.* Translated by R. F. C. Hull, Collected Works, *8*, Princeton, Princeton University, 1960.

Jung, C. G.: *Two Essays on Analytical Psychology.* Translated by R. F. C. Hull, Collected Works, *7*, Princeton, Princeton University, 1953.

Kammerman, M., Bondell, J. A., and Doty, R.: An exploratory investigation into the relationship between self-actualization and modes of experience in sensory deprivation. Unpublished manuscript, United States International University, San Diego, 1973.

Lilly, J. C.: Solitude, isolation and confinement and the scientific method. In Madlow and Snow (Eds.): *The Psychodynamic Implications of Physiological Studies on Sensory Deprivation.* Springfield, Thomas, 1970.

Marks, P. A., Seeman, W., and Haller, D. L.: *The Actuarial Use of the MMPI with Adolescents and Adults.* Baltimore, Williams and Wilkins, 1974.

Rice, D. G.: Rorschach responses and aggressive characteristics of MMPI F 16 scorers. *Journal of Projective Techniques, 32*:253, 1968.

Rosen, A.: Reliability of MMPI scales for a psychiatric population. *Journal of Consulting Psychology, 17*:217, 1953.

Woodworth, D. B., Barron, F., and MacKinnon, D. W.: An analysis of life history interviewers ratings of 100 air force captains. Air Force Personnel and Training Research Center, Research Report, *57*, 1957.

# INTRODUCTION TO THE WATER
# SUSPENSION ISOLATION ENVIRONMENT

**Y**OU are about to have an experience which has been shared by perhaps five hundred or a thousand others in the whole history of the human race.

We have created a new experimental environment that reduces external stimulation to minimum possible levels. The water in this tank is heated to just below body temperature, and epsom salt has been added to increase the specific gravity so you can float easily in only inches of water. The tank is lightproof and soundproof; for the first time in your life, all your thoughts will arise without any stimulation from outside yourself. This experience of isolation from all external stimulation for a brief period is delightful, restful and refreshing for almost all people.

You are now part of one of the most extensive experiments yet conducted in water suspension isolation. Not only will the experience be a rewarding one for you, but what we learn from you will be helpful in developing yet another powerful tool in helping man understand himself and achieve emotional and mental stability.

If for any reason whatsoever you want to leave the tank before your time is up, simply push up on the panel directly over your head and it will swing open, returning you to the world of external stimuli. Your doing so will not in any way compromise the success of the experiment, for that reaction, too, is one which we would wish to tabulate.

### Contents of Taped Message

I am going to show you a very good way to experience this environment. Remember to lie as still as possible. Let yourself relax. Discover that you can relax still more. This is a very comfortable environment where you can relax completely. As you relax, let your thoughts flow. Let your thoughts flow in any direction. Let your thoughts flow to any subject. Let your mind drift where it will. In a moment you will hear some beautiful music that will flow through your body and drift through your mind. Relax and go with it, go with all your thoughts, go with all your feelings.

(Following this message, *Adagio for Strings* by Samuel Barber was played, conducted by Antonio Janigro, recorded by Vanguard.)

# AUTHOR INDEX

## A

Abramson, E. E., 144
Adams, H. B., 116-141, 143, 145, 164, 177-194, 204, 287
Allen, L. H., 216
Angyal, A., 23
Azima, H., 11-28, 76, 83, 87, 204

## B

Barefoot, J. C., 221
Barnard, G. W., 268-276
Bennett, A. M. H., 254
Bernstein, D. A., 220
Bexton, W. H., 11, 21, 48, 87, 254
Bock, R. D., 198
Bombard, A., 244
Bozzett, L. P., 220
Brownfain, J. J., 170
Brownfield, C. A., 117, 142, 143, 177, 190
Butler, J., 89
Byrd, R., 246

## C

Cambareri, J. D., 106, 254
Cameron, D. E., 22, 24
Carson, R. C., 145
Cleveland, S. E., 76-86
Cohen, B. D., 80
Cohen, S. I., 87
Cooper, G. D., 87-115, 117, 120, 137, 138, 142-159, 204
Curtis, G. C., 7

## D

Dahlstrom, W. G., 295
Davison, G. C., 220

## F

Foa, U., 145

## G

Gaines, L. S., 117, 142
Gibby, R. G., 29-46, 76, 79, 81, 84, 85, 87, 97, 99, 117, 120, 121, 145, 168-176, 204, 287
Gibson, W., 243
Gilberstadt, H., 296
Gilford, J. S., 220
Goldberger, L., 47-75, 107, 202
Gough, H. B., 297, 298
Gowan, J. C., 283

## H

Hall, C. S., 297
Harris, A., 30, 44, 76, 84, 85, 87, 204
Harris, R. E., 298
Hathaway, S. R., 296
Head, H., 22
Hebb, D. O., 48, 247
Heider, F., 154
Henrichs, T., 195-203, 295
Heron, W., 48, 105, 195, 268
Holt, R. R., 47, 52, 53, 54, 72
Holtzman, W. H., 83
Horn, D., 65, 219
Hunt, W. A., 220, 228

## I

Ikard, F. F., 221

## J

Janicki, W. P., 216
Jasper, H. H., 22
Jenkins, R. F., 33, 41, 79, 119, 207

305

# SUBJECT INDEX

307